"*This has been a wonderful day!*" *said he, as the Rat shoved off and took to the sculls again. "Do you know. I've never been in a boat in all my life.*"

"*What?*" *cried the Rat, open-mouthed: "Never been in a—you never—well, I—what have you been doing, then?*"

"*Is it so nice as all that?*" *asked the Mole shyly, though he was quite prepared to believe it as he leant back in his seat and surveyed the cushions, the oars, the row-locks, and all the fascinating fittings, and felt the boat sway lightly under him.*

"*Nice? It's the* only *thing,*" *said the Water Rat solemnly, as he leant forward for his stroke. "Believe me, my young friend, there is nothing—absolutely nothing—half so much worth doing as simply messing about in boats.*"

—Kenneth Grahame, *The Wind in the Willows* (1908)

Acknowledgments

I MUST TIP MY ROWING CAP IN THANKS TO THE FOLLOWING GROUP OF gentlemen who formed the editorial committee for this book: William "Bill" Lanouette, Peter Mallory, William "Bill" Miller, and Thomas "Tom" E. Weil—all distinguished American rowing historians. To this group should be added Rick Rinehart, executive editor at Lyons Press/Globe Pequot, also an old oarsman. Rick might not be a historian of aquatic matters per se, but he was in the bow of the Kent School (Connecticut) crew who won the 1972 Princess Elizabeth Challenge Cup (PE) at the prestigious Henley Royal Regatta, so his advice was welcomed as well. It was with the help of this crew that I managed to take the "watercraft"—this coxless straight six, if you will—across the finish line. Of course, other people whom I owe gratitude to are the journalists, authors, and writers who agreed to have their work reprinted in this book. I also would like to thank the publishers, literary agents, and copyright holders who gave me permission to publish works of authors they represent.

Preface

TWO PASSIONS HAVE FOLLOWED ME IN LIFE: BOOKS AND ROWING.

When I was in my younger teens, my friends Per Ekström and Ola Nilsson brought me down to the local rowing club in our hometown of Malmö in Sweden. On a warm and sunny day in May 1973, I found myself sitting in an old, wooden, clinker-built inrigger four with coxswain for my inaugural row on the Malmö canal. Before my 4.5-kilometer-long outing was over, I was infatuated with my new sport. It is incredible to think that it is fifty years ago I took my first stroke.

Although I was captivated by rowing, I must be honest and say that I never became a star. However, my fascination with the sport led me to do things other than racing for Malmö Roddklubb. For numerous years, I was a novice and women's coach at the club. I wrote the club newsletter, I was a member of the board, and in the beginning of the 1990s, I acted as the president of the club, the youngest head of a Swedish rowing club ever at that time. In 1990, Per Ekström and I founded the Swedish Rowing Federation's publication, *Svensk Rodd*, sharing the editorship of the magazine.

My lack of success at the oar turned into something my friend, John Drew, a poet in Cambridge, England, once wrote about his cricket career, paraphrasing George Bernard Shaw. John wrote, "Those who can, do; those who can't, write."

When I was not at the rowing club, I was working as an editor at a small book-publishing company, a job I managed to land after my studies in literature and culture science at Lund University.

To keep on writing articles and to fill the space in the forthcoming issues of the magazine, I decided to purchase rowing books, hoping to find good stories to retell. I already had a couple of old rowing books in Swedish, but I needed more. This being the pre-internet era, I had to visit book shops and antiquarian book dealers and browse their shelves.

It was during a weekend in Gothenburg, when my mother and I had visited my sister, I drove the way downtown to be able to stop at an antiquarian bookshop. I popped in and asked the owner if he had any books on rowing. He climbed up a tall ladder, and from the top shelf he brought down the brown standard trade edition of W. B. Woodgate's *Boating* (1888) in the Badminton Library series, second edition from 1889. He dusted off the book and handed it to me. It was in a very nice condition. I looked at the price. Based on my measly salary as a book editor, it was far and beyond my budget. I thanked the dealer, handed the book back and said sorry it was not within my price range.

When I went back to the car, my mother, who had been waiting in the car, asked if I had found anything. I told her about the Woodgate book and the price. She took out her purse from her handbag, opened it up, found a large bill, gave it to me, and told me to go back to the shop and buy the book.

The owner was surprised to see me again but was probably happy that he would be able to make a bit of cash. While he neatly wrapped the book, I told him that I was an editor of the Swedish rowing magazine and collected material for articles on rowing history. "Very good," he said, but he added, "Oarsmen, do they actually *read?*"

For the sake of the sale of this book, I really hope so!

When I moved from Sweden to Connecticut in 2000, I continued to buy rowing books. They are now in a small room, which my family calls the "Rowing Room." I believe there are now slightly more than five hundred books in my collection (and counting).

I suppose it was my interest in books and rowing—and that I had worked as a book editor—that made Rick Rinehart, executive editor at Lyons Press, ask me to put together fiction and nonfiction stories and poems, verses, songs, and plays to form this anthology. I spent weeks going through my rowing books, magazines, and publications, and I scanned the internet while I made a list of writers and authors whose texts I was interested in reprinting in this book.

Thanks to running the rowing history website Hear The Boat Sing (HTBS), which I founded in 2009, I was lucky to already be in contact with several rowing historians, journalists, and writers. For those for whom I lacked contact information, the rowing historians who formed the editorial committee for this book came to my aid. Some of the more "famous" authors had literary agents whom I approached with my query of permission to include their authors' texts.

Most of the people I reached out to were happily willing to give me permission to use their works and join the crew; a few even wrote stories specially for this anthology. Then there was a small group of publishers and copyright holders who demanded quite a lot of money to reprint the texts of their authors. (These texts are not in this anthology.) There were also a couple of copyright holders and literary agents who did not have the courtesy to reply to my inquiry—their loss, I would like to think.

What you will find assembled in this collection are excerpts of classic rowing stories, rowing on the River Thames and the Charles River, at Henley Royal Regatta, the World Championships and the Olympic Games, professional rowing, the poetic solitude of the single sculler, a Boat Race murder, the downfall of East German rowing, the forgotten center of early British rowing, and the Irish rower who rowed in both women's and men's university crews, and much more.

So are these the greatest rowing stories ever, you ask? Fair question. I guess it all comes down to taste. However, I can promise you one thing—they are very entertaining.

Ready All—READ!

Göran R. Buckhorn
Winter 2022–2023

FICTION

At the Mile

Ralph Henry Barbour

In Ralph H. Barbour's *Captain of the Crew* (1901), Hillton (school) is going to race its archrival St. Eustace on a warm day in June. On the morning of race day, Trevor Nesbitt, Hillton's number four in the eight, wakes up feeling ill. Although there are spares, no one is accustomed to row at four. And Trevor really would like to row in the race, so he tells no one what shape he's in. The race is on, but Trevor is not feeling well. . . .

Splash! Swish! Rattle!

The oars dug into the water venomously, swirled through, emerged dripping and flashing, disappearing again. Brown, sinewy arms shot forward and back, bodies bent and unbent like powerful springs, the water was thrown in little cascades of glistening pearls, and the coxswains, open-mouthed, intense, cried unintelligible things in the uproar, and looked like vindictive little demons crouching for a spring. There was no long, rhythmic swing of the oars now; there was nothing inspiring to the spectators in the quick dashing movements of the sweeps; all seemed without system, incoherent.

Ten—eleven—twelve—thirteen—fourteen strokes! Then the savage struggle was past, and out from the momentary chaos of uproar and turmoil and seething water the Hillton shell shot into the lead, its bobbing cox even with Number Four of the St. Eustace boat.

"Steady all! Lengthen out! Lengthen out!"

The plunging dips of the eight crimson-bladed oars ceased. Stroke, with a quick glance at the other boat, moved back to the full limit of the side, his sweep swirled steadily, almost slowly, through the quieter water, came out square, turned, feathered over yards of racing ripples, and again lost itself under the gleaming surface.

"*Time! Time!*" yelled cox.

And now backs were bending in perfect unison, oarlocks rattled as one, and rowing superbly at thirty-two strokes to the minute, the crimson eight forced the shining cedar craft away until clear water showed between its rudder and the knifelike bow of its rival. Hillton had gained the first trick, and, although the game was by no means yet won, Dick's eyes gleamed with satisfaction, Keene allowed a smile to cross his face, and on the Terrible, racing along in the wake of the speeding shells, Professor Beck and Coach Kirk glanced at each other and nodded. Across the intervening tide came, shrilly, insistent, the cry of the St. Eustace coxswain:

"*Hit her up! Hit her up! Hit her up!*"

In response eight blue-clad bodies bent and strained in an endeavor to place their shell beside Hillton's, and eight blue-tipped oars flashed swiftly back and forth. St. Eustace was rowing thirty-seven. Dick shot a glance of inquiry at Keene. The latter glanced over his right shoulder.

"Can't keep it up," he answered to Stroke's unspoken question. "*Four, you're late!*"

Slowly the bow of the St. Eustace boat crept up on them; now it was abreast of their rudder; a dozen strokes more and it was even with cox; a minute later St. Eustace's bow oar was cutting the water opposite to Dick. But there was no alteration of the latter's stroke. For a minute or two the Blue's boat hung tenaciously to the place it had won; then, inch by inch, it dropped astern again, yet so slowly that it was long before Dick was certain that it was so. The Blue was rowing at thirty-three now, and very wisely husbanding her strength. The half-mile was past, and the race was a quarter over.

Down at the finish crowds lined the shores and stood packed into a restless mass on the great iron bridge that spans the river a few rods below the imaginary line. The scene was a bright one. Overhead the summer sky ached warmly blue, a vast expanse of color unbroken save in the west, where a soft bank of cumulate clouds lay one upon the other like giant pillows. The river reflected the intense azure of the heavens and caught the sunlight on every ripple and wave until from long gazing upon it the eyes were dazzled into temporary blindness. On each side the banks were thickly wooded save that here and there a square or quadrangle of radiant turf stretched from the margin of the stream upward and away to some quiet mansion leaf-embowered in the distance. The western side of the river was deep-toned with shadows for a little space, and there upon the banks the trees held a promise of the twilight in their dark foliage. Up the stream, to the right, Marshall dozed in the afternoon, a picturesque group of white buildings, studded here and there with clumps of green; a long, low factory building stood by the water and glowed warmly red in the sunlight. Across the river and almost opposite to the village St. Eustace Academy sprawled its half-dozen edifices down the southern slope of a gentle hill, but only the higher towers and gables showed above the big elms that stood sentinel about it.

Along the bridge and up and down both shores by the finish crimson flags and streamers shone side by side with the deep blue banners of the rival school. Gay hats and bright-hued dresses pricked out the throngs. Field-glasses now and then gave aid to eager eyes, and everywhere was an atmosphere of impatience and excitement. Many nerves were a-tingle there that afternoon, while far up the river, like thin bright streaks upon the water, the two boats, to all appearances side by side, sped onward toward victory or defeat. It was anybody's race as yet, said the watchers on the bridge; and indeed it looked so, not alone to them, but to the spectators in the launches and tugs that followed the shells, to the officials in their speeding craft, to the occupants of the slender cedar racing-ships themselves—to all save one.

Trevor Nesbitt, toiling over his oar with white, set face, was alone certain that defeat was to be the harvest of the eight heroes in crimson. But although he alone was sure, it is possible that Keene was already scenting disaster, for the coxswain was staring ahead at Trevor with frowning brow and anxious eyes.

"*Brace up, Four! You're late!*"

5

Trevor heard the cry as one half asleep hears the summons to awake; he wondered why cox didn't speak louder; but he brought his wandering thoughts back the next instant and bore doggedly at his oar. Yes, he could still row; one more stroke; now, yet one more; and still another. It seemed as though each must be his last, and yet, when it was done, strength still remained for another, weaker, slower, but still another. Ever since the half-mile had been passed he had been on the verge of collapse. He was faint and weak and dizzy; the blue sky and glistening water were merged in his failing sight into one strange expanse of awful, monotonous blue that revolved behind him in mighty sweeps like a monster cyclorama. Often it was dotted with craft that trailed soft, gray vapor behind them; often the lights were suddenly turned quite out; and the world was left in impenetrable blackness, and he closed his eyes and was glad.

"*Four! Four! What's the matter? Brace up, man!*"

And then he opened his aching eyes again, slowly unwillingly, to find the world for the moment normal; to see the muscles of Water's neck straining like cords; to see a line of crimson bodies working back and forth; to wonder with alarm why he was sitting there motionless when everyone else was at work, and then to suddenly discover that he, too, was going forward and back on the slide, and in time with the other toilers. In one such moment he looked aside and saw a line of blue figures moving like automatons almost even with them. He wondered if they knew—those automatons—that they were going to win. He could tell them, but he wouldn't; not a word. A funny little figure apparently sliding up and down at the stern reminded him of a ridiculous image of a heathen god he had once seen in a museum. It was very funny. He tried to grin—

"*Eyes in the boat, Four!*" shrieked the coxswain shrilly, angrily.

Trevor wondered who he was talking to. Strange that he should talk when they were losing the race; silence—silence like his own—would have been more fitting. There was a sudden jerk at his arms that for the instant brought him back to reality. He didn't know what had happened; possibly he had struck a snag; but he found the time again after a fashion and worked on doggedly, as a machine might work, with neither sensation nor spirit. He had caught a crab, but he didn't know it then. Suddenly an almost overmastering hatred of the tossing blue line across the little breadth of water surged over him. They would win, the beasts, the monsters! And the little heathen image that slid up and down at the end would be happy. And Dick and Keene and all the others would be miserable and heartbroken! Heaven, how he hated those monsters in blue and the little red-haired heathen image!

The cox was talking again now; what was it he said? Water? Cox wanted water; surely someone could get him water? But he had Five, hadn't he? Well, he wasn't Five, and so—What was this? He was wet! Oh, yes, Five was splashing him desperately with water. He wondered why and wished he'd stop; it got into his eyes and mouth and bothered him.

"Four, brace up, can't you? It's almost over!" pleaded cox from a great distance.

What was almost over? Trevor opened his eyes and drew his white, dripping forehead into a puzzled frown. Oh, yes, the race! His mind and vision cleared, and he saw things as they were; saw Keene's eyes looking at him desperately, saw the cox of the St. Eustace boat slide by him and disappear; saw the one mile buoy rush astern; saw himself, huddled over his motionless oar as it dragged, splashing, on the surface. His brain was once more clear. He seized the oar handle, and tried to draw it to him. It was no use. He tried to explain it all to Keene in one long, agonized look. Then he saw the only way by which he could aid, and summoning a semblance of strength, with a deep breath, he reached out, and with trembling, nerveless fingers unlocked his oar and dropped it aside. It was lost to sight on the instant.

"*Careful, Four!*" warned the cox.

Trevor steadied himself with a hand on the gunwale, brought his reluctant body half erect, and then flung himself over the side. He heard the coxswain's voice for an instant.

"*Mind oars, Five and Seven!*"

Then the water closed over his head.

Orm's Beard

Frans G. Bengtsson

THE ACTION IN FRANS G. BENGTSSON'S TWO-VOLUME SWEDISH VIKING saga *Röde Orm* (1941 and 1945; English translation by Michael Meyer, *The Long Ships*, 1954), covers approximately the years 980–1010. At night, a band of Vikings raid a farm on the shoreline of western Scania, which then belonged to Denmark, to steal some sheep. The farm is owned by Toste, and when people at the farmhouse notice what is going on, they set the dogs loose on the thieves. Toste's youngest son, Orm, is quick and catches up with the Vikings, slays one of them, but gets knocked down by the group's leader, Krok. Krok decides to bring the unconscious Orm aboard his ship so the youngster can take the place on the rowing bench of the man he killed. Soon Orm befriends the Vikings and becomes one of them. They sail on adventures that take them to England, Ireland, Spain, and Denmark. It is in Spain that Orm and his comrades get captured by Moors and turned into rowing slaves on one of the Caliph's ships.

They rowed in heat and in fierce rain, and sometimes in a pleasant cool, though it was never cold. They were the caliph's slaves, but they had little knowledge of whither they were rowing or what purpose their labour might be serving. They rowed beside steep coasts and rich lowlands, and toiled pain fully up broad and swiftly flowing river, on the banks of which they saw brown and black men and occasionally, but always at a distance, veiled women. They passed through the Njörva Sound, and journeyed to the limits of the Caliph's dominions, seeing many rich islands and fine cities, the names of which they did not know. They anchored in great harbours, where they were shut up in slave-houses until the time came for them to put out to sea again; and they rowed hard in pursuit of foreign ships till their hearts seemed to be about to burst, and strength to watch raged on the grappling above them.

They felt neither grief nor hope, and cried to no gods, for they had work enough to do minding their oars and keeping a watchful eye open for the man with the whip who supervised their rowing. They hated him with a fierce intensity when he flicked them with his whip, and even more when they were rowing their hearts out and he strode among them with big lumps of bread soaked in wine, which he stuffed into their mouths, for then they knew that they would have to row without rest for as long as their strength sustained them. They could not understand what he said, but they soon learned to know from the tone of his voice how many lashes he was preparing to administer as a reward for negligence and their only comfort was to hope that he would have a hard end, with his windpipe slit or his back flayed until his bones could be seen through the blood.

In his old age, Orm used to say that this period in his life was lengthy to endure, but brief to tell of, for one day resembled another, so that, in a sense, it was as though time was standing still for them. But there were signs to remind him that time was, in fact, passing; and one of these was his beard. When he first became a slave, he was the only one among them so young as to be beardless; but before long, his beard began to grow, becoming redder even than his hair, and in time it grew so long that it swept the handle of his oar as he bowed himself over his stroke. Longer than that it could not grow, for the sweep of his oar curtailed its length; and of all the methods of trimming one's beard, he would say, that was the last that he would choose.

Palais de Justice—A Short Story

Mark Helprin

In a lesser chamber of Suffolk County Courthouse on a day in early August 1965—the hottest day of the year—a Boston judge slammed down his heavy gavel, and its pistol-like report threw the room into disarray. Within a few minutes, everyone had gone—judge, court reporters, blue-shirted police, and a Portuguese family dressed as if for a wedding to witness the trial of their son. The door was shut. Wood and marble remained at attention in dead silence. For quite a while the room must have been doing whatever rooms do when they are completely empty. Perhaps air currents were stabilizing, coming to a halt, or spiders were beginning to crawl about, up high in the woodwork. The silence was beginning to set when the door opened and the defense attorney re-entered to retrieve some papers. He went to his seat, sat down, and ran his hands over the smooth tabletop—no papers. He glanced at the chairs, and then bent to see under the table—no papers. He touched his nose and looked perplexed. "I know I left them here," he said to the empty courtroom. "I thought I left them here. Memory must be going, oh well."

But his memory was excellent, as it had always been. He enjoyed pretending that in his early sixties he was losing his faculties, and he delighted in the puzzlement of where the papers had gone. The first was an opportunity for graceful abstention and serene neutrality, the second a problem designed to fill a former prosecutor's mind as he made his way out of the courthouse, passing through a great hall arched like a cathedral and mitered by hot white shafts of grainy light.

Years before, when he had had his first trial, one could not see the vault of the roof. It was too high and dark. But then they had put up a string of opaque lighting globes, which clung to the paneled arches like risen balloons and lit the curving ceiling.

One day a clerk had been playing a radio so loudly that it echoed through the building. The Mayor of Boston appeared unexpectedly and stood in the middle of the marble floor, emptiness and air rising hundreds of feet above him. "Turn that radio off!" he screamed, but the clerk could not hear him. Alone on the floor with a silent crowd staring from the perimeter, the Mayor turned angrily and scanned halls and galleries trying to find direction for his rage, but could not tell from where the sound came and so pivoted on the smooth stone and filled the chamber with his voice. "I am your mayor. Turn it off, do you hear me, damn you to hell. I am your mayor!" The radio was silenced and all that could be heard was the echo of the Mayor's voice. The defense attorney had looked up as if to see its last remnants rising through rafters of daylight, and had seen several birds, flushed from hidden nesting places, coursing to and fro near the ceiling, threading through the light rays. No one but the defense attorney saw them or the clerk, a homely, frightened woman who, when the Mayor had long gone, came out and carefully peered over a balcony to see where he had stood. It was then that the defense attorney saw the intricate motif of the roof—past the homely woman, the birds, and the light.

Now he went from chamber to chamber, and hall to hall, progressing through layers of rising temperature until he stood on the street in a daze. It was so hot that people moved as if in a baking desert, their expressions as blank and beaten as a Tuareg's mask and impassive eyes. The stonework radiated heat. A view of Charlestown—mountains and forests of red brick, and gray shark-colored warships drawn up row upon row at the Navy Yard—danced in bright waves of air like a mirage. Across the harbor, planes made languid approaches to whitened runways. They glided so slowly it looks as if they were hesitant to come down. Despite the heat there was little haze, even near the sea. A Plains August had grasped New England, and Boston was quiet.

Good, thought the defense attorney, *there won't be a single soul on the river. I'll have it all to myself, and it'll be as smooth as glass.* He had been a great oarsman. Soon it would be half a century of near-silent speed up and down the Charles in thin light racing shells, always alone. The fewer people on the river, the better. He often saw wonderful sights along the banks, even after the new roads and bridges had been built. Somehow, pieces of the countryside held out and the idea of the place stayed much the same, though in form it was a far cry from the hot meadows, dirt roads, and wooden fences he had gazed upon in his best and fastest years. But just days before, he had seen a mother and her infant son sitting on the weir, looking out at the water and at him as he passed. The child was so beautiful as the woman held up his head and pointed his puzzled stare out over river and fields, that the defense attorney had shaken in his boat—having been filled with love for them. Then there were the ducks, who slept standing with heads tucked under their wings. Over fifty years he had learned to imitate them precisely, and often woke them as he passed, oars dipping quietly and powerfully to speed him by. Invariably, they looked up to search for another duck.

"You shouldn't be going out today, Professor," said Pete, who was in charge of the boathouse.

"No one's out. It's too hot."

He was a stocky Dubliner with a dialect strong enough to make plants green. When he carried one end of the narrow craft down the sloping dock to the river he seemed to the defense attorney to resemble the compact engines which push and pull ships in the Panama Canal. Usually the oarsman holding the stern was hardly as graceful or deliberative as Pete, but struggled to avoid getting splinters in his bare feet.

"I haven't seen one boat all of today." Pete looked at him, waiting for him to give up and go home. The defense attorney knew that Pete wanted to call the Department of Athletics and have the boathouse closed at two so he could go to tend his garden. "Really, not one boat. You could get heat stroke you know. I saw it in North Africa during the War—terrible thing, terrible thing. Like putting salt on a leech."

The defense attorney was about to give in, when someone else walked up to the log book and signed so purposefully that Pete changed his strategy, saying to both of them, "If I were you now, I wouldn't stay out too long, not in this weather."

They went as they did each day to get S-40, the best of the old boats. It was the last boat Pat Shea had built for Harvard before he was killed overseas. Though already a full professor in the Law School and over draft age, the defense attorney had volunteered, and did not see his wife or his children for three solid years. When he returned—and those were glorious days when his children were young and suddenly talking, and his wife more beautiful than she had ever been—he went down to the boathouse and there was S-40, gleaming from disuse. Pat Shea was dead in the Pacific, but his boat was as ready as a Thoroughbred in the paddock. For twenty years the defense attorney had rowed loyally in S-40, preferring it to the new boats of unpronounceably named resins—computer designed, from wind tunnels, with riggers lighter than air and self-lubricating ball bearings on the sliding seat, where S-40 had the same brass wheels Pat Shea had used when he had begun building boats in 1919. S-40 had seasoned into a dark blood color, and the defense attorney knew its every whim.

As they carried it from the shadows into blinding light, the defense attorney noticed the other sculler. He could not have been much over twenty, but was so large that he made the two older men feel diminutive. He was lean, muscled, and thick at the neck and shoulders. His face was pitted beneath a dark tan, and his hair long and tied up on his head in an Iroquois topknot. He looked like a Spartan with hair coiled before battle, and was ugly and savage in his stance. Nevertheless, the defense attorney, fond of his students and of his son who had just passed that age, smiled as he passed. He received as recompense a sneer of contempt, and he heard the words "old man" spoken with astonishing hatred.

"Who the hell is that?" asked the defense attorney of Pete as they set S-40 down on the lakelike water.

"I don't know. I never seen him before, and I don't like the looks of him. He brought his own boat, too, one of those new ones. He wants me to help him bring it down. Of course I'll have to. I'll take me time, and you can get a good head start so's you'll be along up river," said Pete, knowing that informal races were common, and that if two boats pulled up even it nearly always became a contest. He wanted to spare the defense attorney the humiliation of being beaten by the unpleasant young man who had meanwhile disappeared into the darkness of the boathouse.

As S-40 pulled out and made slowly for the Anderson Bridge, the young man, whom the defense attorney had already christened "the barbarian," walked down the ramp, with his boat across his shoulders. Even from 100 feet out the defense attorney heard Pete say, "You didn't have to do that. I would have helped you." *No matter*, thought the defense attorney, *by the time he gets it in the water, places his oars, and fine tunes all his allow locks and stretchers, I'll be at the Eliot Bridge and in open water with a nice distance between us.* He had no desire to race, because he knew that although he could not beat a young athlete in a boat half as light as S-40, he would try his best to do so. On such a hot day, racing was out of the question. In fact, he resolved to let the young man pass should he be good enough to catch up. For it was better to be humiliated and alive than dead at the finish line. *He cannot possibly humiliate me anyway*, he thought. A young man in a new-style boat will obviously do better than a man three times his age in a wood shell. *But*, he thought, *this boat and I know the river. I have a good lead. I can pace myself as I watch him, and what I do not have in strength I may very well possess in concentration and skill.*

And so he started at a good pace, sweeping across glass-faced waters in the large swelling of the stream just north of the Anderson Bridge, gauging his speed expertly from the passage of round turbulent spots where the oars had been, and sensing on the periphery of vision the metered transit of tall ranks of sycamores on the Cambridge side. He was the only man on the river, which was glossy and green with a thick tide of beadlike algae. Always driven to the river by great heat, dogs loped along with the gait of trained horses, splashing up a wave as they ran free in the shallows. S-40 had taut blue canvas decking, and oars of lacquered yellow wood with black and white blades. The riggers were silver-colored, an alloy modification, and the only thing modern about the boat. The defense attorney was lean and tanned, with short white hair. His face was kind and quiet, and though small in stature, he was very strong, and looked impressive in his starched white rowing shorts. The blue decking shone against the green water as in a filtered photograph of a sailing regatta.

It seemed to him that the lonely condition upon the river was a true condition. Though he had a lot of love in his life, he knew from innumerable losses and separations that one stands alone or not at all. And yet, he had sought the love of women and the friendship of men as if he were a dog rasping through the bushes in search of birds or game. Women were for him so lovely and central to all he found important that their absence, as in the war, was the stiffest sentence he could imagine, and he pictured hell as being completely without them—although from experience he knew that they must have filled a wing or two there to the brim. Often, as he rowed, he slackened to think of the grace and beauty of girls and women he had known or loved. He remembered how sometime in the middle Twenties, when he was courting his wife, he had passed a great bed of water lilies in the wide bay before Watertown. He grasped one for her as he glided by, and put it in the front of the boat. But when he reached the dock the flower had wilted and died. The next day he stopped his light craft and pulled deep down on a long supple stem. Then he tied it to the riggers and rowed back with the lily dangling in the water so that he was able to preserve it, a justly appreciated rare flower. But people did not "court" anymore.

He resumed his pace, even though, without straining, he was as dripping wet as if he had been in a sauna for five minutes. Rounding the bend before the Eliot Bridge, he saw the young man in his new-style boat, making excellent speed toward him. He had intended to go beyond the Eliot, Arsenal, Street, and North Beacon bridges to the bay where the lilies still grew, where it was easy to turn (although he could turn in place) and then to come back. All told, it was a course of six miles. It would not pay to go fast over that distance in such killing heat. If they were to race, the finish would have to be the last bridge out. By the time he passed under the Eliot Bridge, with two more bridges to go, the young man had closed to within a few hundred yards. His resolutions fell away as if they were light November ice easy to break with oars and prow. Almost automatically, he quickened his pace to that of the young man, who, after a furious initial sprint, had been forced to slow somewhat and retrieve his breath. The defense attorney knew that once he had it he would again pour on speed in the excessive way youth allowed, and so the defense attorney husbanded his strength, going as fast as his opponent but with the greatest possible economy. This he achieved by relaxing, saying to himself, "Easy. Easy. The fight is yet to come. Easy now, easy."

Though the young athlete was a hundred yards down-river the defense attorney could see dark lines of sweat in his knotted hair, and could hear heavy breathing. "I'm a fool," he said, "for racing in this heat. It's over 100 degrees. I have nothing to prove. I'll let him pass, and I'll let him sneer. I don't care. My wisdom is far more powerful than his muscular energy." And yet, his limbs automatically kept up the pace, draining him of water, causing salt to burn his eyes. He simply could not stop.

He remembered Cavafy's *Waiting for the Barbarians*, which he—in a clearly Western way—had originally assumed to be a lament. Upon reading it he discovered that the poet shared in the confusion, for it was indeed a lament, that the barbarians were not still on their way. But for the defense attorney this was unthinkable, for he dearly loved the West and had never thought that to constitute itself it required the expectation of a golden horde. And he believed that if one man were to remain strong and upholding, if just one man were not to wilt, then the light he saw and loved could never be destroyed, despite the barbarism of the war, of soulless materialism, of the self-righteous students who thought to remake this intricate and marvelously fashioned world with one blink of an untutored eye. If a man can be said to grit his teeth over a span of years, then the defense attorney had done just this, knowing that it would both pass and come again, as had the First War, and the Second, in which he had learned the great lessons of his life, in which he had been broken and battered repeatedly—only to rise up again.

He did not want to concede the minor victory of a river race on a hot day in August, not even that, not even such a small thing as that to yet another wave of ignorance and violence. He started with rage in remembering the sneer. Contempt meant an attack against perceived weakness, and did not weakness merit compassion? If this barbarian had thought him weak, he was up against the gates of a city he did not know, a stone-built city of towers and citadels. The defense attorney increased the rapidity of his stroke to meet his opponent's ominously growing speed.

The young man was gaining, but by very small increments. Were the defense attorney to have kept up his pace he would have reached the North Beacon Street Bridge first, even if only by a few feet. But two things were wrong. First, such a close margin afforded no recourse in a final sprint. Because of the unpredictability of the young man's capacities, the defense attorney was forced to build an early lead, which would as well demoralize his rival. Second, not even halfway to the finish, he was beginning to go under. Already breathing extremely hard, he could feel his heart in his chest as if it were a fist pounding on a door.

He was lucky, because he knew the river so well that he had no need of turning to see where he was headed. So precise had the fifty years rendered his navigational sense that he did not even look when he approached bridges, and shot through the arches at full speed always right in the center. However, the young man had to turn for guidance every minute or so to make sure he was not straying from a straight course—which would have meant defeat. That he had to turn was another advantage for the defense attorney, for the young man not only broke his rhythm and sometimes lost his stroke or made a weak stroke when doing so, but he was also forced to observe his adversary still in the lead. If the defense attorney saw the leather thong in the young man's haircomb begin to dip, and saw the muscles in his back uplift a bit, making a slightly different shadow, he knew he was about to turn. This caused the defense attorney to assume an expression of ease and relaxation, as if he were not even racing, and to make sure that his strokes were deep, perfect, and classically executed. He had been in many contests, both ahead and behind.

Though it was a full-blooded race, he realized that he was going no more than half the sustained speed of which he normally was capable. Like a cargo of stone, the heat dragged all movement into viscous slow motion. Time was caught in its own runners, and its elements repeated. Two dogs at the riverside were fighting over a dead carp lapping in the green water.

He saw them clash at the neck. Later, when he looked back, he saw the same scene again. Perhaps because of the blood and the heat and the mist in front of his eyes, the salt-stung world seemed to unpiece in complex dissolution. There was a pattern which the darkness and the immediacy of the race made him unable to decipher. Intensified summer colors drifted one into the other without regard to form, and the laziness was shattered only when a bright white gull, sliding down the air, passed before his sight in a heartening straight line.

Though he felt almost ready to die and thought that he might, the defense attorney decided to implement his final strategy. About a mile was left. They were nearing the Arsenal Street Bridge. Here the river's high walls and banks stopped the wind, and the waters were always smooth. With no breeze whatsoever, it was all the hotter. In this quiet stretch races were won or lost. A completely tranquil surface allowed a burst of energy after the slight rest it provided. Usually a racer determined to begin his build-up just at the bridge. Two boats could not clear the northern arch simultaneously. Thus the rear boat had no hope of passing and usually resolved upon commencement of its grand effort after the natural delineation of the bridge. Knowing it could not be passed, the lead boat rested to get strength before the final stretch. But the defense attorney knew that his position was in great danger. A few hundred yards from the bridge, he was only two or three boat lengths ahead. He could see the young man, glistening and red, breathing as if struggling for life. But his deep breathing had not the patina of weakness the defense attorney sensed in his own. He was certain to maintain his lead to the bridge, though, and beyond it for perhaps a quarter of a mile. But he knew that then the superior strength of the younger man would finally put the lighter boat ahead. If it was to be a contest of endurance, steady and torturesome as it had been, he knew he would not win.

But he had an idea. He would try to demoralize the young man. He would begin his sprint even before the Arsenal Street Bridge, with the benefit of the smooth water and the lead-in of the arch. What he did was to mark out in his mind a closer finish which he made his goal—knowing that there he would have to stop, a good half mile before the last bridge. But with luck the shocking lead so far in advance of all expectations would convince the struggling young man to surrender to his own exhaustion. An experienced man would guess the stratagem. A younger man might, and might not. If he did, he would maintain an even pace and eventually pass the defense attorney dead in the water a good distance before the finish line.

A hundred yards before the Arsenal Street Bridge, the defense attorney began his massive strokes. One after another, they were in clear defiance of the heat and his age. He began to increase his lead. When he passed through the dark shadow of the bridge, he was already five boat lengths ahead. He heard the echo of his heart from the cool concrete, for it was a hollow chamber. Back in bright light, clubbed by the sun, he went even faster. The young man had to turn every few seconds to guide himself through the arch. When he did so he lost much time in weak strokes, adjustments to course, and breaking rhythm. But far more important was what he saw ahead. The old man had begun a powerful sprint, as if up to that point he had only been warming up.

Three-quarters of a mile before the finish, the defense attorney was going full blast. From a distance he looked composed and unruffled, because all his strength was perfectly channeled. Because of this the young man's stroke shattered in panic. The defense attorney beat toward his secret finish, breathing as though he were a woman lost deep in love. The breaths were loud and desperate, abandoned, and raw, as if of birth or a struggle not to die. He was ten boat lengths ahead, and nearing his finish.

He had not time to think of what he had endured in his life, of the loss which had battered him, and beaten him, and reduced him at times to nothing but a shadow of a man. He did not think of the men he had seen killed in war, whose screams were loud enough to echo in his dreams decades after. He did not think of the strength it had taken to love when not loved, to raise faltering children in the world, to see his parents and his friends die and fall away. He did not think of the things he had seen as the century moved on, nor of how he had risen each time to survive in the palace of the world by a good and just fight, by luck, by means he sometimes did not understand. He simply beat the water with his long oars, and propelled himself ahead. One more stroke, he said, and another, and another. He was almost at his end.

He looked back, and a beautiful sight came to his eyes. The young man was bent over and gliding. His oars no longer moved but only brushed the top of the water. Then he began to work his port oar and turn around, for he had given up. He vanished through the bridge.

The defense attorney was alone on the river, in a thickly wooded green stretch full of bent willows. It was so hot that for a moment he forgot exactly who he was or where he was. He rowed slowly to the last bridge. There he rested in the cool shadow of a great and peaceful arch.

The First Meeting of the Crew

Ron Irwin

THIS EARLY CHAPTER FROM RON IRWIN'S NOVEL *FLAT WATER TUESDAY* IS the main character's introduction to elite boarding school crew. It is fall in New England, and Robert "Rob" Carrey, from a working-class background, has been accepted to the prestigious Fenton School on a rowing scholarship. Carrey, a good sculler, is expected to become a member of the school's coxed four, more commonly known as the God Four. The crew's most important race is the annual Tuesday race in April against their archrival boarding school, Warwick. There is great pressure on the God Four, as Warwick has won the race for the last five years.

The boathouse looked like a barn with an elongated top floor. It stood back from the river and was built to appear intimidating. The heavy outside sliding doors opened to the boats and the oars and you walked by them to get to another set of sliding doors that led to the tanks—two stagnant troughs of water with sliding seats and outriggers next to them. Here was where a rower's form was hammered into him, where unforgiving mirrors reflected back every weakness in a place that smelt of dankness and mold and waterborne rot. There was only one window, high up and filthy, that barely let in any light. The way up to the attic rooms was easy to miss, just a simple wooden door, like a cabinet door, that opened to a narrow set of stairs.

 I arrived early, before the others, to the first meeting of FSBC to get my bearings and not look like such a newcomer. At first I thought that the ergometers and weight machines would be up here but soon figured out they were in the basement, a sequestered hell I would come to know all too well. The top floor consisted of the meeting room, such as it was, and Channing's office. His real office. He had a carrel in the English department but this was where he existed. The office looked over the river, and it was the kind of functional room you'd find in an army HQ. A wooden desk. A longer table near the desk. A computer that Channing obviously never turned on, steel filing cabinets. Pictures of the English Henley, banners, posters of races gone by, and a crimson and white wooden oar suspended in the darkness—Channing's captain's oar from Harvard. The pictures and trophies in one of the cabinets looked neglected. He had one entire shelf just for tools. And above and around that, books. Hundreds of them. Huddled black paperbacks, waterlogged leather-bound classics, yellowing cloth-bounds, worn hardcovers. The wisdom of the ages moldering away.

I looked, but didn't dare step inside. Amazingly, his office door just hung open. I had come from a school where everything was locked against the students; offices were protected by steel-clad doors and teachers walked the hallways with keys around their necks. Feared and hated as he was, it probably never occurred to Channing that a student might be insane enough to invade his personal space.

Nothing in his office, aside from the books and that oar, said anything about Channing himself or indicated he had a life outside the school. There were plenty of rumors. One was that he had been a criminal lawyer before Fenton and had quit for any of a thousand reasons: a client had committed suicide, he had insulted his boss, he'd been sued, he'd been disbarred. He lived off campus in an old white farmhouse—that was a fact—and his wife from the scumbag lawyer days was long gone. That was another fact. He had inhabited that office for thirty years and had either never thought to, or purposefully declined to, put anything personal in there.

The meeting room was all raw timber and rising damp and had the distinct feel of a fortress about it. It seemed intentionally stripped of any extravagance and was the kind of room that was always hot and close in the summer and bitterly cold in the winter. Uncomfortable by design, it had been built using the same architectural philosophy that went into constructing a monastery, or an interrogation room.

John Perry, Chris Wadsworth, Ruth Anderson, and Connor came stomping up the stairs for the inaugural meeting. No one said anything to me, but Connor lifted his chin in acknowledgement when he saw me. His mouth was still swollen from our fall, and his torn ear looked crusty and painful. I unconsciously touched my bruised ribs. They were followed by the returning JV four and about a dozen more kids who were going to try to make the team in the spring—sophomores and hopeful juniors from the club boats who only rowed at a recreational level, not competitively against other schools. Other students wanted to be here, but Channing was only interested in the contenders for the JV and Varsity boats. Mid-September and he was already calling us together for a sport that wouldn't start officially until March. For top-level rowers, there was no off-season. Crew was always a reality.

When Channing stalked in, rumpled, mistrustful, and radiating contempt, the room quieted down immediately. He looked like something that had stood up to the elements too long and was starting to fall apart. He was the best coach at Fenton. And the most despised. The way he looked at you, you knew he wasn't missing anything. He was tall, still limber and easy in his movements for his age, which must have been early sixties. He taught a vicious AP English class and was a master of the pop quiz and the brutal exam.

He slapped his briefcase down on the long desk at the front of the room and removed his sheaf of notes, thumbed them for a full minute while he gathered his thoughts and made us sit there scratching, coughing, trying not to look at one another. That torn bouquet of yellow legal sized papers had been stapled together enough times so the top corner looked like it had been chewed. He held these notes by his side while we waited and I could see lines and lines of his penciled handwriting. Even I could see he carried those notes just for show. They hadn't made the school big enough for him. And so we looked at Mr. Charles Channing and he looked back at us and beyond us to the world outside the boat-house and I'm not sure which he liked less.

Seated in a folding metal chair in front of Channing's desk, facing us, was Ruth Anderson, the coxswain of the God Four and the first girl to make the team ever, flouting eighty years of history. She was small, and her hands and wrists were those of an aristocrat; blue veined and bony. The bird-wing ridges of her collar bones were prominent and she had long, dark, feline hair. That year she weighed ninety pounds during the winter and dropped to eighty-four in the racing season. Connor sat next to her and the message was clear. Only the two of them had secure seats on the team. The rest of us would have to fight for them. Nothing was guaranteed.

Channing finally cleared his throat and set the notes down on the table. The gangling bodies in the room hunched forward, as if we were at the start of a session of prayer to a higher power. He began.

"I've called you together to remind you of some of the things you might consider before we gear up for the spring term. It is right that I let the students from the club boats understand how we work here. Some of you may think this meeting is premature. I assure you, it is not."

No other teacher talked like Channing. It took me weeks to realize that he was not being ironic, that this was really the way he spoke. His was the dialect of a lost aristocracy.

He sighed, glanced at Connor and Ruth, rested his eyes on me. "Understand that the first boat at Fenton is a four man shell with cox. As is the second boat. There are no eights, as there are in the clubs." The kids from the club boats—the lower orders—looked on without reaction. They knew this. So did the returners. I wondered if this homily was for my benefit.

"This means there are only eight places in the Fenton School Boat Club. One club rower will be named our spare but will not row with us. So if you do want to make this team, you will have to compete against one another."

I raised my hand as he said this and he smiled. "We should also get to know Mr. Robert Carrey. Whom I had almost forgotten. Please stand, Mr. Carrey. Let's see you."

I stood up and he pulled his spectacles from his jacket pocket. "Mr. Carrey is one of this year's PG recruits and hails from Niccalsetti, New

York. He is a singles sculler, a very successful one. We believe this has prepared him well for rowing in a four."

"That's just it, Coach. It has not," I said.

Channing paused and the room tensed. "Excuse me, Carrey?"

"Rowing in a single is not good preparation for rowing in a four, Mr. Channing. I don't know anything about rowing in a four."

Channing straightened combatively. "Is that so, Mr. Carrey? Could this be an oversight, do you suppose? Let us see. In a single, a sculler—an oarsman—uses two oars. But in a four, the rower uses one large oar. This is the essential difference. Yes, I can see how this might be initially difficult for you to adjust to."

"I didn't mean—"

"No, no, please, this is important. In a four, the coxswain steers from the stern and the oarsmen each have one oar. We also do not row pairs by the way. Students flip pairs, you see, and drown, which is always irritating. Fours are more stable."

"Nobody told me this before and I—"

"Nobody *told* you that we only row fours at Fenton? Even after you were *accepted*?" And then I knew for sure he had prepared this. That Connor had told him about our fight and that Channing meant to finish the argument once and for all. I'd walked right into it.

"Carrey, did you not carefully consult the admission package that was sent to you *to learn what kind of boats were rowed here at Fenton*? Or call the school to enquire? Or examine the school catalogue, which we print at great expense and send out to anyone who asks for it? I am quite sure there are only pictures of fours in that catalogue. We do mention this little affectation of ours. Very clearly."

I waited. I could feel the blood rushing to my head and my hands and willed myself to calm down, to not blow up and have a tantrum. He sensed it and prepared himself.

"Coach, the letter that was sent to me said that I was accepted because of my wins in the single. That was very clear. I could even bring my own boat, it said."

"Well, I am glad we can clarify this for you, Carrey. You are *permitted* to row your single from time to time on my river, when I say so, but my top team is a *four*. It is referred to as the varsity four and some may call it the God Four but there is *only* the four. We have a JV four. We have a club four, yes, and an armada of eights for the clubs as well. But the varsity four is the *only* team that we offer up for competition at Fenton at the varsity level. Is this clear, now? Is there anything I have left out?"

"I won't row in a four." This came out almost as a whisper, because I was trying to keep my voice down.

Channing put a hand to his ear. "Excuse me?"

"I don't row in fours, Coach. I don't row with other people. I'm a single sculler."

"Carrey, I believe you mean you haven't *yet* rowed in a four. Do not be overly concerned. You can easily learn. We have faith in you. We believe you can make the transition from two oars to one and row as part of a crew. Connor Payne, for instance, is a fine single sculler, too, but he is also the stroke seat in the four. I assure you, this is not difficult. Sculling will be a boon."

"Coach, the problem is not me being *able* to do it. I don't *want* to learn to row with three kids I don't know. No offense, but that's not—"

"None taken, Carrey, none taken. Do you think you are offending *us*? You are only offending yourself. We are trying to clarify things for you."

"I'd like to race in the single."

He slammed his hand down on the table. "*In what race*, Carrey? Against *whom*? What boarding school will you race against? Shall we have a special race just for you?"

"I'm sorry, Mr. Channing, but I just don't want to row in the four."

"Then you are welcome to leave." Channing pointed at the narrow staircase. "There's the door, Carrey. Go. You can go right now. But I warn you if you leave this room, you will not be coming back." He said this mildly but he kept his eyes on me. I found myself scooping up my bag to leave and then forced myself to stop. Because Channing meant it. I knew it and everyone else in the room knew it, too.

"If you want to row with us, Carrey, you will have to learn to row in the four. This could be a good change for you. A welcome change. Many single scullers row in the team boats. It is expected. It is not difficult. So think carefully about your next move and *do not sit down*." He turned to the rest of the crew. "The God Four will again be facing Warwick this year."

He took a breath and visibly composed himself. Our exchange had rattled him. He began again. "Every year, as most of you know, we formally challenge Warwick School to a race. And for the last five years, to our perpetual shame, Fenton has failed to win." He said this in the same way he might announce that we had all been diagnosed with terminal cancer.

"For the benefit of those present who were . . . elsewhere . . . last year our disgrace took place at Warwick. This year we race at home and we will not, I repeat *not*, be humiliated on our own river again." Channing waited while every rower shifted in his seat. "As always, we face Warwick on the third Tuesday in April. You should know that the FSBC alumni have made it clear that they hope to see us win." Channing paused. "But they are not us. They are not here. History does not wait for the verdict upon them. All of them wish they had one more crack at victory on the water against that hated place Warwick. This chance is reserved for we few." Another pause. He was quite the showman. "Listen."

We listened. Outside, you could hear the shouts and whistles on the fields around us, pulses of noise. "The armorers, accomplishing the knights, with busy hammers closing rivets up, give dreadful note of preparation."

I had no idea what Channing was talking about, but I had the sense of it.

"And preparation for rowing is indeed dreadful. Mr. Perry, let's start with you."

John Perry was riding his chair backwards. He sat like a chained beast, his blue letter jacket buttoned precariously over his bulk. He looked up at Channing with tiny blinking eyes.

"You *are* John Perry, yes?"

Perry looked at all of us for support and we looked back at him. Connor interlaced his fingers behind his head and examined Perry while Ruth looked politely away, at some spot on the floor to my left.

"Coach?" Perry was flustered. "I mean . . . you know who I am, Mr. Channing—"

"John Perry from the losing first boat of last year? This is you?"

Perry tried to smile. "Yeah, okay, it's me—"

"I ask because you look like his fatter, slower twin. Perry, you are too heavy for my boat. Your task is to lose weight and become stronger and gain endurance. This does not mean eating pizzas at the Fenton Pizza Garden or grappling with idiots from Taft on the football field."

Wadsworth snickered under his baseball cap. Seated in a window seat, he was framed by the late afternoon light, his legs dangling into space. Channing turned on him immediately. "Chris Wadsworth. Another survivor from the disastrous boat of last year. Have you been thinking how you will make amends? You have work to do."

He turned to the board and wrote the number 7 in the middle. "You have seven months, gentlemen—and lady—until the Tuesday race against Warwick School. Less than that until the season starts." He took off his glasses. "I cannot call formal practices until the spring, but Mr. Payne and Ms. Anderson will be keeping track of who is working. This means that while I cannot *force* you to begin training now, I can *ask* that you start thinking about the fact that no rower's position here is secure and I can *urge* you to make every preparation necessary for what lies ahead. You will all be tested and some of you shall be found wanting."

He turned the full force of his gaze on me and I knew he was getting ready for his final delivery. "Carrey, you have never seen what awaits you this spring. You need to understand that right now you are just . . . the raw material. You are merely breathing potential. The tabula rasa where Fenton's history will be written. Did you seriously think we would tremble before your abilities? *You*, a PG mercenary who is already a disciplinary case two weeks into the start of the school year because—"

"Come on. That was not my fault, I—"

"We do not care to give hearing to your explanations or alibis, Carrey. We care about getting ready for a race that will define us. Will define you. We care about crossing the finish line ahead of the other boat. We care about winning. This is all we care about. And we cannot win if you are being disciplined, or if you have been expelled. So, Carrey, I ask that you be not afraid of greatness: some are born great, some achieve greatness and some have greatness thrust upon them. Don't query the form in which greatness comes. Am I clear?"

"Yeah."

"Yeah? Do you mean 'yea'? As in, 'Yea, though I walk through the valley of the shadow of death, I will fear no evil: for thou art with me; thy rod and thy staff they comfort me?'"

"Yes."

"No, Carrey. No. I offer none of you comfort. I offer you no protection from evil. This you will fashion yourself or be beaten. Opportunities for glory are flying around all of you like bullets. And some of you, Carrey, are crawling upon the ground with helmets on. Have you made your decision? We all await."

My head was spinning with rage. *Do it*, I thought. *Leave this crap. Walk out the door.*

I grit my teeth. Screw this for a laugh, as Wendy would say. Walk out. Walk out and go . . . where?

Home?

I took a breath.

"I'll do it." And felt like I was betraying everything I'd come from and suffered through to stand there. A Judas for a bunch of prepsters.

"You will do what, exactly?"

"Try out for the four."

"And suffer the slings and arrows of outrageous fortune with the rest of us?"

"Whatever."

Triumphant, Channing stared at the others, all of them looking away from me as I stood there, defeated. "Seven months. Connor will be ensuring that you begin your preparations. Dismissed."

You never saw a room full of kids clear out so fast, all shoulders and gangly arms squeezing through the door and pounding down the stairs. Connor and Ruth conferred briefly then got up and left. I put my bag over my shoulder and started to follow.

Channing caught me at the door. "Mr. Carrey. A word."

Connor glanced back at me and grinned, shut the door behind him.

Channing put his glasses back on and it occurred to me they might also be a prop. He dug around in the mess of his briefcase and pulled out a folder, licked his thumb, opened it. He read for about three seconds to himself, then looked at me. "It says, in summary, Robert Carrey. PG student. Championship-level rower with decent grades. Hails from the Niccalsetti Senior School, an institution of learning I was unfamiliar with until you appeared here. Your grades are surprisingly high—are you hiding a brain from us, young Carrey?"

It was my turn to look out at the trees sloping up the sides of Mt. Algo and just breathe. There were millions of those trees. I was barely holding it together. It was a farce—being my age and dealing with this crazy old man.

"Mr. Carrey, a recent missive from our mutual friend the dean informs me you have been caught destroying school property and fighting with one of our associates in the Rowing Cottage."

"I tried to tell you. Connor deserved it. If you start in on me you might as well go get him, too."

"Connor Payne might have deserved it but you have both been punished for it. Did you deserve to be punished?"

"He was asking for it."

"Connor Payne asked you to hit him and you complied?"

"I didn't hit him, I just wanted him to get out of the way."

"Be that as it may, you now owe the school twenty hours of work, and you will be working for me. Off campus. I happen to need a painter. Can you paint?"

"I can paint."

"Are you sure? The school does offer free labor to its senior teachers but I have found in the past it is often not the most qualified or intelligent or diligent labor."

"I've painted stuff for my father since I was eight. If I finish early, will you let me out of whatever's left?"

"There will be plenty for you to do."

"All right. I get it."

"Meet me at my home at four next week on Monday, once you have recovered from your injuries sustained in your . . . altercation . . . with the captain of my first boat."

"What about Connor?"

"What about him?"

"Does he have to paint your house?"

"He does not. I am not his advisor. I have no idea what he will be doing to work off his hours. He may wind up raking leaves, or shoveling mulch, or cleaning bathrooms."

"I hope he gets the bathrooms."

"I shall keep you apprised."

"I'd hate to think you'd make me do a job like this because I'm a scholarship kid, Mr. Channing. Just to put me down."

"No, no, Carrey. Rest assured we'd have contempt for you even if you paid full fees."

"Does the school supply you with paints too?"

"No. But I do have the use of its sandpaper and tools."

"Free labor and equipment."

"Teaching is notorious for its many benefits. This is why I entered the profession."

"I thought you used to be a lawyer. Plenty of perks there."

"You are misinformed."

"They say you got fired."

"Fired or disbarred? I never can keep track."

"Is it true?"

"With all this free labor and sandpaper and such at my disposal, Carrey, why would I ever consider the law as a profession? Meet me at my house on Monday. 4 p.m. sharp. Wear your work clothes. Try not to assault anyone on your way."

"Where do you live?"

"Walk down River Road until you see a white house. Can you remember that?"

"I can."

"Good. Go. Learn."

Early Boating Recollections

Jerome K. Jerome

One of the funniest books on boating is Jerome K. Jerome's *Three Men in a Boat (To Say Nothing of the Dog)*, which was published as a book in 1889. Three friends, "J" (Jerome, the narrator), George (Wingrave), and "Harris" (Carl Hentechel) and J's dog, Montmorency (which is totally fictional) go on a two-week river adventure on the Thames from Kingston-upon-Thames to Oxford and back to Kingston. J reminisces about his and his friends' earlier boating experiences.

I devoted some three months to rafting, and, being then as proficient as there was any need to be at that branch of the art, I determined to go in for rowing proper, and joined one of the Lea boating clubs.

Being out in a boat on the River Lea, especially on Saturday afternoons, soon makes you smart at handling a craft, and spry at escaping being run down by roughs or swamped by barges; and it also affords plenty of opportunity for acquiring the most prompt and graceful method of lying down flat at the bottom of the boat so as to avoid being chucked out into the river by passing tow-lines.

But it does not give you style. It was not till I came to the Thames that I got style. My style of rowing is very much admired now. People say it is so quaint.

George never went near the water until he was sixteen. Then he and eight other gentlemen of about the same age went down in a body to Kew one Saturday, with the idea of hiring a boat there, and pulling to

Richmond and back; one of their number, a shock-headed youth, named Joskins, who had once or twice taken out a boat on the Serpentine, told them it was jolly fun, boating!

The tide was running out pretty rapidly when they reached the landing-stage, and there was a stiff breeze blowing across the river, but this did not trouble them at all, and they proceeded to select their boat.

There was an eight-oared racing outrigger drawn up on the stage; that was the one that took their fancy. They said they'd have that one, please. The boatman was away, and only his boy was in charge. The boy tried to damp their ardour for the outrigger, and showed them two or three very comfortable-looking boats of the family party build, but those would not do at all; the outrigger was the boat they thought they would look best in.

So the boy launched it, and they took off their coats and prepared to take their seats. The boy suggested that George, who, even in those days, was always the heavy man of any party, should be number four. George said he should be happy to be number four, and promptly stepped into bow's place, and sat down with his back to the stern. They got him into his proper position at last, and then the others followed.

A particularly nervous boy was appointed cox, and the steering principle explained to him by Joskins. Joskins himself took stroke. He told the others that it was simple enough; all they had to do was to follow him.

They said they were ready, and the boy on the landing stage took a boat-hook and shoved him off.

What then followed George is unable to describe in detail. He has a confused recollection of having, immediately on starting, received a violent blow in the small of the back from the butt-end of number five's scull, at the same time that his own seat seemed to disappear from under him by magic, and leave him sitting on the boards. He also noticed, as a curious circumstance, that number two was at the same instant lying on his back at the bottom of the boat, with his legs in the air, apparently in a fit.

They passed under Kew Bridge, broadside, at the rate of eight miles an hour. Joskins being the only one who was rowing. George, on recovering his seat, tried to help him, but, on dipping his oar into the water, it immediately, to his intense surprise, disappeared under the boat, and nearly took him with it.

And then "cox" threw both rudder lines over-board, and burst into tears.

How they got back George never knew, but it took them just forty minutes. A dense crowd watched the entertainment from Kew Bridge with much interest, and everybody shouted out to them different directions. Three times they managed to get the boat back through the arch, and three times they were carried under it again, and every time "cox" looked up and saw the bridge above him he broke out into renewed sobs.

George said he little thought that afternoon that he should ever come to really like boating.

Harris is more accustomed to sea rowing than to river work, and says that, as an exercise, he prefers it. I don't. I remember taking a small boat out at Eastbourne last summer; I used to do a good deal of sea rowing years ago, and I thought I should be all right; but I found I had forgotten the art entirely. When one scull was deep down underneath the water, the other would be flourishing wildly about in the air. To get a grip of the water with both at the same time I had to stand up. The Parade was crowded with nobility and gentry, and I had to pull past them in this ridiculous fashion. I landed half-way down the beach, and secured the services of an old boatman to take me back.

I like to watch an old boatman rowing, especially one who has been hired by the hour. There is something so beautifully calm and restful about his method. It is so free from that fretful haste, that vehement striving, that is every day becoming more and more the bane of nineteenth-century life. He is not for ever straining himself to pass all the other boats. If another boat overtakes him and passes him it does not annoy him; as a matter of fact, they all do overtake him and pass him—all those that are going his way. This would trouble and irritate some people; the sublime equanimity of the hired boatman under the ordeal affords us a beautiful lesson against ambition and uppishness.

Plain practical rowing of the get-the-boat-along order is not a very difficult art to acquire, but it takes a good deal of practice before a man feels comfortable, when rowing past girls. It is the "time" that worries a youngster. "It's jolly funny," he says, as for the twentieth time within five minutes he disentangles his sculls from yours: "I can get on all right when I'm by myself!"

To see two novices try to keep time with one another is very amusing. Bow finds it impossible to keep pace with stroke, because stroke rows in such an extraordinary fashion. Stroke is intensely indignant at this, and explains that what he has been endeavouring to do for the last ten minutes is to adapt his method to bow's limited capacity. Bow, in turn, then becomes insulted, and requests stroke not to trouble his head about him (bow), but to devote his mind to setting a sensible stroke.

"Or, shall *I* take stroke?" he adds, with the evident idea that that would at once put the whole matter right.

They splash along for another hundred yards with still moderate success, and then the whole secret of their trouble bursts upon stroke like a flash of inspiration.

"I tell you what it is: you've got my sculls," he cries, turning to bow; "pass yours over."

"Well, do you know, I've been wondering how it was I couldn't get on with these," answers bow, quite brightening up, and most willingly assisting in the exchange. "*Now* we shall be all right."

But they are not—not even then. Stroke has to stretch his arms nearly out of their sockets to reach his sculls now; while bow's pair, at each recovery, hit him a violent blow in the chest. So they change back again, and come to the conclusion that the man has given them the wrong set altogether; and over their mutual abuse of this man they become quite friendly and sympathetic.

One Hundred Years from Now

Robert Treharne Jones

IT IS THE YEAR 2107 AND ONCE AGAIN THE WORLD OF SPORT KEENLY anticipates the Boat Race, the annual clash of the titans between the athletes from China and the European Republic.

The Europeans are this year determined to break the stranglehold which the Chinese have held on this event—a dominance which has seen them record the longest winning streak since the race became a play-off between East and West. This year it's the turn of Germany to captain the team and try and reverse the Europeans' fortune—they've been fortunate to recruit the coaching services of Andreas Hacker, whose great-grandfather was an Olympic sculling champion in the last century.

The crews will shortly make the long trip to the Global Rowing Venue in India, where the combination of skilled, cheap labour and neutral territory proved a winning formula when the idea of the 2000 metre indoor venue was first mooted.

The complete lack of wind or current is agreed to provide the fairest of conditions possible, but following pressure from the health and safety lobby the depth of the lake has had to be further reduced. The inspectors originally regarded any water, no matter how shallow, as too hazardous for use but rigorous safety plans now include a lakebed mounted on a hydraulic platform which can be raised within minutes should any athlete or spectator suffer a mishap.

It's all a far cry from the old days of the 21st century when students from the Oxford and Cambridge city academies used to race each year over a four-mile course of the former River Thames in London, in the north-western corner of the European Republic.

But following the disqualification in 2035 a disgruntled athlete took his case to the Court of Human Rights who ruled that the event was both discriminatory and unfair. The crews at that time were selected from just two former universities, but the spring cyclones which became so regular following the two-degree rise in global temperature, coupled with the unpredictable stream across the Thames Lake, made the race a lottery, at least according to the judges.

In its place a selection tournament was held to determine who would contest the final, with the winners meeting similar crews from across Europe. But the standard never grew high enough to challenge the dominance of China, and so the Europeans clubbed together to form a crew capable of winning the race.

The history books provide a wealth of information on the race which has gone through so many changes since the first contest almost 293 years ago. Reading the tide used to be the key to success, but when the government of the time failed to heed warning signals and install a second Thames Barrier early last century the result was almost inevitable.

The Big Ben clock tower, Westminster Abbey, and the Tower of London were just some of the historical sites which were damaged irreversibly by flooding, and large areas of central parts of the city had to be rebuilt.

The Boat Race course had already lost much of the sentimental attraction which had proved such a draw for so many years. The destruction of one of the historic bridges by a terrorist attack was the last straw for the authorities, who did their best to make sure that the public stayed away from the riverside walkways on Race Day.

The race in India will be behind closed doors, as usual, because the costs of policing the event had proved too much. Rowing has never achieved global popularity as a sport, but interest in the Race has always been high, for reasons which the press has never really been able to fathom. And that's why almost one billion people have registered to receive the plasma-cast directly onto their contact lens, while some luddites will stay at home and watch the race on their computer screen.

And all across the world groups of men and women will gather together to celebrate and recall the day *they* won the Race!

The Boat Race Murder

David Winser

FOR THE THREE WEEKS BEFORE THE BOAT RACE THE OXFORD CREW generally lives at Ranelagh. This costs quite a penny, though it is conveniently close to the boat houses, but the question of money doesn't much worry the rowing authorities. The reason for this is that rowing, like every other Oxford sport, is more or less entirely supported by the gate receipts of the Rugger Club. So there we lived, in Edwardian comfort, and played croquet on the immaculate croquet lawns in the special croquet galoshes they give you and admired the birds and the ruins. They also fed us remarkably well considering we were in training.

All kinds of things occurred. There was one peacock, an amorous bird, which had a crush on the president, who rowed two. It used to come and display its tail in front of him and wait for him to submit. He never did, though.

But at Ranelagh, in spite of the way they'd sometimes put our names in the papers, we led a completely reporterless life, if that's the word I want. We didn't like the sort of stories that got told about rowing, such as the one which held that the crew that won after Barnes all died in the next five years (they're actually mostly alive still). So what with the O.U.B.C. and Ranelagh, and the fact that all the rowing reporters were friends of ours and of rowing, you didn't hear much. But, now, I think this story needs telling. In fact I more or less have to tell it.

You must try and picture a fizz night at Ranelagh. Someone, the coach or some other old Blue, had suddenly produced a dozen bottles of champagne and the coach has said that the crew's been going so well that it damn well deserves the filthy stuff. Actually, as he and everyone else knows, the main purpose of fizz is to stop the crew getting stale. But the tradition's always the same: it's supposed to be a reward for hard work. On this particular night the coach and an old Blue between them had produced *two* dozen bottles, because the second crew, the *Isis*, was coming over to dinner from Richmond.

Perhaps you can imagine the rest already. Solly Johnstone leaning back in his chair and laughing so hard at his own jokes that everyone else is laughing. Once I saw the president try to stop him making jokes because it was hurting him terribly to go on laughing so hard, but Solly didn't stop. And then, after dinner, two crews milling about in the big games room, the president taking cine-camera pictures with an enormous searchlight affair, the *Isis* crew taking on the varsity at billiards and ping-pong, Ronnie playing the piano and someone singing, the gramophone playing "The Donkey Serenade," Solly still making his incredible jokes, and somewhere over in the corner Melvin Green talking about rowing to Dr. Jeffreys, who coached the crew for the first part of training. The noise, and the general tohu-bohu, as Solly said, were both considerable.

I was watching this with a benevolent and yet slightly mildewed eye, because I had a feeling that I didn't deserve to be quite as cheerful as the rest of them. I was the cox, and furthermore I had had some very bad news. And again, when people like Jon Peters and Harry Whitteredge were slightly out of control, their fourteen stone made walking dangerous for coxes. No one who saw them that night would have credited them with the dignity, the dignity which only their genius stopped short of ponderousness, with which they sent that boat along in the race. They looked about as dignified as a bull on skates. But I happened to know that they were going to get as bad a shock as I had, nearly as bad a shock as Jim Matthews. Jim Matthews was the stroke, and he was going to find himself out of the crew.

Now this may not sound especially serious. Jim Matthews never had the reputation of Brocklebank, or Lawrie, or Sutcliffe, or Bryan Hodgson. You didn't read in the papers that he was going to pull off the race all by himself. And in a way he wasn't. But I heard a conversation once between Jon and Harry, who were wonderful oarsmen in their day, and it was rather significant.

"That fellow Matthews," Jon said, or words to this effect, "doesn't look much, and he doesn't do much, and doesn't talk much. Also I don't like him particularly. But I'm damned if there's anyone else who gives me time to come forward."

"The trouble with us, Jon," Harry said, "is that we need such a hell of a lot of time."

"Yes, but Jim gives it to us. If we have Jim we'll win this race."

"Don't you think we will anyway?"

"Not without Jim."

"I know. Nor do I."

I don't suppose it matters much to you who wins the Boat Race. But, for the purposes of this story, to get the record straight, you have to realize that ten or eleven men think of practically nothing else, for twelve whole weeks of training, than getting into the crew and seeing Oxford win. It becomes an obsession, a continual idea at the back of one's mind. Jon had a baby car, and once, when the crew was travelling by car from Oxford to Henley, Jon and Harry took an omen. If they could pass and *touch with their hands* every other O.U.B.C. car, Oxford would win the Boat Race. So, at considerable risk to their lives (and Oxford wouldn't have won without them), they touched every car. It was that sort of thing every day. And now the coaches were going to drop Jim Matthews, and those two wouldn't have time to come forward. When that happened all their dignity and poise over the stretcher went with the wind and they became more of a hindrance than a help, charging backwards and forwards in the boat. So, not for you or Oxford perhaps, but for those men who rowed in the crew, Jim's going was a real tragedy. Everyone knew that once they'd put in Davis, the dark-haired short-built *Isis* stroke, they'd leave him there. And Davis, who had plenty of guts and rowed as hard as he could, was hopelessly short in the water. There'd be hell to pay.

As for Jim, I knew a bit how he felt. I'd been in and out of the crew myself, because the *Isis* cox was at least as good as I was and knew the river even better. I wouldn't have been a bit surprised at anything Jim had done. But, as soon as the coaches told him, he'd frozen up completely. He hadn't said anything to them, which was stupid of him. They hadn't wanted to make the change; his own carelessness, which we knew was designed to save himself for one of those terrific races he'd row, looked sloppy. The coaches were worried, and the rowing correspondents started saying Oxford was stale. Hence the fizz, and hence Davis.

And all Jim said, in front of the coaches, he said to me. "Come on, Peter," he said. "I'm going to scare the Alacrity bird."

So Jon and I took him back to Ranelagh in my small M.G. and dropped him near the Alacrity bird's usual haunt; the bird was a crane which flew when you chased it. Then I let Jon drive the car into its garage. He wasn't allowed his car or his pipe during the last six weeks of training, and he needed a few luxuries like that. He joined me again before I reached the main house and we walked in together.

"Your petrol's low," he said. He didn't know about Jim yet but he sounded depressed, as if he knew something of the sort was afoot.

"There's enough for to-morrow, isn't there?"

"Provided the gauge is right, you've got half a gallon."

"That's all right then. Don't worry about the outing, Jon. Fizz night to-night."

Somewhere outside in the garden poor Jim Matthews was walking. I think the Alacrity bird was only an excuse because he wanted to be by himself. I was sorry for Jim. He'd have one more outing, with Davis rowing two, and then he'd go.

Next day, as might be expected after a fizz night, everything went wrong. To begin with I left it too late to get down to the river in time, thinking I'd take my car. I was the only one of the crew allowed to go into shops, because the others were thought to be especially susceptible to flu at that stage of training, so I used to take my car with me and go out shopping after the outing. But that morning I found there wasn't any petrol after all, so I had to run all the way across the polo grounds. They were just getting the boat out when I came, with a little boy doing my work. I pushed him aside without saying thanks, and behaved in a thoroughly bad manner. And then Davis, who was pardonably nervous, paddled on hard when I told him to touch her gently and the boat just missed drifting on to a buoy. Jim Matthews, like everyone else, sat there doing nothing, while I swore. The only incident of interest was that Jon and Harry swore back, being apparently by now aware that Davis was coming up to stroke. Davis rowed too fast. They got tired, and the coaches would accuse them of bucketing, and the boat would start stopping. I didn't blame them for swearing. I swore too.

The coach picked up his megaphone. "Ready, cox?" he asked. He didn't ask out of kindness.

I said yes.

"Paddle on down to the Eyot," he said. "Jim, make them work it up a bit once or twice."

Now the Eyot is a good fifteen minutes' paddle from the boat houses, and Jim, I suppose because it was his last time at stroke, took them along really hard. When he worked it up he worked it right up, nearly to forty, and kept it there for a full minute. Then, not so long afterwards, he did it again. And to end up with he put in a terrific burst of rowing. All the time he was steady, swinging them easily along. I could see the great green holes in the water Jon and Harry made. The boat travelled. I wondered whether the coaches were going to change their mind. No one will know that now, not even Jim. I noticed Davis's blade wasn't coming through very well at the end of the paddle, but I hadn't thought anything else about it. When we'd eased, he leant forward over his oar and stayed there, but again this wasn't very unusual; it had been about as hard work as a paddle like that can be. After a rest I gave the order to come half forward, because we were going to do a rowing start. But Davis didn't move.

"Half forward, two!" I said, still angrily.

Then apparently bow leant forward and touched him, because his body slumped forward, slid over the gunnel, and went into the water. I don't know when he died, but he was dead when the launch reached him. Luckily Dr. Jeffreys was on the spot, waiting to see what difference the change would make. Well, he'd seen.

If I'd ever doubted whether the coaches deserved their positions, and during training you doubt most things, I was all wrong. They took the launch on up to the London University boat house, where no one ever went during the mornings, got Solly's car round there, put Davis's body in it, brought it to Ranelagh without either the crew or the press or the secretary of Ranelagh seeing, and before lunch they'd got the whole crew together, and Dr. Joe Jeffreys was talking to them. One of the chief duties of the coaches was to keep the crew feeling happy.

"Well," said Joe, "you all saw what happened. Poor young Davis died of heart failure. I know how you feel, and you know how I feel. But there's one thing you ought to understand clearly. The reason he died was that his heart was dicky before he started. I never tested it, but I know it was, because your heart doesn't fail at the end of a paddle unless it *is* dicky. And I know all your hearts are damn sound, because I *did* test them. Just to make sure I'm going to test them again to-day."

And he did. And he was quite right; there was nothing wrong with any of the toughs.

But in the middle, when Jon had just gone out and Solly, Joe and I were alone in the room, Joe suddenly stopped.

"I *did* test Davis's heart," he said.

Well, Solly made a rather typical crack about the value of tests, but apparently this was a pretty sound test. Anyway we went and rang up the police.

"That kid was murdered," said Joe. I suppose Solly thought he was just humouring him. Another of the duties of coaches is to keep the other coaches feeling happy. Those last weeks of training are the devil all round.

It was rather typical of the way the Boat Race gets a grip on people that the crew went out that afternoon. Solly insisted he was only doing it to allay any suspicion about Davis in the minds of the press. But anyway the boat went out, and, with Jim stroking beautifully, they rowed the best two minutes they'd ever done, clearing their wash by yards at thirty-six. When Jim was there, that was as good a crew as any.

The police were around when we got back, but that didn't bother us much. You see, we all knew each other pretty well; you don't have murderers rowing with you. Murderers are professionals, probably, as they've worked with their hands. Anyway, you don't.

Well, they found out what had killed Davis. We'll call it diphenyl tyrosine; Jim and I knew what its real name was because we happened to be medical students. Joe Jeffreys knew it too, of course. The odd thing about it is that it's a component of quite a common patent medicine. That's all right, because it only quickens up your heart for a day or so; but when you start with a quickened heart and then row hard in a Boat Race crew your heart gets very quick indeed, so quick that it doesn't really function adequately. It starts to jump about a bit, and then it starts to fibrillate, to quiver all over in a rather a useless way. Then, if it's the ventricle fibrillating, you die. Davis had plenty of guts; he went on just as long as his heart did. He had the guts of a good stroke, but he wasn't Jim Matthews. I was sorry for Davis, but, for the crew's sake, I was glad Jim was safe. The funny thing was that whoever killed Davis must have known that he'd got guts.

Now they started in on a long investigation of the crew's movements during the day before. It had to be the day before because they'd got a very interesting bit of evidence. A man had come into a chemist's in Putney and he'd asked for this patent medicine, as no doubt men did every day. He'd worn a mackintosh and an old hat.

But underneath the mackintosh the chemist had noticed he was wearing those queer white blanket trousers the crew wear out of the boat.

The policeman who was doing the detective work then had two very frustrating conversations which he described to us with fair relish.

He'd asked the chemist if the purchaser in the white trousers had been a big man. The chemist said Yes.

"Bigger than me?"

'Well, maybe.'

"Sure he wasn't fairly small?"

The chemist considered. "Well," he said, "you might call him small."

"Could you draw a line against the wall showing just his height?"

The chemist stepped forward confidently, stopped, tried to think, and then said:—

"No. Not exactly, somehow."

"What colour was his hair then?"

"Oh," said the chemist, "if I noticed the colour of all my customers' hair I'd be in a pretty state." He became a little irritable. "All I know is," he said, "he had white trousers on."

The other conversation was the sequel to the discovery that Jon and I brought my car back when the rest of the crew came in. They wanted to find if anyone went *out* of Ranelagh in a car like mine.

The detective people went to the porters at the two gates. "Did you see a small black sports car go out of the grounds?" they asked. "After 5.30."

Those were the days when Hornets and M.G.'s were as common as sneezing. One porter said he'd seen four, colour unnoticed; the other had seen seven, three of them black or dark-brown.

"Well," said the fellows, "did you see any coming back again?"

"Those seven," said the porter who wasn't colour-blind, "was going both ways." He wasn't shaken from this peculiar belief. In short they didn't get any change out of porters or chemists. Someone in the crew *did* buy this patent medicine and someone *could* have gone out in my car. They never found the bottle, of course. There were hundreds of ways to get rid of it—you might put it down the lavatory and pull the plug, for instance. It was one of those small bottles. You'll be guessing its name in a minute but, luckily, you'll guess wrong.

Then, also in front of me, someone realized that if the chemist had been at all an efficient man he'd have made the fellow in the mackintosh sign for the medicine, simply because, technically, it was poison if you had a whole bottleful. So one of them went off to find out if the chemist was as efficient as all that, and the other started to find out where we'd all been.

Now the curious thing about all this investigation was that it had taken a very short time. It was still only the day of the murder. As soon as they knew it was murder they'd started thinking about heart drugs, the sort you might mix up in someone's milk as they went to bed, or drop in a glass of fizz; so they thought of diphenyl tyrosine and, sure enough, there it was when they did an autopsy on Davis. No one knew when he'd taken it; but they'd decided it must have been in his fizz. Personally the mechanism of this seems pretty difficult to me, but that's what they said. I suppose they'd had experience of that sort of thing. Anyway he'd certainly not have been looking out for it; very few people expect to be poisoned in the middle of a fizz night. They seemed so certain about it all, quite rightly as it turned out, that we didn't like to doubt their word. So we were all terribly efficient when it came to describing our movements.

They only wanted to know about the time between 5.30, when we all came back from the outing, and six. The chemist said the purchaser in the white trousers had come in at about 5.45, and the reason he knew was that it was a quarter of an hour before he closed at 6, and the fact that no other customers had come in afterwards had made him think he'd been a sap not to close quarter of an hour earlier. This looked pretty good evidence to me, and the detective fellows liked it a lot.

Most of the crew had been together from 5.30 till six, all in the big games room. Jon, Jim and I hadn't been there at first. We knew where Jim was, outside with the Alacrity bird. The three of us got back from the outing a little later than the rest of them because of that talk with the coaches, and Jim had come into the house again at ten to six. We were sure of that, or very nearly sure, because by six o'clock, when the news came on, he'd played a complete game of ping-pong with Ronnie. That left quarter of an hour of Jim unaccounted for.

Jon said he had been in his room all the time till six, when he came down for the news.

I said I hadn't been in the games room at all. First of all I'd done the crossword and then I'd been signing autographs for the crew.

"How do you mean 'for the crew'?" one of them asked.

I told him that the rest of them could never be bothered to sign autograph books. All the coxes after Peter Bryan's time had had to forge the signatures of everyone else; it was one of their duties. So long as you had two or three different nibs and patience you could make a very good job of it indeed.

"Oh," they said, laughing. "That's dangerous."

I said not so dangerous as they thought.

Well, one of the detectives walked to the chemist's and back. It took twenty-five minutes, walking hard. That meant that Jon or I could have gone on our feet or by car, while Jim could only have gone by car. On his way there he met the detective who'd been to see if anyone signed. Someone had, all right, but it was probably not his name. *A. G. Gallimage*, someone had written.

They went to work on this clue, rather ingeniously. The detective said he wanted a genuine autograph, and went round to each member of the crew with some sentimental story about his daughter being ill in bed and only needing a genuine autograph to recover. It's wonderful what rowing men will swallow. Jim was the only one who made a fuss. He was playing ping-pong again and he said, as rudely as usual:—

"The cox can forge mine."

The detective said he knew that. His daughter wanted a real one. After that Jim signed, a bit grudgingly; and went on playing.

He signed in a writing very like Gallimage's.

This more or less meant Jim or me. I forgot to say that they'd checked up on Jon and found that a maid has seen him in his room between 5.40 and 5.50. She didn't say so, but I expect he went up there for a smoke. He thought it improved *his* rowing but nobody else's. So Jim and I were left, and the signature did very well for either of us. It was typical of the effect of the Boat Race atmosphere that the detectives came and asked Solly if they could arrest both of us. I know they did because I was in the room at the time.

"Would you mind if we arrested Matthews and your cox?" they asked.

"Yes, old chap," said Solly. "We can get another cox, but we haven't any more strokes. Leave them both if you can."

The detective looked serious. "Evidence is bad," he said.

Solly leant back in his chair. "Trot it out," he said. "The cox and I will spoil it. The cox does the crossword in half an hour every morning."

"Twenty-five minutes with Jon," I said. "That was two days ago."

Then I shut up.

The detective trotted out the evidence. At the end I pointed out a flaw. It wasn't half as hard as the *Times* crossword, let alone Torquemada.

"But if Jim went," I said, "he must have used the car."

"Yes."

"But there wasn't any petrol in the car."

"Sure?"

"Quite sure. You see Jon and I both saw the gauge reading half a gallon. Only next morning is still read half a gallon and there wasn't any petrol in her. It foxed me completely."

"It certainly did," said Solly.

"You realize what you're saying?" asked the detective.

"No," I said.

"If Jim Matthews didn't take your car, then someone walked to the shop. That means you walked, because Jim didn't have time."

"He could have run," I said.

"Ah," said the detective. "There's where you're wrong. *He wasn't out of breath.*"

I suppose I looked pretty shaken by this bit of information, because Solly patted me on the back in a very kindly way. "That's all right," he said. "It'll turn out not to been either of you. Glad you remembered about the petrol."

I was a good deal comforted by this. "Well," I said, "that fellow who coxes the *Isis* is a damn fine cox, and I've got one Blue already. I know we'll win. But I wish they had wireless sets in prison."

"We'll try and let you know all about it," said the detective. This seemed to me a pretty decent way to speak to a murderer.

That isn't all, and it won't be all either. Oxford won, of course, with one of Jim's beautifully timed spurts. He couldn't have made it without Harry and Jon and they couldn't have made it if he hadn't been there, swinging them along so steadily and easily that you'd have thought they were paddling. That is, until you saw how the boat moved.

Furthermore those detectives forgot one thing. Perhaps you saw what it was. Of course my petrol gauge is a bit odd; they can easily test it and show *that it sticks on the half-gallon mark.*

49

I'm sorry for Jim. I wish it hadn't happened. To be honest, I don't see any other way we could have won; but even Jim, who was a casual ambitious fellow, didn't mean to pay that price for it. He thought Davis would feel ill and give up in the middle of the paddle. But Davis went on rowing till his heart stopped.

NONFICTION

The Pineapple Cup

Aquil Abdullah (with Chris Ingraham)

DURING HIS ROWING CAREER, AQUIL ABDULLAH WROTE HISTORY BY becoming the first African American male to win the US National Championships in the single sculls. He would also be the first Black man to race in the Diamond Challenge Sculls at Henley Royal Regatta, in 1999. At his second try to take the Diamonds, the following year, he won the Pineapple Cup, which he writes about in his rowing autobiography *Perfect Balance* (written together with journalist Chris Ingraham), which was published in 2001. In 2000, Aquil experienced his largest disappointment in rowing by losing the Olympic Trials in the single sculls by 0.33 second to Don Smith.

Looking back on how I felt after racing Don Smith at the 2000 Olympic Rowing Trials almost brings me to tears. I didn't feel like crying when I lost; I was still in a state of shock. I had just raced the most strenuous, and one of the fastest races of my life, and I could only think that Don was one tough man. I had tossed everything at him, and he still didn't cave. It wasn't until I looked at my mother standing on the shores of the Cooper River that my eyes began to swell with tears and my throat began to hurt as I choked back wave after wave of primal screams. Alone was the only thing that I wanted to be, alone in my single, alone on the water, as I had been so many mornings on Lake Carnegie. I didn't practice alone, but for some reason I always felt alone. Even with an extended family as big as mine, I felt alone. With the throngs of people giving me support and telling me how proud they were of my performance, I felt alone. In the arms of a beautiful woman, I felt alone. Even with the encouraging words of my godfather, or with the tears of one of my best friends, who knew the same pain, I felt alone. I felt this way because my defeat was singular. There was only one other person who could possibly understand, and he was the victor of the race. Don crossed the finish line 33 hundredths of a second ahead of me, and for that he had won the right to represent the United States of America in the 2000 Olympic Games in Sydney, Australia.

And so in the wake of my loss, even much later, I reflect on my experience at the Olympic Trials. The multitude of emotions is strong. They still choke me up today as I try to make new National Teams however I can. The bottom line is that I felt like a loser. I felt like a wimp and a failure. No matter how many times I was told that I raced an incredible race, I would remain a wimp in my own mind until I redeemed myself. In a way, this book is that redemption. It is my story. This is for all of those who, like myself, have felt alone after defeat.

Where do we go after defeat? What should I do next? What more was there to be done? After finishing that race and realizing I'd lost, I was nonplussed. I learned sometime later that my mother didn't know what to do either. She wanted to console me, but had no idea what words or gestures would convey the strength of emotions needed in such a cat-astrophic time. She asked Ken Dryfuss, my coach from Potomac Boat Club, "*What do I say to him?*" The truth is words and consolation came no easier for me than they did for her. I had given my life to the pursuit of making the Olympic Rowing Team, and now that I failed to reach that goal, it felt in many respects like I had nothing left.

One thing that I failed to look at when I first lost was the fact that I had only really trained hard for two years. It takes eight years to become a doctor, it takes three years to become a lawyer and it takes numerous years to do anything worthwhile. If we look at people who excel in any arena, it is very easy to talk about how much natural talent they have. What we do not see is the countless number of hours they have spent honing the skills they have and gaining the skills that they do not have in order to reach the point where everything they do seems effortless. It would be foolish for me to believe that I could be as good as Tiger Woods in golf or Michael Jordan in basketball, or even Steven Redgrave in rowing. The one thing that I could do was require of myself the same amount of dedication, commitment and effort as those who excel in any area of life.

I tried to remember that talented people work really hard to excel in their area of expertise, but in most cases, they work really hard at everything else too. Michael Jordan is now a successful businessman. Former professional wrestler Jesse "The Body" Ventura is now an elected politician in Minnesota. There are numerous other examples of athletes who are successful outside of their sport. One quality that distinguishes the ordinary from the excellent is a sense of balance found in those who reach the top.

Placing one's entire self into the determined pursuit of a single aim can be a blind and risky business. How do we get to the point where we place all of our self-worth in one thing? How do we become blind? I had always believed single-minded determination was necessary in the pursuit of excellence, whether in sports or in any other aspect of life, but now my perspective has changed. We need balance. Great value can be found in devoting oneself to a specific purpose, and much can be gained through the pursuit of that aim. Anyone who wants and attempts to master a certain skill or to reach a high level of excellence in a given field deserves commendation. Excellence and mastery do not come easily for anyone, no matter how much natural talent a person possesses. While I cannot condemn working hard for a single goal, losing the Olympic Trials against Don really made me realize the importance of living a life with balanced passions and pursuits. A balanced life makes for well-rounded, fascinating human beings.

Some sports may require athletes to train six hours a day and some sports do not allow the athletes to focus on anything other than the sport for long periods of time. Although the training for rowing is intense, it allows oarsmen the chance to engage in other endeavors. Consider the distinguished careers of athletes like Steven Redgrave, Bob Kahler, and Jeff Klepacki. Each has managed to build a successful rowing career and business career. In my life, at least since 1998, rowing has taken precedence above all other interests. Nevertheless, I shudder to think what a limited person I would be, if, given my love of the saxophone and my success in the work place, I let these interests slip away from the wholeness of my personality.

The subject I presently address is tricky territory because I understand the importance of being excellent at something, and I also understand—all too well—how hard one has to work to reach the level of excellence. The Olympic Trials taught me a valuable lesson about balancing my life. I would shudder to see that lesson mistaken as a suggested path of diverse mediocrity. Finding reconciliation between the single-minded dedication required of excellence and the benefits of embracing a variety of interests can be a difficult task. Perhaps the best way to do so is to examine why we undertake an endeavor in the first place. What do we seek to gain from those activities we choose to occupy our lives?

In the case of sports, I believe all athletes participate in sports because, to varying degrees, they value the combination of a physical and mental challenge that sports provides. Measuring ourselves physically and mentally against others who attempt to do the same is rewarding insofar as the competition involved in taking these measurements helps build physical prowess, mental toughness and ideally, a stronger character. Outside sports, what reasons do we have for undertaking an endeavor? At the most fundamental level, we probably choose to do what we do because in some sense we stand to gain from that decision. Whether that means taking a prestigious job to earn money, playing music to tap into the soul or drinking booze because it makes you feel good, most things we do are done because they give us some sort of benefit. Given the infinite number of courses we can choose for our lives, great arguments can surround which activities and undertakings are more productive, useful, or healthy than others. In some cases, as with illegal drugs, for example, society on a whole would probably agree that there are more meaningful and healthy ways to live. Everyone must choose his or her own path, and although some paths may be widely recognized as better or worse than others, ultimately, the only right path for each person is the one he or she actively and independently chooses.

It seems to me, what we make of our resources and what we do with our time determines how successful we are as people. I may never be a superb saxophonist, but I can be a superb rower and a good saxophonist if I structure my time right. Likewise, I may never be a superb businessman, but I can be a superb rower and good businessman. For some people, pursuing one end to the point of excellence may be the best decision. For others, sampling from a more diverse plate of interests may be more appropriate. Diversity allows one to appreciate what is truly important in one's life. I don't think that I ever have been or ever will be the type of person capable of pursuing a single goal while totally ignoring every other aspect of my life. I have learned to be the type of person who structures his time wisely and gets the most out of every opportunity.

Finding a balanced life is tough for people who strive to be the best at what they do. In sports, our society places a high premium on being the one to stand on the highest medal platform. From being the best we gain accolades from friends and family, fame from adoring fans, a validation of who we are and what we do. Very easily, the pursuit of the gold becomes a pursuit of ourselves, we believe that the glory defines who we are. So what happens when we don't win the gold? If we are to maintain our self-esteem, we must change how we define who we are. In the pursuit of excellence, we can easily arrive at a narrow measurement of our worth, and this happens in all aspects of life. No matter what we do, our society places a great amount of importance on trophies, medals, icons and awards because they symbolize the excellence that we strive to achieve. Although these symbols are useful as viable and tangible emblems of success, I believe it is valuable to remember that they are merely symbols. The gold medal is just a symbol of my love for my sport; it is a symbol of my commitment, a symbol of my determination, a symbol of my desire to win. But in the end it is merely a symbol that says I was the best on one day at one moment in time. It says nothing about what I will be or do for the rest of my life. Far more important is the work and love involved in obtaining it. Every time we train, our training is another symbol indicating our love for our sport. Intense training can often lead to an unbalanced and single-minded life. Whether or not this is best for any given person I cannot say. Most important is what we gain through our training. As I can personally attest, not everyone comes home with the gold. Those who do are winners, without a doubt, but they are not the only ones who emerge from their efforts with something gained.

What have I gained by not winning the Olympic Trials? The question is actually very shallow, because it only looks at one event in the past three years. I think the better question to ask is, "What have I gained from training to be an Olympic caliber sculler?" That question is more relevant, and easier to answer. It is a question that I believe all athletes who attempt to achieve Olympic glory should ask of themselves. If your goal is to achieve something different than the Olympics, be it a strong relationship, a closeness to God, a promotion at work, a mastery of Scrabble, whatever it happens to be, you ought always to ask yourself what you have gained from trying to reach your goals.

It's easy to say what you win if you attain your goals. If you achieve Olympic glory, you can say, "I have a gold medal" or "I have done something that has never been done before." But those who don't actually make it to the Olympics and those who don't make the medal stands may have a harder time determining what they have gained from all their training. In the end, we must remember the age-old wisdom that no matter the goal, those who try persistently and rigorously to achieve something always gain a lot from trying. The challenge—particularly when one falls short of his or her objective—is to have a perspective that will enable one to see all he or she has gained in the process, and to correct those decisions that deterred the achievement of the goal in the first place. This can be difficult when one fixes so resolutely on a single aim and operates with the mentality that suggests anything shy of that aim is a failure. In my case, once I saw through that narrow focus, I realized that what I have gained has enriched my life and made me an immensely better person. I can say that I am in the best shape of my life. I can say that I am one of the best scullers in the United States, that I have met some of the greatest human beings in the world, that the support shown to me by friends and family through my training shows me how much I am loved. I can say that I was part of one of the greatest dual races in American history, and I can say that on one day in my life, I gave my best. I could go on listing what I've gained, but the important fact is my life has been enriched so much as a result of training to be an Olympic caliber sculler. Achieving my goal of becoming an Olympian was merely the carrot that helped me along the path to becoming a better person. And although I would obviously have preferred to win that race against Don and reach my actual goal, what I did win is a greater understanding of why I do what I do, and how I can work more wisely to achieve other goals in my life.

If we take enough time to look at our lives and ask what we gain in the pursuit of something, we will all become better, more honest people and thus do our part in making a positive contribution to society. Those who we label as winners get the momentary recognition of being the best, and being the best is one of the few differences between first place, second place, third, fourth and all the others who finish below the top. When the challenge is over, though, only one person can reach that top level. Don and I raced incredible races at the 2000 Olympic Trials. Reporters likened it to a prize fight bout between two evenly matched boxers. But the course ended when it did, and at that time, Don was ahead. Someone always has to win in racing sports, and because someone always has to win, someone else always has to lose. In 2000, I was that loser. Did that make me unsuccessful? I don't think so.

I have spent many hours wondering what it means to be successful. Is our success in sport defined solely by the results of a race, or is it measured by how much we improve from where we started? In the Olympic Trials I had a personal goal to row 6:51. I beat my goal, yet it was not enough. Were my efforts a success since I accomplished my performance goal? I'd set a target and hit it as planned. *Of course I was a success*, I thought. Then I realized: *No I wasn't, I lost*. When I thought some more I discovered what seems to me the best explanation of success. I believe that success in life is determined by the extent to which we use our experiences, both good and bad, to learn the lessons that make us better people. True winners rebound after a tragic experience. Although more people fail to reach the top than those who succeed, we can all be winners if we make a concerted effort to learn from every experience in our lives. Unfortunately, this is easier in theory than in practice. In reality, profound emotions are involved. It hurts bitterly to try your hardest and still not finish first. What do we learn as athletes, as human beings, when we are not first? The answer depends on how much we try to learn. Certainly, if we seek to turn a sour outcome into a positive experience, we will head in the right direction, but so often in sports, work or other parts of our lives, we forget why we started an endeavor. Finding a positive outcome from a seemingly negative experience then seems impossible.

As I mentioned before, we often choose to undertake the various activities in our lives because we stand to benefit from them in some fundamental way. Enjoyment alone proves this point. For instance, when a child first kicks a soccer ball, she does so because it's fun. Next, the child wants to score a goal. After the child scores her first goal, she wants to score another, because it felt good to accomplish something. Only after this, when other people want to score goals too, does the thought of winning become an issue. It may take longer, but the child starts to hone her skills in order to improve, to play like Mia Hamm. Eventually, perhaps, the child grows into a woman who plays soccer passionately and holds the sport as an inextricable part of her existence. In the more veteran stages of participation in sport, that original joy at kicking the ball becomes clouded by all the other dynamics involved in being a high caliber athlete. If we take a moment to remember the original and most fundamental reason we do what we do, I would imagine that nine times in ten, we will realize—win or lose—we've had what we wanted all along. This is not to suggest we shouldn't keep score in sports, because keeping score helps us measure our own improvement. Rather, people should always try to remember the original reasons why they began participating in any endeavor, regardless of the scores they earn along the way.

Now, as I reflect on why I began rowing, I would like to introduce the idea of the Pineapple Cup. The Pineapple Cup is the prize given to the winner of the Diamond Challenge Sculls at Henley Royal Regatta. Here I use the term "Pineapple Cup" as a metaphor for those important goals we all have in our lives. For me, it was becoming an Olympic caliber sculler and making the Olympic Team in 2000. For others, the Pineapple Cup may be to become president of a company, to make the varsity basketball team as a sophomore in high school or to be elected as a congressman. Everyone's Pineapple Cup signifies some different objective, but we all have a Pineapple Cup for which we strive. Regardless of how important (or unimportant) achieving an objective might be for each individual person, I believe we all covet positive reinforcement from the people around us. There aren't many cheers for losers. The desire to be applauded and well received can, as I have learned from my personal experience, lead people to define their self-worth by their capacity to achieve the Pineapple Cup. If I place my entire self-worth on achieving that goal, what does it say about me that I failed to do so? Does it say I am worthless? Of course not! Rather, it simply says that I cannot achieve the Pineapple Cup. It does not mean I cannot achieve different goals, and equally challenging ones at that. The problem, though, is standing up after you've been knocked down.

Looking back on my rowing career, I shudder at the fondness of my memories. I am still young, so my nostalgia may seem premature. The point, I suppose, is that I will never "get over" losing the Olympic Trials in 2000, but I will move past it. That loss, under those circumstances, will always be a source of ire for me, as long as I live. But I have learned not to wallow in my disappointment or in what might easily be perceived as a failure. By not making the 2000 U.S. Olympic Rowing Team, I gained a better understanding of who I am, and a better perspective on the roles my various interests play in my life. It occurred to me, given some time to reflect, that growing as people is the most important victory we can ever achieve in our lives. I have found that one of the hardest things for me to do is to change negative patterns in my life. I have also found that once I have changed those patterns everything else becomes much easier. If I can go through every experience life hands me and use it to learn something that improves me as a person—something that makes me more pleasant to be around, more of a positive influence on the world, more of a role model—then I will always be a winner. This is the validation I have discovered for the work I have put into an endeavor that otherwise may seem to have left me empty-handed.

The Legend of the Japanese Eight

Andy Anderson (a.k.a. Dr. Rowing)

Part I

Walk into any boathouse in the country and sooner or later someone will draw you aside and tell you the story of the Japanese crew that rowed at such a high rating that they died after the race. It is probably rowing's most common legend. But is it true? Or is it an urban legend—a story that everyone has heard, usually from a friend who knew someone who knew someone who was there?

Accounts vary, of course: most of the time this is supposed to have happened at the Tokyo Olympics in 1964; usually the stroke rate is said to be "in the 50's," although I have heard it told as high as 65. Most versions of the story are fairly similar about what happened to these oarsmen: two men died in the boat, two on the dock, and the rest in hospitals within the next few months. Many would-be rowers hear the story about the time that they are introduced to racing starts, a scary enough prospect even without thinking about death as a possible consequence.

Could such a dramatic tragedy really be true?

In 1990 I coached the crews at Hitotsubashi University, one of Japan's oldest rowing schools. Chief among my interests that summer was investigating this most famous rowing story. Surely here at Toda, the Olympic basin, I would be able to uncover the dark truth.

The guys who rowed in my crews had never heard this story, I soon discovered. *Well, you know, kids have no sense of history today*, I thought. Pressing the issue with my interpreter, Ryo, a graduate in his late twenties, I learned that he had not heard of this most famous Japanese crew either.

Maybe there had been a cover-up. Of course, they probably wouldn't admit it to a foreigner. I'd have to gain their trust. Ryo told me that soon I could ask some of the old boys (as graduates are known). I was invited to their monthly banquet.

After the dinner and the speeches were over, there followed a lively discussion. Ryo had told me that as a guest coach I would be asked some questions. I told him that was fine; I had one of my own to ask. The first came from an older man with shaggy white hair. "Mr. Anderson," he started hesitantly in English, "What, please, is your philosophy of outward pitch?"

I'd never been asked to articulate a *philosophy* of outward pitch before, but I labored through an explanation of the relevant angles at the catch and finish and the way that great force being applied at the catch might drive the oar deep, etc. I was politely listened to. Then a firestorm of Japanese broke out. It was obvious that the room was deeply divided about pitch. There was heated debate, fueled by free-flowing beer and *sake*.

When the pitch discussion died down after about fifteen minutes, a second question arose. What did I think about breaking the arms right after the catch? Absolutely not, I replied. This met with shouts of approval. (There was a forest of liter bottles of Kirin on the table by now.) Apparently a popular modern technique had been to use the arms right away. Much loud discussion followed.

And so the evening went. These men were passionate in their devotion to rowing. Every technical point drew forth their verbal sparring. I soon found myself in the club's bar drinking a cognac. The group had dwindled to seven or eight. Now was my chance.

"There is a story," I started, cursing myself for the overly loud and overly slow voice that was coming out of my mouth—the foreigner voice, "that in the Tokyo Olympics a Japanese eight rowed very high—fifty beats per minute—and after the race, many of the men died. Do any of you know about this story?"

Dead silence. I shifted nervously from foot to foot and sipped at my drink.

Finally, Mr. Okamura said, "We know of no such story." He looked around the group for confirmation. "The German eight rowed very high. Do you mean the German eight?"

"No, the story that everyone tells is of a Japanese eight. Most of the crew died because they had rowed so high." Long pause. "I've never believed it," I added.

"This is not a true story." He looked at me with steely eyes. "What do you think it means?"

"I'm not sure," I stammered. I'm your friend, I wanted to say. I love coaching here. I'm not making this up.

"Maybe Kamikaze idea? We Japanese would row to kill ourself?"

"Maybe that's it. So this story is not true? Now I can tell everyone in America."

"Do you remember the man who asked you the question about pitch?" my friend Mr. Ito asked. "That man rowed in the Olympic 8." He paused and looked around the group. "He was alive, *neh*?"

When I left Toda at the end of the summer, one of my going-away gifts was a videotape of the 1964 Olympics. No, there is certainly not anyone dying out on the water.

So where did this story come from? How many of us have repeated it, or at least let it be told in our boathouses to emphasize the importance of settling? It is certainly one of rowing's urban legends—a bizarre but believable story that we delight in telling and hearing (like the famous Poodle in the Microwave). Rowing has a rich trove of folklore. It's time to search out and write down rowing's great legends. Our sport needs someone to look into its past. And I'm just the man to do it.

Part II

It seems that everyone treasures the legend of the Japanese eight. Since my first column, I've heard a Chinese version of the tale, had people claim that the story must be true because it is mentioned in *The Shell Game*, and had it asserted that the Japanese have always used miniature equipment—short oars and cut down boats. Best of all, I've been offered help in identifying the sources of this popular legend. After many nights burning the midnight oil, I can add to my earlier piece. In case you've just joined us, I refer, of course, to the story of the Japanese crew that rowed at such a high rate that the oarsmen died.

Hart Perry alerted me to a crew from Tokyo Imperial University that competed at Henley Royal Regatta in the Grand Challenge Cup in 1936. They amazed the crowds at Henley in their race against Quintin Boat Club of London. As the official record of the regatta puts it,

Quintin went off at 41 to the 40 of Tokyo and the race was level past the Barrier, but the Japanese had half a length at Fawley. Below the mile, with a spurt at 50, Tokyo took a length. With another spurt at 56, the Japanese won by two lengths.

Mr. George Moody of England wrote to verify the events:

I saw the race at Henley and followed them from the start on a bicycle (possible in those days). I was rowing in the Regatta and we paid the Japanese a courtesy visit one evening. They were staying near us at the top of St. Mark's Road. There was not much verbal communication between us other than "Good luck." They had brought their own provisions with them.

Mr. Moody notes that the same crew had raced at the Marlow Regatta earlier in the summer, where perhaps owing to the course's shorter distance (1,600 meters, as compared with Henley's 1 mile 550 yards [2,112 meters]), they had maintained a rate of 52 for the majority of the race.

The Japanese lost their second race at Henley to the eventual winners of the Grand, Zurich Rowing Club, by the verdict of "Easily." They competed later in the summer at the Berlin Olympics, failing to make the finals.

Mr. Joe Burk of the Pennsylvania Athletic Club won the Diamond Sculls in 1938 and wrote to say, "Undoubtedly the performance of the high-stroking Imperial University crew at the 1936 Henley was the source of the legend." He goes on to note that everyone was still talking about this high stroking crew two years later. "Things like that don't die quickly."

Well, so now we have established that there was a Japanese crew that rowed at seemingly impossible rates. What about the second half of the legend, the dying part? It seems likely that the reports of incredible stroke rates merged with another much-publicized, incomprehensible feat, the Kamikaze flights of the Japanese Zero pilots in the Second World War. Even a cursory reading of newspapers and magazines of the war years reminds us of the extent to which the western press fanned the flames of anti-Japanese feeling. The Japanese were portrayed as a people that did not value human life, willing to do anything to win, even to the extent of suicide. Is it any wonder that the two events became linked and that we heard about a crew that would sacrifice anything to win?

My correspondent, Mr. Moody, a trustee of the National Rowing Foundation and donor of his collection of rowing books to the Moody Book Collection at Mystic Seaport Museum, raises one more interesting point. In the nineteenth century there were persistent rumors that rowing was bad for one's health and led to early death. Perhaps even now you may come across someone who tells you that "rowing enlarges the heart." Fine for one's active youth, the rumor goes, but when middle age sets in, and that muscle turns to fat, *presto*, heart trouble. This was the original rowing-causes-death legend. A famous study was done of Harvard oarsmen at the turn of the century that concluded that the contrary was true: oarsmen lived longer than other college men.

The best legends, the ones that live on despite having truth flung in their face, are those that speak to deeply ingrained hopes or fears. Certainly we all think about "dying during a piece" or "flying and dying." Is it so surprising that these fears have been transmuted into tales of literal death?

I have no doubt that despite my efforts to get at the truth behind this one, some fine spring afternoon I will walk into Bingham Boathouse here at Groton and hear someone begin in solemn tones "Hey, did you know that there was once a Japanese crew. . . ."

Training with Harry Parker

Toby Ayer

SPENDING THE ACADEMIC YEAR 2007–2008 FOLLOWING HARRY PARKER and his Harvard squad, Toby Ayer got up close and personal with Parker and his crew. In 2016, Ayer published *The Sphinx of the Charles: A Year at Harvard with Harry Parker*. In the following excerpt, Ayer is in the launch with Parker on the Charles River during an outing in March 2008.

For several years the canonical way to imitate Harry Parker's voice was a sort of gruff sing-song. With a deep tone, sometimes with the throat slightly restricted, the official contour of every sentence was flat, then slightly down, then gradually up to a peak, then down to finish the last syllable or two. You would hear it when the rowers bantered with each other, when alums told stories, and during the nightly skits at Red Top (the training quarters where Harvard prepares for the Race against Yale), when someone took the role of Harry for the week. This standard Voice was passed down and adopted, immediately recognizable as HP. The best thing about it was that it did not sound like Harry.

There is the deep bass, used in a quiet room, almost monotone but with the occasional word emphasized. Sometimes a long sentence fades out, so you lean in to catch the last few words. There is the barking tenor, used in the megaphone, typically a few words at a time: a name, a comment, and a quick fix. There is the happy cheerleader, exclamatory and perky, used with recruits, high school campers, and anyone who needs to be impressed. There is the growl, used during competitive pieces: a single phrase, a single word, repeated two or three times, with two exclamation points to drive the point home, to plant these phrases in the rowers' heads. Drive it through!! Stay strong!!

Despite what everyone has said about him for more than forty years, Harry says a lot to his rowers. The appealing myth, perpetuated by reporters, authors, other coaches, and even his own athletes, is that Harry hardly ever says anything. When words do come, they are prized and scrutinized. "The Alan Greenspan of rowing," according to one. Yet Ted Washburn '65, coxswain and longtime fellow coach, says "it would never have occurred to me" to describe Harry as a silent coach. In contrast, he is "very active," but with the gift of being "comfortable in silence, letting a boat row."

It is the first week of March. The notice on the board now says "7 6 5 weeks until race day #1." Harry leaves his original piece of paper on the board, crosses out each number, and squeezes in the new one next to it with a Sharpie.

Two eights do some very close racing on Monday afternoon, three-minute pieces, always finishing within a few seats of each other. Harry loves it. At 7:30 Tuesday morning he walks into the lounge to talk to the whole squad. He tells them that when they sign up for practice they should indicate when they are actually available, not just times that he has typically scheduled crews. (One year he informed the team that "in case you didn't know it, your day belongs to me.") He specifically wants to get crews on the water earlier if possible: 4:15 is becoming a time when "you practically can't do any work" on the river, because of all the other crews out there. MIT is finally on the water, and BU, and Northeastern, and the high schools are starting up too. If we can't get out before then, he says, we're better off rowing after 5:00.

He reads off the crews from his list, muttering that he hopes he gets it right. There are three eights and a four scribbled on his paper, and he has shuffled crews slightly from the day before. He stands with the paper held just above waist height, head bent over it, and reads in a low voice. As he progresses through each crew list his voice loses volume, and the last few names are almost inaudible. It is a scene easily parodied in a Red Top skit.

It's windy but warm today, the warmest day since Florida. Wayne Berger takes the four on its own, and Harry follows the three eights upstream. Pulling away from the dock, Harry sees two hawks overhead. "Look at those hawks," he says. "Awesome." He takes out his cell phone and calls Wayne, who is not far upstream. "Look at the hawks circling above me!"

If not for the wind, Harry would have had the eights do two ten-minute pieces at twenty-six, but instead he opts for a lower intensity. Once they have warmed up he just tells them to go to three-quarter power, and they head all the way to the top of the rowable river by the Newton Yacht Club, where four large pleasure boats sit wrapped in white plastic at the deserted docks. There is a wide open stretch of water here, and today it is rough. Harry says the southwest wind would normally be blocked by the trees and leave this water calm, but now there are no leaves.

They turn, row two bridges downstream, about eight minutes at three-quarter pressure, come back up to the top, then down again all the way to Eliot—five minutes longer than before—before finally paddling home. On the upstream pieces there is a headwind, and Harry tells them repeatedly how to deal with the conditions: square the blade up late to get full compression before squaring, so the blade isn't being pushed back by the wind. When they turn he reminds them about the reversed wind direction and how to adjust their rowing. Spend more time on the slide, he says, and "don't get anxious" on the way forward.

Harry is getting impatient with his technical calls. One rower is over-reaching and he tells him to be "steady with the shoulders," not to hunch them over or reach more after reaching the front of the slide. "C'mon ... change it!" he says. He still focuses mostly on the squaring and catch sequence. He tells another rower to "loosen your grip in the inside hand, square it later." The bow seat of one boat, the same one Harry switched last week between two eights, doesn't really get hold of the water. Harry tells him he needs to put the blade in before changing directions at the catch. In the launch he points out that this rower is strong—strong enough to be in the varsity. "But it depends on whether he figures this out ... he's very wound up." He is tight in his hamstrings and calves, but also "wound up emotionally."

Crew selection is on everyone's mind. The small, tough Irishman and his close friends have often made guesses during the spring about the racing lineups. At this time last year, they got five out of eight correct for the varsity, and by spring break, before seat-racing, it was seven out of eight. They scrutinize the daily lineups, and especially the opposite seats when two crews go out together (since they are the most likely to be switched between boats in a seat-race), and who ends up in the stern fours.

They also try to guess the workout each day while they stretch in the lounge beforehand. There are some predictable patterns, or at least a set of possibilities, and a general sense that they will rotate between them. Before practice today, one of the varsity lightweights passes one of Harry's guys who was once a lightweight, and asks what they are doing today. The answer comes with a shrug and a smile: "Probably hard pieces of some sort."

A couple of days later Harry has one eight on its own early in the afternoon. After the warmup, when they stop just below Weeks, Harry tells them they will do some twenties to warm up more, and then "some thirties, forties, and fifties" at rate thirty-four, so they get used to maintaining good bladework at the higher rate. The wind is nearly due west, and on many stretches of the river that means a direct headwind or tailwind and choppy water. They stay in the Powerhouse Stretch, doing two pieces in each direction and then spinning. On each lap they start from the catch, and do five strokes at two-thirds slide before lengthening out.

Once again, given the early start time, they are the only crew on the river for the first half of practice, and Harry relishes it. A Radcliffe four appears at one point and disappears into the Basin, and a few high school crews are launching from Riverside near the end of the session. The west side of the river is protected from the wind, and after the second trip downstream, Harry tells the coxswain that "as long as we're the only ones out here, let's go up the Boston arches." This is a complete violation of the normal traffic pattern, which on the Charles is as on the road: you must stay on the right-hand half of the river, which means the Cambridge side going upstream. Two laps later, the coxswain asks if he should still go up the Boston side, and Harry says yes, "we'll pretend it's our river."

Harry tells me he only recently realized that the Powerhouse Stretch is rowable when a west wind blows. The protection on the Boston side comes from buildings: a hotel, a biotech company, the newer additions to the Harvard Business School. But none of these was here when Harry first came to Boston. Back then a west wind would make the Powerhouse choppy and unpleasant, so he always took crews upstream from Newell in those conditions. If we had a few more buildings, he says, we'd have a great stretch of river here!

(The Powerhouse Stretch is so named because of the Blackstone Steam Plant, located near the top end of the straight, on the corner of Western Avenue and Memorial Drive. It was built in 1901 to run the new electric lighting in Cambridge, and started supplying steam to heat Harvard's buildings in 1930. The university now owns the facility, whose manager, Nick Peters, was not aware that his plant's identity has been invoked, however unknowingly, by the many thousands of rowers who have rowed up that kilometer of river.)

As it is the gusts are intermittent, and as the boats head roughly north or south, the wind hits them from one side or the other and feels like a headwind either way. It's another opportunity to practice headwind-style bladework, says Harry. "Keep the blades feathered until you are at full compression," he tells them. That way the wind can't slow them down.

The strong, "wound up" starboard is in the bow seat again, and for the most part Harry is happy with him. He seems to be Harry's "project" for the year, a strong but unstable oarsman who needs attention if he is to meet his own potential. Harry thinks he might make the varsity—he was in the "B" four at the Tail of the Charles in November, and is one of the strongest members of the squad. But his movements are a little stiff, his blade not always in time, not always taking hold of the water well enough. Harry puts him in the bow, and gives him a lot of attention.

But today it is the four-seat who gets most of Harry's coaching. His hands move away from the finish slowly, so his oar lags behind the other ports on the way forward, and then he has a sudden reach just before the catch, so his blade nearly catches up—but not quite. Mainly Harry talks to him about how he squares his blade. "You're making it harder for your-self," he says, "by squaring it too early. Leave it on the feather until the end, then square it just before the catch." On each piece, the four-seat's blade will start out in sync with the rest of the blades on his side, and then a few strokes later it starts squaring early, halfway through the recovery. "Loosen the grip with your thumb," Harry tells him. A tight grip with the inside hand, which controls the squaring, often leads to a slow turn of the handle. On every piece, every time they spin the boat, Harry talks to the four-seat about his blade. He tells two others their blades are rising too high off the water before they come down for the catch, and tells them to "reach out, rather than down." As he speaks, Harry's gloved left hand makes a little outwards swooping motion, mimicking the motion he wants to see.

"Some" pieces turns out to be: three thirties, two forties, two more thirties, a forty, a thirty, a forty, three more thirties, and one final forty. For the thirties the coxswain counts the strokes, but for the longer pieces Harry times a minute and fifteen seconds on his watch and calls out the moment to start counting the last ten strokes.

In his technical calls he focuses on the catch sequence, but reminds them often to be "solid in the water." For these pieces he says not to put a maximum effort into each stroke, but rather to focus on a solid push from the catch to the finish, to be consistent with this at the higher rate. After three laps he asks the four-seat how his bad knee is holding up, and the seven-seat about his back. All is well, so they keep going.

The oarsmen are clearly exhausted at the day's effort—intense work that adds up in time to more than three full 2,000-meter races—and they are visibly gasping after each piece on the last two laps. The very last piece is a "forty," and Harry almost forgets to call the last ten. A coach can lose track of time, and a coxswain will often lose count, but the rowers are aware of every stroke they take. That last piece was forty-four strokes, they say afterward. The others were forty-three.

Henley behind the Scenes

Mark Blandford-Baker

As anyone who has been to the world's most famous regatta knows, Henley has many aspects of uniqueness. One of those is the way the entire operation runs seamlessly, perhaps invisibly, for competitors and spectators alike. None of that happens without a lot of work that goes on quietly behind the scenes.

The Regatta has a professional team of full-time and seasonal staff who work under the broad direction of the Stewards' Committee of Management; they are joined by volunteers in the run up to the Regatta and throughout the week.

I've been privileged to be one of those helpers, in my case being responsible for proof-reading the daily programme. Each day there is a freshly printed programme containing the timetable of racing and the details of all the crew competing, along with the results of the previous days' racing, the draw chart, and a host of other information. Being Henley, this has to be to 'Regatta standard', which basically means it must be perfect.

That standard means that every person's details have to be checked to ensure a complete set of initials, and the spelling of their name is correct. Date of birth is required in order to create a unique record—it has been known for a coach to put down any old date only for it to be queried when it looks like someone who has competed before! Foreign names of clubs and competitors require care to ensure accents and shortened forms are correct. Club colours are checked, some change them, and others may be new clubs to the Regatta. Once crews have weighed in, seat orders and steersmen confirm that crew is ready for insertion in the daily programme. This makes it an organic task as crews arrive in Henley, those not competing until later in the week have to be tracked to ensure they are given the same care and attention.

By Tuesday morning this information is ready for the Wednesday programme which is printed that afternoon. Once the Regatta is under-way, the bulk of the work is done in the evening after racing. Within a few minutes of the National Anthem the results pages and draw chart are coming over from the printers who have been preparing them throughout the day. Once the timetable for the following day has been finalised, that is sent to the printers, and later the first proof of that and the main pages with the crew details arrive. A small team of dedicated and hawk-eyed volunteers help me with the proof-reading. Working in pairs to ensure accuracy, everything is checked, from the smallest spelling corrections that may have been noticed, to the big picture of ensuring the right day and date and running order are correct. All done in an open office with others bringing back equipment or doing other tasks to close the day and prepare for the next. On Wednesday evening I hope to be able to call the printers to roll the presses by about 10.15pm; as the week goes on and the number of races reduces, it gets earlier. With luck, Saturday evening can be all done by 8pm.

This is all very good, but the stories are in what can go wrong or needs a pause for consideration. How often, for example, is a dead heat not re-rowed on the same day? When that happens, how does the result get displayed in the results pages? The answer was that we couldn't find a precedent so you work out what seems right and go and see the Chair-man to get it approved. When someone has to withdraw from competi-tion after the Draw, how is that portrayed? That was relatively easy, the Chairman remembered when it had happened to him and you reach for the record books. Continuity of style is important, but sometimes changes occur. Did you notice that in 2017 'Holland' was replaced with 'Nether-lands' for the first time in the history of the Regatta? Why? Well 'Hol-land' is only a part of the country called 'Netherlands' and the latter is the correct form as well as being the style used by FISA and the IOC. "Change?!" you shout, well yes, just occasionally, and when it is the right thing to do.

It gives great satisfaction to do something and get it right, and for a pedant like me that is important. Sometimes it can give others particular pleasure. A few years ago (I've been fortunate to be doing this job for nine regattas as of this year) I came back into the Secretary's tent where I have a desk during racing and one of the staff on reception warned me there was an irate lady waiting for me. Her son had been rowing in a school crew and his surname was incorrectly spelt in the programme. After apologising profusely I set about looking into why that was. It was an unusual name and the coach had written it on the entry form clearly but inaccurately. Since it was his first time competing there was no reason to query it. His mother was all for hanging the coach out to dry when I looked at the weighing-in sheet which had been signed by the competitor (who is asked to verify their name and initials for just this purpose). I commented that he had just won his race and so I would ensure it was corrected for the following day's programme. The lady was so chuffed she brought me a bottle of champagne the following day. That crew went on to win the Princess Elizabeth Cup that year and so it mattered even more that his name was now right as it is engraved on the base. I'd love to know who got the bigger blast from her, coach or son.

Along the way there are other jobs that need to be done and fit with these other duties. Helping the Steward in charge of entries double-check the draw slips prior to going to the Town Hall for the Draw is crucial. Only those who have qualified, or did not need to, less any withdrawals and adding in any one moved up as a result, separating selected crews which are drawn first, right event in the right envelope. . . . There's a board facing the main entrance to the Enclosure that states the time racing begins the following day. Changing that late in the evening so it reads for the day after tomorrow is not too difficult, but there's usually a member of the team who can be persuaded on Saturday night to go and put a time on there, just so long as I remember to take it off again before I go. There won't be any racing on Monday, and early on Sunday that board will be removed by one of the grounds team. Detail, Henley style.

Some volunteers help in other areas once the Regatta is underway. For over 25 years now I've been a race reporter on the back of an umpire's launch. This is the second best view of the race after the umpire and requires speed and accuracy, giving the key information back to the commentary team for broadcast. In the enclosures the voice you hear is not the person on the launch but someone else, away from engine noise and radio interference, and for the first two and a half days, that team has to deal with two races on the course at a time. Now in this age of the television images it is even more important the reporting is swift and accurate. There is a separate team of commentators for the broadcast, but in the Stewards' Enclosure spectators can see the screens but hear the general commentary.

More recently I have taken on arranging the Regatta Church Service. Did you know there was one? Well of course there is, this is Henley. 9.30am on Finals Day in the Parish Church. A short (40 minutes) service with a bit of singing and a jolly (usually) preacher. Usually, the details can be all done and dusted around Easter so the order of service can be printed. HQ likes to get things done in good time, it's part of the great efficiency that pervades the whole operation. The church is filled with Stewards and their guests and other supporters of the Regatta, not to mention the locals whose usual service has been sort of usurped. Overseas schoolboy crews that have had the misfortune to be knocked out before then take the collection. By 10.30am everyone is in the enclosures drinking coffee or something stronger and waiting in anticipation of the first final to thunder down the course.

On the Friday before the Regatta the qualifying races are held for those events that are oversubscribed. For many this will be the only time they race down the course, at least that year, but it is a great experience for them and part of what inspires people to strive to compete at Henley another year. Marshalling all those boats takes a large number of Stewards and volunteers over several hours on your feet, but who would rather be at work instead? Not me; it's the start of HRR for another year and there's nothing else I'd rather be doing for the next ten days.

The Red Rose Crew

Daniel J. Boyne

IN 1975, A GROUP OF AMERICAN WOMEN WERE SELECTED TO ROW IN the eight at the World Championships at the Holme Pierpont National Water Sports Centre in Nottingham, England. The crew was coached by Harry Parker. It had not been a smooth ride for these women. At home, they had to battle sexual prejudice, bureaucracy, and male dominance, Daniel J. Boyne writes in his *The Red Rose Crew: A True Story of Women, Winning, and the Water* (2000). The following is an excerpt from chapter 16, where the Americans were to meet the best female crews from East Germany, West Germany, Romania, the Netherlands, and the Soviet Union.

The wind was waiting for the American women when they arrived at the Holme Pierpont course on Sunday, along with their five adversaries: Romania, W. Germany, Holland, Russia, and East Germany. Wind added an element of chaos to rowing that favored the more experienced crews. Rowing in heavy wind was like walking a tightrope while someone continuously shook the rope or kept hitting your balancing pole. The wind, and the waves that it created, buffeted a crew shell and threatened to throw it off keel. When the balance went off, the blades could hit the water between strokes and wreak further havoc with the balance or "set." And when the set went off, the rowing itself got sloppy, slowing the hull speed of the boat down even more.

The women's eight final was slated to start at five o'clock, the last event of the day. As the biggest and fastest boats on the water, eights were always left for the finale. At this point the few American spectators in the stands hadn't had much to see. All the other U.S. women's crews that rowed earlier had failed to get any medals. The Vesper four had finished last, the quad from Long Beach fifth. The double and the pair hadn't even made the final, and rowed in a second-tier race called the "petites." Even Joan Lind, the talented U.S. sculler, had only managed fifth. So far, the American boats were turning in typical, sub-par performances. The eight was not only the last boat, but the last hope.

The rowers quietly took their wooden boat off its rack, shouldered it, and walked it down to the dock. When they rolled it over and down to the water, a pleasant surprise lay within it. One of the managers from the Long Beach squad named Debbie D'Angelis had tied a single red rose into the laces of each of their shoes. It was a small, wonderful gesture that almost made up for the silly leotards, and a perfect way to launch their last race together. The red roses were the same color as their uniforms, and they decided to keep them in the boat for the race. No matter what happened, they had already gained recognition and a sense of achievement for going further than any American women's eight had gone before. The result of the final was up to fate.

The crews were sent out briefly and then called back in. The wind was simply too strong. It was rare to postpone a regatta. A crew race would be held in rain or snow, but if the race was held in high winds, there was the possibility of swamping. When a boat swamped, things could get messy. The crew generally wasn't at risk unless the water was cold or someone couldn't swim. The wooden boat and oars floated, and if the rowers stayed with the boat, there was generally no real danger.

Chris Ernst and Anne Warner knew about a boy who had died at Yale when his crew had hit an old water-ski ramp. It was October, and he'd tried to swim ashore, but in the cold water he'd cramped up and never made it. While at Radcliffe, Wiki Royden had swamped once at Canadian Henley, just before her crew made it to the finish line. As the strongest swimmer in the boat, she'd promised to save the coxswain, whose own ability to float was in question. Once a boat filled with water, it would hover just below the surface, turning into a floating bathtub. A swamped crew was more of a nuisance for the race officials, who would have to rescue the rowers without damaging their boats. And six swamped boats would cause a huge delay.

While they were waiting for the wind to die down, the Americans placed their boat on the grass beside the race course, upsidedown in low slings. Wiki and Anne lay under the overturned boat, gazing at the roses tied into the shoes, and using it as a makeshift cabana against the sun. To combat further illness, they were all popping vitamin C tablets like candy, and swallowing glycerin drops to keep their mouths from going dry. These may not have been as good as steroids, but they were a useful placebo nonetheless.

The time spent waiting passed slowly. Despite what the mind tried to convince the heart and body to do, a racing situation triggered the body's primitive reflexes—the flow of adrenaline and the fight-or-flight survival mechanism. Ironically, Gail Pierson, who had more racing experience than anyone, seemed to actually be suffering the worst. Her heart rate had started to skyrocket, causing her breathing to get short, and her mind was in a state of near panic. She went off alone to try to calm down with some breathing exercises that she'd found useful in the past. Harry Parker, too, had disappeared, leaving the team to deal with their own demons.

Wiki looked at the roses to pass the time and chatted casually with Anne Warner. The two college rivals had become close over the summer, especially as roommates during their stay at Henley. And Carie Graves had found an odd diversion for herself—she went around pulling the balls off of everyone's team-issued tennis peds. When the call finally came for them to race and the boat was again made ready, Carie strode up to Chris Ernst in the bow seat and threw the pompoms into her lap.

"Here, have some extra balls!" she said. "Become a member of the extra balls rowing club!"

To Chris, who was always a bundle of nerves up in the bow, it was just about the best thing anyone could say.

It was six o'clock before the U.S. team finally shoved off, the last crew to depart from the dock. The wind had subsided and was now westerly at two knots, providing a light tail wind that would actually make the rowing easier. The late summer sun had already begun to set over the finish line, and it cast a golden, hazy glow over the man-made hummocks along the banks and on the backs of the rowers as they came down the course.

It wasn't until they were well out onto the practice lane, doing their warm-up starts, that Gail Pierson realized something was wrong. Where were the other boats? Quickly she glanced over her shoulder and saw them lining up for the final, backing into the anchored stake boats.

The stake boats that the British had built weren't boats at all, but an ingenious row of six moveable finger piers, all of which connected to a main dock that nearly ran across the entire width of the course. At the end of each finger dock was a plank, extending out like a low diving board. A boy dressed in jeans and a white shirt lay down on each plank and reached out to grasp the stern of each crew, to hold it there until the starting commands were given. Because the boats weren't exactly the same length, the starter then instructed a second boy to extend or pull in the moveable finger dock, thus lining up the bows of the crews perfectly.

While this alignment was happening, the coxswain of each crew was busy keeping their boat on point, centered in their own lane. In windy conditions, this task was particularly challenging, and if an eight went off the line crooked, the coxswain would immediately lose time and speed correcting the boat's course. Thus, just before the race began, the coxswains who were still adjusting their course held their hands aloft, indicating to the starter they weren't quite ready. When all the hands were down, the race would begin.

When Gail glanced back and saw the hands of the coxswains held aloft, readying themselves like bronco riders, she knew that they were in trouble.

"WAY ENOUGH AND TURN US AROUND!" she yelled at Lynn. "WE'RE GOING TO MISS THE RACE!"

The Americans had been so distracted by the delay of the race that they hadn't heard the call to the line. Quickly, they spun the boat around, the port side backstroking and the starboards rowing. A sixty-foot-long shell, however, isn't designed to turn in place, and the maneuver seemed to take forever. As they sped off toward the starting line, Gail could only hope the other crews were having trouble settling into the stake boats. God, this was the last thing the crew needed before the final. If they hadn't been on pins and needles already, rushing down to the start made certain they would be.

But surely they wouldn't start the race without them, would they?

Nearing the line, she saw that this was exactly what was going to happen. The five other boats were all lined up; the starter was calling out to each of them. No one seemed to care that the Americans weren't there in the empty lane. In good FISA fashion, they were going to start on time—with or without them.

To come this far and not to race. *It was impossible*, Gail thought. The crew would forever be a laughing stock, the ones who had literally missed the boat. Something had to be done. But what? Even rowing at full tilt, they were still a good thirty or forty strokes from the line; and in the time it would take them to circle around and come up into place, the three-minute race would practically be over. Then she came up with a radical idea.

"CUT ACROSS THE COURSE!" she instructed Lynn.

Using the small rudder that controlled the boat's steering, Lynn swung them diagonally across the race course, directly in front of the other boats. Turned sideways, the long boat suddenly presented a formidable obstacle for at least two of the lanes—and forced the starter to abandon his effort to begin the race without them. A brief moment of confusion followed, and then the starter yelled at them to quickly pull into position.

For interrupting the race, they were assessed one false start. Two false starts and a crew would be disqualified. That meant they would have to go off the line conservatively, but that was all right. At least they would race.

The U.S. strategy was basic: come off the line at forty strokes a minute, settle twice (to make sure that Carie actually *did* settle), and row the body of the race at a 36. They'd stay long and powerful and not get rushed. Then for the last twenty strokes, they'd crank up the stroke rating again, when Lynn gave the command, "Do it now!" That's when they'd take a crack at the Russians. Perhaps they'd surprise them this time.

The boats were lined up, the rowers poised and silent. Their torsos leaned forward over their bent legs, arms outstretched, like sprinters waiting for a gun to go off. And if only there was a gun, instead of the formal French commands that seemed to take forever to be spoken. Then their still legs would become pistons, burning from the exertion of driving down 100 times without relent. But at least after that it would all be over. The waiting was far worse than the race itself.

"ÊTES-VOUS PRÊTES . . . ," the starter's voice began. But before he finished, the Russian crew jumped off the start, taking a few other crews along with them. Now the boats had to all be lined up again. It was another delay, and it made things even more nerve-wracking. But at least now the Americans weren't the only ones who had to be careful going off the line.

When the crews were realigned, the starter tried again. "ÊTES-VOUS PRÊTES . . . PARTEZ!" It was a clean start.

On either side of the course, the coaches watched as the orderly array of six crews suddenly broke into a jumble of forty-eight swinging bodies and oars, churning up the water behind them. The boats themselves slid back and forward against each other, trading the lead on every stroke. It was like watching the start of a marathon, just a mass of bodies jostling to break free.

Inside each crew, there was a controlled frenzy, an effort to block out the surrounding chaos and keep the focus within the boat. The Americans especially, who had so little experience together as a crew, could not forget this was their main task. A 1,000-meter race, with an average stroke rating between 36 and 40, amounted to a mere 120 strokes to sum up all of one's skill and effort, the hundreds of miles of training, the relentless battling among the members of the crew. With so few strokes in which to prove oneself, each one had to count—each had to have both intensity and precision. Unlike in many other sports, where there was always an opportunity to get back in the game, rowing had a real finality to it. A few bad strokes could easily cost you the whole race.

Something had clearly happened to the Russians, for after the first forty strokes they weren't even in the picture. Perhaps their false start had made them begin too cautiously. Perhaps they were trying a new strategy. In any case, they sat about a boat length behind the Americans, who had come off the line without restraint. And a boat length was a hard distance to make up, even for a strong crew.

By 500 meters, or the halfway mark, the six-boat field had separated into two distinct races. The Russians, the West Germans, and the Dutch, in lanes 1, 2, and 3, had all slid back to nearly a boat length behind the leaders: East Germany, the United States, and Romania. Romania was clearly in third place, but unless you were actually rowing in the boat, it was hard to tell who the leader was, East Germany or the United States.

Wiki Royden had always felt that she could look out of the boat and still stay in time with the rest of her teammates. As a sculler, she had needed to look out and see where she was going, and the habit had become ingrained. Anne Warner, rowing behind her in the four seat, would sometimes yell at her when she looked out of the boat. But it really didn't matter, she thought; besides, Gail Pierson sometimes looked out too. One of the drills that Harry made them do was to actually close their eyes and *feel* the rest of the boat, not to rely on the eyes to keep in time. If she could row blind, she thought, then she could certainly use her eyes to peek over at the East Germans.

When she glanced over to her right, only twenty feet away, she found herself looking directly across at the seven seat of the East German boat. *One seat down*, she thought. That was less than one second. Lynn had told them as much, but to see it for herself—the boat they had to beat— helped her turn the race into a personal, one-on-one battle that a single sculler loved. That's what motivated her the most.

The danger of focusing on the East Germans, of course, was that the Romanians, just off to their left, were still within striking distance going into the final sprint. They seldom missed getting a medal at the Worlds. But now, psychologically at least, the race had turned into a two-boat battle, the US against the East Germans. No one else mattered, and both crews knew it. Mentally they had locked horns and were drawing energy from each other—pushing themselves to the breaking point and beyond the reach of the other crews.

Carie Graves never looked out of the boat, especially not during such a close battle. When things got tough, she put her head down and went deep down into the basement of her mind. It was a place where she could draw enormous power, but it sometimes frightened her because of the visions that surfaced. Arthur Grace had captured Carie's striking, intense look many times—the clenched teeth, the piercing dark eyes—but even he hadn't guessed the nightmarish reality that she could enter. Sometimes she hallucinated that she was a soldier, stalking the Khmer Rouge through a marshy grassland, a gun slung over her shoulder. Her thoughts became trained on her own survival, and anger, not fear, was the emotion that ruled her.

She wanted not to run from this enemy, but to kill it. And she barely heard Lynn Silliman's command.

"DO IT NOW!" she shouted. The final sprint.

The wooden boat surged, trying to follow Carie's lead and shift into a higher gear. But they were already at the limits of their power. Their lungs felt like they were on fire, their quadriceps felt the icepick-like pain, and a sickening nausea had entered their stomachs. This should have been the breaking point for one of the crews, but both refused to give up the fight—the connection to one another. From the grandstand the boats seemed to cross the finish line together—one crew overlaid almost perfectly against the other. Even spectators standing right at the finish line, looking across the course, could barely distinguish the members of one crew from the other.

Then, like two boxers going into a clinch, the rowers suddenly ceased all motion and let their bodies slump over idle oars. Their boats continued to drift aimlessly forward until they came to a slow halt. All poise abandoned, some of the women fell back into each other's laps, while others let go of their oars and grasped the gunnels, mouths open wide, trying to find a comfortable way to rest while their chests heaved and their hearts continued to race, their bodies screaming for lost oxygen.

Neither crew had delivered the knockout punch, but this time the East Germans would get the clock's judgment—1.6 seconds ahead of the Americans.

Crew races end too soon, like a dream interrupted. But for the rowers who row the race, it is a moment of pure salvation. Some collapse, others shout for joy, and some close their eyes in silent prayer. In the slow seconds that passed while they waited to paddle into the awards dock and receive their medals, Wiki Royden gazed out of the boat at the diminishing waves. Her breathing and the wild beating of her heart had finally almost returned to normal. Now she was completely free to look out, to let her mind wander, without the reprimand of the coxswain or the coach, without the critique from one of her teammates.

After the frenzy of the race, it felt good to just sit there and do nothing but stare out at the waves. Each individual wave, she thought, looked like any other, and the waves were like the days that had gone by this summer—days of rowing and training hard that were now all mixed up in her mind and indistinguishable from one another. This day, she concluded, that had passed by so quickly was like one of the many waves that now danced around the boat. It was just a day, like any other. But at some point in the future, she sensed it would rise up and stand much higher than all the rest—like a mountain in her life.

At present, however, there were still so many questions that kept running through her mind. They had come so far so soon, and now it was suddenly all over. The electronic scoreboard displayed the race results with a cold and formal finality. Would they row into the dock and put the boat away and never see each other again? Or would this just be the beginning of things, a preview of the first Olympics next year. And what would Harry think, back at the dock? Was second place good enough for him?

All of these doubts were put aside for the moment as the team rowed up to the awards platform. There Thomi Keller, the head of FISA, was standing on the dock looking absolutely radiant, dressed in a navy blazer and white cotton trousers. The Americans weren't clowns anymore in his or anyone's eyes, but one of the best crews in the world—perhaps *the* best, if you believed that the East Germans had used steroids. Cameras flashed as Keller carefully hung the silver medals around their necks. As each one of their heads bowed in turn, they looked like they were being knighted. Then, he formally shook their hands. Apparently Keller had become fast friends with Nancy Storrs' father, who had taken the red-eye to London and then driven straight on to Nottingham to see his daughter row. With no sleep and a few beers in him, Storrs now felt giddy enough to rush onto the dock, steal a kiss from Lynn Silliman, and then pretend to nearly push Keller into the water. At this, the women broke up into laughter.

They shoved away, put on their white warm-up shirts, and then joined the other five finalists for a victory paddle over the last part of the course. The boats were supposed to finish in order of the way they had just placed, so that more photos could be taken for the local papers. Only the Germans noticed, too late, that somehow the American boat had edged by them, crossing over the finish line first. Had Carie Graves been able to speak German, she might have told them that she never paddled easy; it made her butt hurt.

Back at the dock, a small band of supporters waited for them: Sy Cromwell, Bernie Horton, Lynn's mother Ann, and of course, Harry Parker. Their quiet, reserved coach didn't quite know what to do. Usually, his victorious Harvard crews grinned and shook hands with one another, or slapped each other on the back—an occasional whoop or holler might be heard. But as soon as his women got out of the boat, they immediately ran around screaming and hugging each other, eyes welling up with tears. Even Gail Pierson, the elder statesman of the group, suddenly sprang into a handstand on the dock.

As Parker stiffly embraced each one of them in turn, a very unParker-like expression slowly began to spread across his face. It began with a huge grin, which grew bigger and bigger until it broke into an unbridled, toothy smile. It was a look of almost pure joy, and it mirrored what he saw in his team's eyes.

Meeting a Rowing Superstar

Göran R. Buckhorn

THE FIRST TIME THERE WAS A FISA (Fédération internationale des sociétés d'aviron, the international governing body for rowing, now called World Rowing) event in Sweden was in July 1984 when the Swedes organised FISA's 7th Junior Championships in the city of Jönköping. My rowing coach at Malmö Rowing Club, Tore Persson, went to Jönköping to help out. During the regatta, among other things, he drove FISA President Thomi Keller around in a launch on Lake Munksjön.

Persson, a multi-time Swedish champion in the single sculls and double sculls in the 1950s, had a limited knowledge of English, but during those days on the lake, Keller and Persson understood each other perfectly well in a way that only old oarsmen do. Both being regatta organisers, they shared the thought that a regatta is foremost for the *rowers*.

"Nice fellow," Persson would later say about Keller.

Between 1990 and 1995, FISA organised World Cup regattas for elite single scullers. The competing athletes received points at each regatta, and at the end of the season the top-ranking scullers received cash prizes. The World Cup was a way for FISA to market the sport of rowing and try to increase sponsorship and presence on TV and in media.

One of the largest regattas in the Nordic countries in the 1990s was the Scandinavian Open, which welcomed not only Nordic crews but also crews from Europe and beyond. The organisers from Denmark, Finland, Norway, and Sweden had arranged with FISA that one of the World Cup events should be included in each year's Scandinavian Open regatta. In 1991, the Scandinavian Open and World Cup were going to be held on Lake Hjelmsjön in the small village of Örkelljunga in the province of Scania in the south of Sweden. The organiser for the regatta was the regional rowing association, the Scania Rowing Federation, presided over by Tore Persson.

As one of the editors of the Swedish rowing magazine, *Svensk Rodd*, I suddenly found myself appointed the press officer for the regatta by "Regatta General" Tore Persson. However, before the regatta began on 31 May 1991, I was also to act as an all-around fellow. Therefore, I was not surprised when one of the ladies at the Swedish Rowing Federation's office in Stockholm called me one evening a few days prior to the regatta informing me that I was to meet up with one of the top international scullers in Malmö and drive her to the regatta in Örkelljunga. I asked who she was? Elisabeta Lipă, came the answer.

I knew that Lipă was an Olympic champion and a World Champion and probably had a heap of rowing medals hanging on a wall in her home in Romania.

"What languages does she speak?" I asked the Swedish Rowing Federation lady at the other end of the phone. "Well, according to the information I have," came the reply, "she speaks Romanian and French." "Okay, good," I said, "I will brush up my school French."

At noon the next day, I was standing at the bus stop outside the railway station in Malmö waiting for the bus from Copenhagen Airport. At that time, there was no bridge between Malmö and Copenhagen, so from the airport, you had to take a bus which then rolled onto a ferry which crossed the Öresund, the sound which is the border between Denmark and Sweden. Once on the Swedish side, the bus drove to the Malmö railway station to drop off the passengers.

I had practiced my school French the evening before: "Welcome to Sweden. My name is Göran and I will drive you to the regatta . . ." and so on.

But what does Lipă look like?, I thought, while I was standing there at the bus stop. I need not have worried. When the bus stopped and the travellers flooded out from the bus, there was one person a head taller than the rest. I waved while I approached Lipă, who looked down on me. I smiled, reached out my hand and said in my best French (*which would have made my old French teacher proud*, I thought): "Bienvenue en

Suède. Je m'appelle Göran et je vais vous conduire à la régate." Big smile from me.

Lipă looked puzzled. I tried again: "Bienvenue en Suède. Je m'appe—." Lipă lifted her right hand and said, "No, no. . . ." She pointed at herself. "Română, rusă" and then in another language that sounded like "rumynskiy, russkiy"—Romanian, Russian. She smiled. I smiled back. I pointed towards my car, which was parked across the street from the bus stop. I put her large bag in the boot. When Lipă sat down in the passenger seat in my small, mustard-yellow German car, she had to step out so I could adjust the seat, trying to push it as far back as possible. She sat down on the passenger seat again—she still sat with her knees up to her ears. . . .

I smiled nervously and shrugged my shoulders. Lipă smiled back. It was going to be a long drive to Hjelmsjön.

We were driving along the Malmö Canal, and we passed my rowing club. I pointed toward the club house while with one hand I made a circling motion like pulling on an oar. Then I pointed at me. Lipă nodded.

Well on the motorway, I tried to get a doomed conversation started despite no knowledge of any Romanian or Russian. I don't know why, but I said, "Ceauşescu." Lipă looked at me, appalled. "Ceauşescu bad," she said gravely. Now I nodded. One and a half years earlier, the Romanian president, the communist leader Nicolae Ceauşescu and his wife Elena had been put in front of a wall and executed by some soldiers after a brief "show trial." The video of the killings had run on every European TV channel for days just after Christmas 1989, showing what could happen when the people get tired of a dictator and decide to get rid of him.

It was a lovely, warm day. We looked out the car windows at several beautiful rapeseed fields and wheat fields we passed along the motorway. Scania is known as the breadbasket of Sweden, but I did not know how to convey this to Lipă, so I said nothing.

As we had both run out of topics to discuss, in total silence, we drove north for an hour to Lipă's motel, which was close to the regatta course. Before I left the motel, Lipă started digging in her large bag. She fished out a Romanian doll in a folk costume, smiled, and handed it to me. I smiled back and shook her hand.

At the Scandinavian Open/FISA World Cup regatta on Hjelmsjön, Elisabeta Lipă won the A-final in the women's single sculls race, followed by Silken Laumann, of Canada, and with Maria Brandin, of Sweden, in third place. Thomas Lange, of Germany, won the men's race by managing to just squeeze by Václav Chalupa of Czechoslovakia. The bronze medal went to Jesus Posse of Uruguay.

A TV team wanted to interview Lipă after her victory. After some panic at first, I managed to find a young woman who rowed in a four for one of the Baltic states and who knew some Russian and some English. The TV team got their interview.

Elisabeta Lipă would continue to take medals. During her active years as a rower, she won a total of five gold medals, two silver medals, and one bronze medal at five consecutive Olympic Games. Not even Sir Steve managed to do that. She also holds another record among rowers—20 years passed between her first and last Olympic gold medal, 1984 to 2004. Added to her Olympic medals are 13 World Championship medals in the single sculls, double sculls, quadruple sculls, coxless pairs and eights.

In 2008, World Rowing awarded Lipă with the Thomas Keller Medal, the highest honour in the sport of rowing. The award was presented the first time in 1990, the year after Keller's sudden death at age 64.

Since November 2015, Lipă has been the Romanian Minister of Youth and Sport.

Lipă's doll now stands in the prize cabinet at the rowing club in Malmö. I think few of the members know where it comes from.

My Potential Achieved

Rebecca Caroe

I WAS NEVER GOING TO BE AN OLYMPIC ATHLETE. EARLY ON IN MY ROW-ing career I did have dreams of making the first eight and was rather surprised to find that this was not the coach's plan for me. I quickly learned how to spot the capability of the other crew members, comparing them with my own. Whether it was in technique, in lifting weights, or times on the rowing machine. I realised that the things I could do something about were my fitness and my rowing technique.

However, my god-given body had limitations. First off, it took me a while to learn about what they were—and then, I had to test those limits.

My club rowing career took me through several different clubs as I moved for work. This was always interesting. I learned to blend in with new people on a new river in new crews. But did I actually achieve my potential? I believe this is the ultimate question for everyone who aspires to be an athlete. I have pondered it many times. I know that there were good races that I had with results that appeared to be better than my capabilities. And I also knew the reverse—that there were races that we threw away through poor decision making, or a lack of endeavour.

Do I know if I once in my sporting life achieved my potential? Yes, I do.

I hold this very dear to my heart.

It all started in 1999. I was part of a large women's training group at Tideway Scullers School in London. The club specialised in sculling, single sculling in particular, and as a result, we were all individually fit. We were used to going out and doing pack rows where we chased each other down and up the river.

I knew that if I could steer well, if I could manage the eddies around the bridges and if I could outsmart my crewmates with fitness and technical skill, there were times when I could achieve good results against people who were much better athletes than me, physiologically and psychologically.

The year was 2002. It was the first year that the Henley Stewards had named the women's eights competition as the Remenham Challenge Cup, and we were determined to enter. It was always going to be a tough competition for a club crew. Women's events at Henley in those days were only ever open classes. That meant that an international crew could enter. And you could find yourself racing World and Olympic champions. Despite this, there was no way Tideway Scullers School women were going to miss out on this opportunity.

As luck would have it, there weren't any internationals that year because the Lucerne Regatta was on the same weekend.

During the preparation for the regatta it seemed that good fortune was not on our side. It was the same year as the Commonwealth Regatta which meant that England, Scotland, Ireland and Wales all held selection camps to pick out the best possible athletes for their squads. For those of you not from Great Britain, we compete for our "home" country in Commonwealth events. So, if you were born in Wales or Scotland, you would definitely go and compete for them rather than try out for your club crew at Henley.

I was already in my 30s and likely too old to make the squad—I went to the trials and was not picked. Two girls from our club crew were successful. They both were extremely strong and had seven-minute ergos, but they were less experienced in the boat.

The rest of us formed an eight and did our best training together to make a fast boat.

We were tremendously excited when the draw for Henley Royal Regatta came out. We found that in the first round Tideway Scullers was picked to race the selected England crew with our two former crew mates sitting in that boat.

I remember going out on the water for that first race with our coach telling us firmly that we had nothing to lose, that we needed to do our best possible performance and to race it as if it was the final.

This led us to have no fear.

We paddled down the course as we did our warm up and we arrived at the starting blocks. I cannot remember the weather; I cannot remember being confident or nervous; I cannot remember much about the beginning of the race.

I know we went out hard though. We went out hard because we had to. We went out hard because we had a target to beat. And we went out hard because match racing is psychologically challenging. If you can get in front it's much, much more difficult for the other crew to beat you.

We drew the Berkshire station closest to the towpath where the spectators follow the race. The Club Captain had confidently told us that this gave us an advantage in the first third of the race because we were out of the stream.

The Henley race course is straight, laid out across a gentle bend in the river. The current moves from being closest to the Berkshire station to being closest to the Buckinghamshire station at different places on the course.

As a result, we knew that through the middle third of the race, the advantage was with the other crew. Our goal was to hold them as far as we were able through that middle third. The Captain had told us that if we could be within two thirds of a length when we came into the final third of the race, the advantage switched to us. He called it "the travelator." He said, "If you can stay in touch with the crew, as you come into the enclosures, there's a very good chance that you can beat them."

How he knew this I do not know, but we took confidence from his statement and had decided that this was going to be part of our race plan.

In the lead-up week we had managed to train only a couple of times. One member of the crew was an anaesthetist and she had a very intense work schedule. And as a result, we had trained on Monday and Tuesday but failed to get an outing together for Wednesday or Thursday and came together two days before the actual race for our last practice on our home waters.

Years later, when talking to the legendary coach Harry Mahon, he described a peaking program that he used for his athletes, which included a rest on the Wednesday and extremely light training on the Thursday with some sharp pieces of 500 meters and 250 meters on the Friday, the day before racing on a Saturday. And by good fortune, we had followed the exact same pattern.

Back to the race. It developed pretty much as the Captain had told us. The England crew led from the start. They were much stronger than us. We did our best to hold on to them and not let them get too far ahead.

Our coxswain, Julie, had an incredible skill; she could steer absolutely straight down the booms without deviation. She was able to keep us as far as possible to the left-hand side of the race course, so that we were little affected by the stream. This is an extreme skill, and trust me, there are a few coxes who can do this.

Coming past the Remenham clubhouse Julie told us to get ready for the last third of the race. And we attacked hard. The England crew had only been together for a few weeks and probably had had fewer practices in their boat than we had in ours. We used this knowledge as a measure of confidence in ourselves. We were a club crew who had been training together all year (although not always in an eight).

As we moved into the last third of the race, Julie called us to a supreme endeavour. And we started to push and the England lead started closing. In classic coxswain style she was telling us how close we were to the other crew. She was calling down the numbers in the boat saying that she was level with their cox and then she was level with the stroke girl.

I remember how hard I worked as we went into the travelator and then all of a sudden, as we were going past the enclosures, I found that I could not tell how hard I was working. I carried on rowing and I had an out-of-body experience—I thought I could see myself from above. I thought I could see how I was rowing. I was paying attention to how my arm was extending after the oar had come out of the water. How my shoulders followed it. And I rolled forward around my pin to place the blade in at full length and full compression and then to drive my legs. And I didn't notice the stroke rate we were going at. I could not tell if I was tired or not.

I heard Julie continuing to call us down the other crew and tell us again and again that we were gaining ground. We were moving through the opposition.

I did not allow myself time to think, I did not allow myself to dream, I did not allow myself to deviate in any way except from delivering one stroke after another and another and doing my utmost to match Kate, sitting in front of me in the two seat. We had to be the best bow pair that we could be in order to give the crew the best possible chance. This was the mindset of everybody who was in the boat that day.

As the finish line came closer, our boat continued to stride away. Suzanne, the stroke, set a stunning rate and her rhythm was long and emphatic. She was backed up with an extremely strong middle four. And all of us had this rhythm and swing which made the boat surge through the water with more economy than the opposing crew could muster.

This was one of those days when the less favoured crew got a resounding victory.

As we crossed the line, one length ahead, we knew that we had beaten the England eight and their selectors were going to be worried.

We continued through the regatta and ended up losing in the final. There, we were out-gunned by the Oxford Brookes University crew containing many former British international athletes. I never got to collect a medal. But I absolutely did know that in that race I had achieved the ultimate and my rowing career was at its peak.

After that first heat, we discussed what had happened. And it was extraordinary. Virtually every member of the crew had had a peak experience where they could not tell how hard they were rowing. They were feeling like super women and able to deliver an amazing amount of power, energy and effort without feeling that it was making us out of breath or forcing a performance from us that we were not capable of delivering.

Few athletes ever have that sort of a peak performance feeling. And even Kate, who had been to two Olympic Games, said it was the first time she had ever felt it.

Whether you are headed to the Olympic Games, or working to fulfil your potential as an athlete, I encourage you to do your best, your very, very best, and to keep an eye on how your performance is going. Because if you can have a peak performance feeling like I did that day, you will be satisfied for the rest of your racing life.

I had definitely achieved my potential.

Why a Sliding Seat

Frank Cunningham

THE SCENE IS MY LIVING ROOM, A SMALLISH, CLUTTERED HAVEN WHOSE décor is defined by forty years' accumulation of memorabilia. Conspicuous over the picture window is my Great Uncle Charles Lemuel's oar from the Harvard Class Race of 1890. I have a visitor, his bulky form outlined by a wall of books. He is sitting in a low, uncomfortable wooden chair that creaks as he shifts his weight in it. He comes quickly to the point. He says he is a karate champion and he wants to learn how to scull so that he can win a gold medal at the Olympic games.

Wrenching the smile from my face before it can betray me, I ask him how old he is.

"Thirty-nine."

"Done much rowing?"

"None."

"Canoeing, kayaking."

"None to speak of."

I had begun to be aware of something in his manner, something terribly earnest. I decided to be as businesslike and straightforward as possible. Very simply, he wanted to know how he should go about learning how to scull, and how long I thought it would take him to be competitive. What should I say? Should I be encouraging, or should I tell him to forget about it? It was becoming increasingly clear that he had absolutely no sense of humor.

I thought he should acquire a wherry and start right away getting used to it. I gave him a handful of instructional articles I had written—rather good, actually—to prepare him for what was ahead. Even so, they would hardly be enough to precipitate him into the ranks of world class scullers, so I suggested that we meet at mutually convenient times over the next several months. We chatted a bit more; then, apparently satisfied, he thanked me sincerely and, fixing his inner gaze on future Olympic laurels, stepped past my threshold into the night.

I never saw or heard from him again.

Then there were the two bike racers. Young, athletic, brimming with bonhomie. They were fascinated by the idea of sculling. It was so much like bike racing: dependent on good legs, endurance, etc. When can we start?

I pushed through their application for membership in the Lake Washington Rowing Club, gave them their safety checks in the wherry, sent them off with a few shouted instructions and stood on the dock watching two future champions paddle out the waterway.

Three weeks later I had seen one of them twice—not in rowing togs, incidentally—the other, not at all. Then, without a good-bye, they were gone. Could it have been something I said? Hardly. They gave up because they were embarrassed. They had made fools of themselves with their airy assumption that sculling was enough like riding a bike to master easily.

The kayak racer was different. He stuck to it long enough to be pretty good. But when the opportunity to make the U.S. National team as a kayak racer arose, he departed from the rowing club and, as far as I know, from rowing.

The rugby player never felt quite comfortable in a sport that carried no risk of grievous bodily harm. He soldiered along for about four months and then went back to mayhem on rain-soaked turf.

I hardly think that the reader will identify him or herself with any of these. Each one represents a special case. Not surprisingly, they were all very strong men. I admit to a little disappointment, then, because I allowed myself to think that at least some of them would do well in the sport. And if, in the fullness of time, they had actually made names for themselves, well, would it be impossible that a little bit of their success might touch me? But there it is. I have frequently found myself trying to help someone to obtain the sort of satisfaction that I have enjoyed in my fifty-five years in the sport, only to discover that they really had no interest in it—were, after all, interested in something quite different.

Many people regard rowing as primarily exercise. The sliding seat for them is just a device that makes it convenient to condition the legs at the same time the back and arms are being toned and strengthened. Like the fellow, forty-ish, who, after struggling for three or four weeks to get the hang of a wherry, asked me how long it would take before he was going to be able to work up a sweat. My answer, I'll admit, was shaped by the fact that he really wasn't enjoying his experience at all. I said, "Three months, maybe four." And I never saw HIM again.

Rowing is plying oars to move a boat. The thousands of people around the world who make their living moving all sorts of vessels, large and small, by working an oar certainly don't do it for the exercise, or fun. But I think I can understand the way they feel about the skill they have acquired through years of toil. It is a means to an end, to be sure, but I would be very surprised to learn that they don't take pride in their skill. And these are the fellows to watch. Talk about grace, efficient movement, and the mastery of a tool! Next time you have a chance to see primitive people working oars on the waterways of the world, say on National Geographic TV programs, pay close attention to the way they slide their blades in and out of the water, and the way they use their body weight to the fullest. Only in this way can they carry on hour after hour. The idea that we regard rowing as a sport would strike them as ludicrous. But to watch them is to realize that they possess artistry.

So, why row in a boat with a sliding seat? To learn artistry, of course. What better reason? Toil if you must—and I grant you that rowing can be strenuous fun—but row to achieve mastery of the oar. Sliding-seat craft are extremely sensitive and responsive to their crew. They demand good performance. Embrace the opportunity they provide to achieve a skill you can be proud of, a skill that compares with—what? I leave it to you. The appropriate analogy will spring to mind one day when you are out in a boat enjoying the water, the air, and the artistry of your blade work.

The Curious Case of Doctor Dillon

Greg Denieffe

IN BRITAIN AND IRELAND, SPORTING COLOURS ARE AWARDS MADE TO students of educational establishments who have excelled in their chosen sport. Rowing types will be familiar with Oxbridge 'Blues' and, perhaps, London 'Purples'. Often, the award is simply referred to as *Colours* and the criteria for gaining them varies from making the university/college/ school top team to gaining international recognition while still a student.

For years, the myth that a *rower* had been awarded a 'Blue' in both women's and men's university rowing has spread via the internet, popped up in magazine articles, and even gained 'credibility' in a television documentary.

The Women's Boat Race in question is the one between the boat clubs of two of England's finest collegiate universities: Oxford and Cambridge; the men's equivalent is the race for The Gannon Cup between the boat clubs of Dublin University and its near neighbour, University College Dublin.

As you would expect with an introduction like that, there is more to this story than mere rowing. In the 1940s, three extraordinary people, two patients and a surgeon, became pioneers in the still-emerging field of sex reassignment surgery. One was Laura Maude Dillon, who hailed from Irish nobility and was the first person to undergo surgical treatment to transition from female to male; one was Robert Cowell, a Spitfire pilot and a celebrated racing driver, who transitioned from male to female; and the third was a pioneering surgeon, Sir Harold Gilles, who performed most of the difficult surgeries on them.

Dillon was born in London on 1 May 1915. Just ten days later, her Australian mother died, leaving her in the care of her alcoholic father, Robert Dillon. He was heir to the Irish baronetcy of Lismullen in County Meath. Laura was raised by her father's unmarried sisters on the English south coast. When she was ten years old, her brother, also Robert, inherited the baronetcy from their uncle, John Fox Dillon, and for the next four years, the siblings spent a fortnight of their school holidays on the Lismullen Estate.

Laura attended Brampton Down School for Girls in Folkestone, and in 1934, she went up to Oxford, initially to study theology at the Society of Oxford Home-Students, later to become St. Anne's College.

It was here that Dillon began rowing, an outlet that allowed her to give vent to her masculinity. She cut her hair short and began dressing like a man. In 1935, she rowed in the two-seat of the Oxford University Women's Boat Club crew that beat the Cambridge representatives, Newnham College Boat Club. In 1936, she stroked the University crew to victory over Cambridge, again represented by Newnham College, and won a second Blue.

The 1935 race was a timed event, Oxford winning by six seconds over a half-mile course on the Tideway. As president of O.U.W.B.C., Dillon introduced a programme of reform, bringing in a coach, an old Leander man called Danks, and was instrumental in changing the way the race was run. As a result of these reforms, the 1936 race, held on the Isis, was the first side-by-side race between the universities, allowing a verdict of 'half-a-length' in Oxford's favour to be recorded.

Cambridge University Women's Boat Club was founded in 1941, while Oxford University Women's Boat Club had come into being in 1926. This allowed Oxford to select crews from more than a single college and to award colours. I cannot find any record of Dillon racing in 1937 but in 1938 the O.U.W.B.C. was unbeaten. Dillon stroked the crew to victories over London University Boat Club, Civil Service Boat Club, and King's College London Boat Club. However, she was denied a third Blue when the race against Cambridge could not be held owing to the illness of one of the 'Light Blue' crew.

As well as competitive rowing, Dillon once rowed a coxless pair with another girl, from Oxford to Putney, putting up in hotels overnight. She graduated in 1938, and the decade that followed was fateful but before leaving Oxford for good, she joined up with three other girls, crossed the English Channel and raced at Amsterdam and Frankfurt regattas, albeit without success.

Having moved to Bristol to work as a laboratory technician, Dillon began a testosterone course and in 1942, a house surgeon at the Bristol Royal Infirmary carried out a double mastectomy on her. The rowing connection endured in Bristol as Dillon coached the women's boat club at the local university. The war dragged on, and Dillon, now working in a motor garage, began to pass permanently as a man. In 1944, 'she' officially became 'he' when the name on Dillon's birth certificate was changed to 'Lawrence Michael' and the sex on the document was changed to 'male'.

These changes would eventually cause Michael the most awful rejection by his family. As 'male', he was the presumptive heir to the Baronetcy held by his brother who ostracized him when he found out about the operation and the new name. However, according to Teresa Stokes, a long-time supporter of the rowing history website Hear The Boat Sing, Dillon would not have been able to inherit a title because he was born a woman.

As well as continuing his transition and working in the garage in Bristol, Michael began studying science at The Merchant Venturers' Technical College. This preparatory course was enough for him to win a place at Trinity College, Dublin (1945–1951), beginning with their pre-medical year before moving on to read medicine. Having passed the university entry interview, he faced a second by his brother, who he called Bobby, now resident in Lismullen, 26 miles north of Dublin. They agreed that Michael would never admit to any relationship with him for fear of causing a scandal.

The temptation to join the Dublin University Boat Club was great and in doing so, he used membership of the Brasenose College 'Second Eight' to explain his previous rowing experience. In his first season with the club, he bypassed the maiden (now called novice) grade and raced as a junior (now called intermediate) at several regattas, winning eights and fours at the prestigious Trinity Regatta. This allowed him to claim Junior Eight Colours but in his own words: "My particular brand of humour demanded that after my Oxford 'Blue' I would be satisfied with nothing less than Senior Eight Colours."

His appearance on the upper reaches of the Liffey warranted an honourable mention in the club's history, *In Black & White*, published in 1991: "The war is now over, and the chorus is strengthened by the addition of a couple of ex-servicemen, and by a chap called Dillon, reputedly the subject of the first sex-change operation."

1947 appears to be a 'fallow' year, more than likely because Dillon was undergoing and recovering from treatment received in England. His autobiography, *Out of the Ordinary: A Life of Gender and Spiritual Transitions* (2016), states that he was rowing in the autumn of 1947 (training for the 1948 season).

The Irish Amateur Rowing Union introduced Umpires Licences in the 1970s. Before that, clubs nominated a list of starters, umpires, and judges and the Union published these in what became known as *The Blue Book*. In 1948, Trinity Regatta was a two-day event beginning on a Friday afternoon and concluding the following day. The Regatta Returns submitted to the Union list "Dillon—D.U.B.C." as the starter for five races on Friday 4 June. Dillon was nicely settled into the Dublin rowing scene, if not wholly in agreement with the style of rowing practised by the coaches as this quote from his autobiography demonstrates:

> [T]here was a further problem, less easily solved. Oxford rowed the orthodox style while Trinity favoured a rather spurious type of Fairbairnism. Rowing men will know that the gulf between the bigoted adherents of each style is as rigid as that between Roman Catholic and Protestant. If I rowed, it would have to be Fairbairn which was anathema to me.

On the second day of the regatta, Dillon swapped the starter's flag for the stroke seat of the D.U.B.C. 2nd Senior IV, lost the race to U.C.D., and despite having a further three years of study left, never wore the club's black and white stripey zephyr again. None of these races qualified him for a Dublin University 'Pink', the equivalent of an Oxbridge 'Blue'.

However, Dillon's rowing days were not over. The second three years of his studies in Dublin (Autumn 1948 to Summer 1951) were spent working as a trainee in the city's hospitals but that wouldn't necessarily have excluded him from membership of the University Boat Club. Nevertheless, the next time he appeared on the banks of the upper Liffey at Islandbridge, he was a member of Neptune Rowing Club. His first appearance as a member of the 'Green and Blacks' was as the official starter for the first six races of the 1949 Trinity Regatta. Neptune R.C. is just upstream of D.U.B.C. but on the other side of the river, and Dillon was not only one of their regatta officials but raced in their top senior crews for two seasons, 1948/49 and 1949/50.

Over a period of one month in the summer of 1949, he raced on four consecutive weeks with mixed results. On 7 July, a Thursday, he raced at Galway Regatta in the Irish Senior VIII Championship. Rowing in the two-seat, his Neptune crew lost to his old pals from across the river. The 1949 D.U.B.C. crew was considered fast enough to challenge for the Ladies' Plate at Henley Royal Regatta where they always race as Trinity College, Dublin (T.C.D.). Fate dealt them a poor hand when they were drawn in a preliminary race against the outstanding Lady Margaret Boat Club (L.M.B.C.) crew from Saint John's College, Cambridge. L.M.B.C. had seven Blues in their crew and a one-and-a-half length verdict sent the Dublin club home to think again whilst the winners went on to set a new course record in the semi-final. No other crew came as close to Lady Margaret as Trinity had in that first race but that was a scant reward for the coaches who had plotted Trinity's bid for Henley glory. Days later, Neptune, with Dillon onboard, led them by two lengths in the semi-final of the Irish Championship before the students reeled them in and crossed the finish line barely a length to the good.

The following week, at Dublin Metropolitan Regatta, the result was the same. However, D.U.B.C. did not travel to Cork Regatta, where on Saturday 23 July, Michael Dillon, once again Neptune's two-man, won the prestigious Leander Trophy. At the end of that month, Dillon and the rest of the Neptune seniors set off for a bank holiday weekend in the west of Ireland, taking in Carrick-on-Shannon Regatta. They had a good day, winning the Senior IV and the Senior VIII events. In total, he had six races on that August bank holiday Monday. The regatta ran a little over time with the last race, the Senior VIII final, finishing at 8.10 p.m. Later that evening, the Regatta Dance—a staple of the Irish rowing scene—was held in The Gaiety Ballroom with live music provided by Frank Murray & His Band. The dance started at 10 p.m. and finished at 3 a.m. The pubs got the early business before the crowd moved on to the Ballroom of Romance, which was 'soft drinks only'.

Dillon started the 1950 season in the stroke seat of the Neptune Senior VIII but failed to hold his place. With only one change in personnel, M. J. Moore coming into the crew at four and J. F. Swanton moving from four to stroke, Neptune was victorious at Dublin Metropolitan, Cork, Limerick, and Carrick-on-Shannon regattas.

Despite Neptune's successes, D.U.B.C. remained the top Irish crew in 1950. They reached the final of the Ladies' Plate at Henley taking the scalps of the Cambridge crews from Jesus and Pembroke colleges in the quarter-final and semi-final, respectively. New College, Oxford, held off a late challenge in the final to claim victory over Trinity, who once again returned from Henley and became Irish champions.

It was the discovery that Dillon had raced for Neptune R.C. that prompted me to seek out a copy of his autobiography to try and find the reason for the move away from D.U.B.C. According to, Chapter 6, 'Medical Student', Dillon did remarkably well in the Trial Eights for the 1948 season. His crew, composed of second and third VIII men, beat an old boys' crew and they were asked to race again immediately against the first VIII, who they beat by two lengths. The next term he was in the Senior VIII, but it was discovered that he would not be eligible for the Ladies' Plate at Henley, since an Edwardian rule forbade any oarsman who had been matriculated more than five years from taking part. Not being eligible for the Henley crew meant he was out of the crew. However, in the Summer of 1948, he was 'given' a four to stroke to allow him to receive his Senior Colours. This was the 2nd Senior IV race at Trinity Regatta on 5 June which D.U.B.C lost to their rivals U.C.D. It is probably the revelation of this nice gesture by the club that has given wings to the rumour that Dillon won university 'Blues' as both a man and as a woman.

The 1936 Regulations for D.U.B.C. allow the boat club to award Colours for Maiden, Junior, and Senior VIIIs. They are not comparable to the 'Blues' awarded by Oxford University which are awarded by the independent Oxford University Blues Committee.

Despite his successes rowing with Neptune R.C., Dillon mentions them only once in his autobiography:

> [B]ut if I could not go to Henley, I could not row in the Senior Eight anymore, for this was the peak of the rowing endeavour each year. Next year, therefore, I joined Neptune Boat Club [sic], a town club, and viewed the College regattas through the eyes of the town boys who regarded the undergraduates as "snooty" in the extreme.

However, it also explains why he lost his seat in their 1950 crew:

> On Friday and Saturday nights the ambulance would bring in an assortment of drunks with various head injuries whom they had picked up off the streets after they had consumed their week's pay. . . .
>
> But what was resented most was been woken up for a toothache, which could have gone to the dentist and had not, or the extracted tooth that continue to bleed or the pain that "I've had for days doctor." For we went to bed hopeful of a quiet night always.
>
> Once I fell foul of my colleagues, two Belfast men and one Austra-lian student, because they would come to bed at one in the morning and not put any restraint on the noise they made, shouting or singing as if it were day. In the fracas that followed I had my left elbow momentarily dislocated, and the ulnar nerve torn, which necessitated two operations by "my marn" and added to the toll of Rooksdown with which I had not yet finished and also put an end to my rowing for that year.

As Dillon progressed with his medical studies in Dublin, he underwent a series of genital reconstructive operations by Gilles at Rooksdown House, Basingstoke (1945–1949). Following his graduation from Trinity, he found work in a small hospital north of Dublin as a Resident Medical Officer (1951–1952). In time, he was contacted by Roberta Cowell (previously

Robert Cowell, a former racing driver) who had read his 1946 book *Self: A Study in Ethics and Endocrinology*. Cowell was interested in Dillon's sympathetic medical contacts, but Dillon fell in love with her and got his heart broken. Devastated, Dillon left Ireland and joined the Merchant Navy, signing up as a ship's surgeon (1952–1958). If Facebook existed at the time, I think Michael's relationship status would have read 'It's complicated'.

Alas, the contentment felt by Dillon didn't last. In 1954, the magazine, *Picture Post*, published an article on Cowell and shortly after, her autobiography, *Roberta Cowell's Story*, was released to a readership looking for sensationalism. It led to Michael Dillon being identified as the doctor that had carried out the illegal (at the time) orchiectomy on Cowell. The media publicity surrounding the news caused Dillon to flee. In May 1958, the *Sunday Express* printed an article containing an interview with Dillon's brother Robert; either someone had triggered that *Debrett's* and *Burke's* peerages differed by referring to Michael as 'brother' and 'sister' respectively, or they were tipped off by Cowell.

Dillon resigned his post as ship's surgeon and disembarked in Kolkata (at the time Calcutta). For the next four years, he practised Buddhism, became a monk (of sorts), and changed his name to Lobzang Jivaka. He died on 15 May 1962 at the young age of forty-seven having suffered from malnutrition and pneumonia. His autobiography, *Out of the Ordinary: A Life of Gender and Spiritual Transitions* was finally published by Fordham University Press (New York) in 2017. His brother, Sir Robert William Charlier Dillon, 8th Baron of Lismullen, had wanted the original draft from 1962 destroyed but Michael's London literary agent, John Johnson, successfully defended all legal attempts to make him hand it over. The Lismullen Baronetcy became extinct on the death of Sir Robert who died on Christmas Day 1982.

In 2015, Channel 4 Television broadcast *The Sex Change Spitfire Ace*, a reference to Roberta Cowell, in their *Secret History* series. It covered Dillon's life and relationship with Cowell and is well worth watching because it has the only known video of Laura Dillon rowing.

After reviewing all the evidence, I declare the result of the Colours argument as Blues 2—Pinks 0. Honourable mention for D.U.B.C. Senior Colours. Leave to Appeal granted.

Downfall of Rowing's Master Class

Christopher Dodd

THE HUBBUB IN THE SUMPTUOUS COLUMBIA CLUB CHANGED ABRUPTLY to gasps and cheers when a steward rolled a giant TV set into the room and announced that something sensational was going on. It was Thursday 9 November 1989 at a reception for the FISA coaches' conference in Indianapolis. The assembled company watched agog as men and women set about tearing down the hated Wall separating East and West Berlin.

Wilfried Hofmann, president of the East German rowing federation and stalwart of Dynamo Berlin, the police sports club, was wedged in an armchair in pole position before the box. I watched his jaw drop to an unprecedented depth as his ginger complexion turned white. By breakfast time, Hofmann had vanished.

This is how the hierarchy of FISA, the Fédération des sociétés d'aviron (now known as World Rowing), learned of momentous changes that were to compound the federation's internal turmoil. The tumult began when Thomi Keller, long-standing president of FISA, died suddenly a few days after its 1989 congress in Bled had elected him president once more for what would have been his final year in office.

The swallowing of the Democratic Republic by Federal Germany occurred in a haste that would have been described as unseemly if the DDR could claim significant numbers of mourners. The immediate consequence for FISA was to make provision for two German teams to compete in the world championships a year hence. The two German rowing federations merged after East and West crews crossed the finish line for the last time deep in the Tasmanian forest at Lake Barrington for the 1990 World Championships.

I was in Indianapolis because I had just begun research for *The Story of World Rowing* (Stanley Paul, 1992). The collapse of the Wall made my planned visit to Germany urgent and poignant. Thus, in January 1990, I found myself in Hofmann's austere office at the German Gymnastics and Sports Association in East Berlin. It was a tidy room with a large bare desk and a heavy-duty bookcase along one wall. There may have been a portrait of head of state Erich Honecker on the wall, but perhaps I'm imagining it.

The atmosphere was bleak and made bleaker by our mutual lack of common vocabulary. I asked the president of East Germany's rowing federation what contribution the Deutsche Demokratische Republik (DDR) had made to the sport, and what did the future hold? 'The training system is no good for the new political system,' Hofmann said after a pause. 'There will be less time for training, less money, new motivation . . . coaches, sportsmen and functionaries must find another way.' Another, longer pause. 'The old system is finished.' Then Hofmann wept as he gestured to the bookcase, the closed glass doors of which somehow signified an era's end. 'The whole history of DDR rowing and its achievements is in that case,' he blubbed. 'The West Germans will destroy it.'

I found a much happier scene beside the Spree at the yard of VEB boats, where a trailer from Britain was loading racing shells. Klaus Filter of the DDR's research lab for development of materials for sports equipment (Forschung und Entwicklungsstelle für Sportgeräte) shook my hand warmly across his desk, a desk top as empty at Hofmann's but for a marketing manual in English. The portrait on naval architect Filter's wall was of Che Guevara. Here was a man who already knew that what he had created at the old Pirsch yard was marketable. He took me off to a posh tearoom on the eastern side of the Brandenburg Gate to celebrate being able to go to a posh tearoom.

At Grünau, the rowing headquarters of East Germany and site of the 1936 Olympic regatta, Helmut Pohlenz relaxed in the Liebig café. He was chief doc to the DDR rowing federation and a member of FISA's medical commission, and was pleased that he and his family would now be able to visit relatives in Hamburg, and drive a Volkswagen to get there instead of the Trabant that was his on a ten-year waiting list. But his professional life was in jeopardy because the Federal Republic did not recognise East Germany's medical qualifications.

I took the train to Leipzig (where free bananas were being thrown from trucks to passers-by) and knocked on the unmarked door of the university medical laboratory to talk to its director, Dr Professor Buhl. This was sparked by a tiny news agency report in the *Guardian* quoting Buhl's confession to the existence of a doping programme—the significance being that he was the first East German to do so while remaining in post.

When I told Buhl I was from the *Guardian* and I wanted to interview him about doping, he replied that he was very busy. I said I was in Leipzig for four days. He said please come back at five-o-clock. When I returned he took my photographer colleague and myself to his home for dinner and talked freely of his laboratory's work on the nervous system. He described how they were now able to give an athlete a map of how his or her body performed and how stimulants might change that performance. He said that the laboratory never administered drugs—that was down to coaches. Was there any research or advice on side effects? No, he said, that unfortunately wasn't in the government's remit. I asked him what would have happened if he refused this work. 'I would be sent to a rural clinic as a general practitioner', he said.

Dr Buhl came over as a high-minded scientist who was aware that his work had been abused, trapped into reaching for the 'I was only following orders' conundrum. I felt sympathy for him. When I asked what he hoped for in the new Germany, he said that his family looked forward to using the pool at the university where he worked.

While the hundreds of coaches and employees in East German rowing were contemplating their future, FISA was struggling into a new order. After Keller's death, Denis Oswald found himself thrust into the deep end at the beginning of his presidency, while the new professional director, John Boultbee, was still wet behind the ears. New media and marketing commissions were set-up, and other commissions updated. The development programme turned its attention to east Europe.

In May 1990, Oswald appealed for that good old left-wing sentiment, solidarity, in *Regatta*, Britain's rowing magazine. He wrote that the reduction in financial support for rowing in Eastern Europe means that if we don't keep high standards in those countries, we will lose some variety and strength. He asked where women's rowing would be in 1990 if it weren't for the eastern bloc countries. 'We're all in the same boat, after all,' Oswald concluded. FISA's new buzz word was 'universality'.

During Henley Regatta in 1990, the *Guardian* was first to report a significant sighting at Leander Club, home of the pair-oar Steve Redgrave and Matt Pinsent whose eyes were focussed on gold at the 1992 Olympics in Barcelona. They were seeking a coach because their guru Mike Spracklen was with the Americans in California. So on that day in Henley, Jürgen Gröbler and his family were being entertained by the 'Pink Palace's' captain 'while the Groblers studied the natives before deciding to accept the post of pro coach for a salary worth millions of oestmarks,' as *Regatta* magazine put it later. Thus, a new life began for a man who coached 37 East German crews to Olympic or World medals. By now, incidentally, Gorbachev's *perestroika* in the Soviet Union resulted in CCCP strip joining DDR strip as premium items in the rowers' redundant-apparel exchange market.

On the whole, Oswald's prayers were answered. The Cold War was over and the Rowing Wall was rubble. By 1991 there were former East German coaches at work in Australia, Austria, Belgium, France, Italy, the Netherlands, USA, and Britain. Secrecy had been blown out of the water. Werner Berg, the little Stasi spy who always travelled with DDR teams, was redundant (the western press enjoyed putting technical rowing questions to the eavesdropping Berg, knowing full well that he hadn't a clue what makes a boat go faster). Happily, Hofmann's gloomy forecast of destruction of DDR history did not come about, and some years later Hofmann co-curated a marvellous exhibition of rowing club history that toured the new, united, Germany.

The February/March 1991 issue of *Regatta* magazine printed an obituary of DDR rowing and its achievement of 153 gold medals, 74 silvers, and 42 bronzes in European, World and Olympic regattas from 1966 to 1990 (total golds awarded in those events equals 334). The last word belonged to Bruce Grainger, at that time Britain's performance director. Grainger studied under Karl Adam at West Germany's Ratzeburg academy and was a translator of *Rudern*, Ernst Herberger's DDR manual of rowing. Grainger acted as Wilfried Hofmann's interpreter and translator on FISA's youth commission. His conclusion after the Berlin Wall fell:

> *It's right to acknowledge the contributions of the East Germans over the years because they have set a tremendous standard for the sport. For the last seven or eight years crews from other countries have been able to match those standards, and I'm glad that this has happened because if we'd never met that challenge before the Berlin Wall came down we'd never have been able to turn round and say we'd done it.*

Hear, hear!

A Different Symphony

Stephen Kiesling

Rowing at Yale, Stephen Kiesling (class of 1980) decided to write his senior thesis on rowing while attempting to qualify for the 1980 Olympics. *The Shell Game* (1982) is his journey from racing against Harvard to the World Championships and finally to the Olympic Team. This chapter begins at the US national team selection camp during a seat-racing duel with Harvard stroke Gordie Gardiner, fighting to earn the last seat in the straight four to compete at the 1979 World Championships in Bled, Yugoslavia.

Grace, in another form, also gave Gordie a second chance. Immediately after the practice, he argued that the results of the seat racing were not reliable because the boats had been so erratic in the previous practices. In any case, he argued, we had been at the camp so long that the results of any one practice should not be decisive. Before the next practice, Findley Meislahn, the coach of the straight four, told me that there was some possibility that I would be switched again. I knew then that when the boats were pulled together, Gordie and I would be the only changes.

Why would they let him try again unless they wanted him to win? I thought to myself as I went down to practice. Findley told me that because I had won the first time I would be given the seat unless there was a dramatic reversal from the previous practice, but I was nervous and frightened. It occurred to me that the coaches might want to keep Gordie rowing with us until the remainder of the four was selected, but that seemed unlikely. After all, Gordie was from Harvard, and the Harvard coach, Harry Parker, was head coach of the National Team.

When we went down to row, the business with the oars continued. I never saw Marcella until the boats were pulled together and Gordie and I were told to switch. Once again, he refused to give it up. My four had won the first race, but I was not thinking clearly and had wasted most of my reserve energy trying to increase the margin in the last few strokes. As we switched seats, I was scared. I wanted to reach out and grab Marcella, just to deprive him of it.

Gordie, more than anyone other than Harry Parker, had engineered our loss at the Ferry; and now a strange, unreasoning dread told me once again that something was badly wrong—although rationally I believed I was where I wanted to be. Because my boat had won the first race, I needed only to tie the second to win.

A five-minute seat race is a long way, almost a mile, and only one minute short of the standard 2,000 meters. Five minutes seemed infinitely more painful than the four-minute pieces of the day before, and five strokes into the piece I realized that I did not have the concentration. Powered by hatred and fear, I could not relax. *Just like the Harvard race,* I thought in a wave of nausea, but when I tried to relax, the boat became sluggish. Gordie's boat began inching away.

The other four appeared to be moving away faster than it actually was because the boats were converging slightly. Because our boat tended to pull a bit to the starboard side and the other boat pulled a little to port, soon the blades from the two shells were only inches apart, and we were two seats down and then three. Coming into the last minute, though, we pulled back and finished even. Once again victory was mine, but the margin was smaller. I prayed that the coach would switch another pair of oarsmen to indicate that my victory had been telling, but instead he made us line up for the next piece. I had won three times, but one loss would throw the entire series into question.

Two minutes into the next piece, the boats were even but my body was giving way. A muscle in my chest which I had pulled early in the season began to knot and then my legs started to cramp. The shirt on the man in front of me melted in a swirl of red and blue revolving in the flow of oars. My head, which was usually erect and focused on the shoulders of the man in front, lolled from side to side. With two minutes left in the piece, it occurred to me with an impersonal clarity that I did not have seventy strokes left in me—maybe ten and maybe twenty, but not a full two minutes' worth. I was going to lose that piece and any subsequent piece I would row.

The four was again veering to starboard only a few feet from the blade tips of the other boat when mine began to fall back. *I have only ten more strokes*, I thought in despair. Ten more strokes. . . . Instantly, I changed my technique. As we became more tired, we tended to decrease the length of our strokes, but now I reached out beyond the normal limit and then gave what I thought was a tremendous surge at the end of the stroke. I counted these strange new strokes as once again the shells faded into the whirl of color. One, two, three. The boat staggered. At any moment it would die. Four, five. I glanced over to starboard but could not focus. I could hear the coach yelling directions frantically from the launch. Our bowman awoke to the danger and called for the port side to ease, but he too must have seen the escape because he did not turn the rudder. Nine, and then on the tenth stroke, the blades of the two boats tangled in a splintering crash—dead even with one minute left in the race. That night Gordie packed his bags.

A week later, Paul Prioleau, Dave Kehoe, John (Twig) Terwilliger, our coach Findley Meislahn, and I put our four on the trailer and drove to the trials at Princeton to race the University of Pennsylvania and Vesper Boat Club for the right to go to the World Championships. In the other straight fours were members of previous national teams who, having been cut from the camp, returned to their clubs to train for the trials. They began practicing two weeks before our four had even been selected, but having survived the camp, we knew that we should win. Tired of uncertainty and annoyed that we had to race against oarsmen whom we had beaten individually at the camp, we stenciled on the backs of our racing shirts our new logo—a picture of two vultures and the words PATIENCE MY ASS, WE'RE GONNA KILL SOMETHING! Five hundred meters into the race we led by a seat. At a thousand meters, when we already led by a length of open water, we raised the rating and then raised it again with five hundred meters to go. We won by six boat lengths, a "time zone," and paddled back to the deck to be outfitted with the blue shirts with red-and-white sashes of the United States National Rowing team.

John Terwilliger, the three man of the straight four, came from nowhere and made the team. A large, lean cowboy from Wyoming, Twig decided that he wasn't working hard enough at the nearly nonexistent rowing program at Seattle Pacific University, so he packed himself into his car, turned on the tape deck, and headed east. He arrived in Boston in the middle of May because he had heard that Harry planned to coach a group in preparation for the national camp. Everyone else in the group had heard of everyone else at least by reputation, but no one had yet heard of the Twig.

Harry took him out for a few practices in Cambridge and then told him to try again the next year, but because Twig had driven three thousand miles, Harry led him down to the Harvard rowing tanks to show him some technical points to work on back in Seattle. Twig took a seat in the vacant tank room and started to row. After twenty minutes Harry left to coach the next practice. Several hours later, when Harry was in his office finishing up, an oarsman came to the door. Someone, he told Harry, was rowing in the tanks and wanted to know if he could stop. No one is sure how long Twig rowed that day, but if he had been on a straight course, he might have made it back to Wyoming. Harry told him to show up for practice the next morning.

John Biglow, who had initially hated me for being inexperienced, considered Twig's success outside the realm of decency. Initially, there was little contact between the two because John stayed with the eight, but only a few days after we arrived in Yugoslavia, John fell ill with a sudden virus. He turned pale, lost weight, and eventually had to be replaced by one of the spare oarsmen. For fear of infecting anyone else, he roomed alone and often dined at his own table. I don't know if his sudden vulnerability made him recede into himself or whether he felt that the team abandoned him as soon as he could no longer row; whatever the reason, the illness took the heart out of him. After a couple of attempts to get back in the boat, he resigned himself to life on the bank. That was when he, Dave Kehoe, Twig, and I began our nightly hearts game.

John and I had often played hearts, a card game somewhat like bridge, before races at Yale, and we convinced Twig and Dave to join us. The object of the game was not to take any hearts unless one managed to take all the hearts and the queen of spades. All was well so long as Twig sat quietly losing, but once he shot the moon and beat us all. It was after the first hand on our second night of play when I asked Dave how many hearts he had.

"None."

"John, how many do you have?"

"None."

"Well, I don't have any either," I said in disbelief, looking over at Twig, who was counting his cards.

"I have thirteen hearts and I picked up the queen," he said ruefully. "How many points is that?"

"Twig, that means you won."

John stalked off in a rage. Thrashing Twig at cards had been one way for John to emphasize subtly that Twig was an outsider and to ease his own mounting frustration at not being able to row. To be beaten by me at cards was bad, but to be beaten by Twig was too much. For the remainder of the trip John went out of his way to prod Twig's already short temper, until the night after the finals Twig finally lost control and punched him in the nose.

Before he went to the camp, John thought that the national team would be the ultimate team, that we would have so much in common that the individuals would be a more cohesive group than even the Yale crew had been. The national team boats were rowed so well that we could use the pronouns "I" and "we" interchangeably when describing a set of strokes. When we rowed, I wasn't conscious of others; instead, I was conscious of the amplification of my own strength by the others, but John thought that we would have that same unity outside the shells. At the camp and especially after he got sick, John learned that the intimacy he expected was more commonly a single-minded dedication to looking after ourselves. Because Twig was different from the rest of us, his presence exemplified the failure of John's expectations. John hated Twig because he didn't seem to know how to look out for himself; however, when I was arrested by the militia while climbing the flagpole, Twig stayed close to make sure nothing happened to me.

As I followed Twig and the others up the stairs to our rooms one night after another hearts game, I thought of how different we were from the Yale crew. We were better oarsmen with higher expectations, but we hadn't grown up together. We came together fully formed and served one another as the next step toward a personal excellence. Being in the company of the best would bring out the best in us individually, but we were all too conscious of ourselves to be melded into a whole greater than the sum of its parts. We raced together on that clear mountain lake in Bled with the castle on the cliff and the island with the little Romanesque chapel, but we didn't know what or whom we were racing for. My goal had been to make the team, and I had never thought beyond that. Against Gordie I had carried the banner of Yale, but afterward I had earned a place on this new team, a team which, rather than providing a direction, provided only a vehicle for our own individual directions.

Halfway through our first heat in the World Championships we were in second place and moving on the leading four, but when the time came to sprint we lost heart and dropped back to third. On the following day, a crab in the start of the repechage heat, our second chance to qualify for the semifinals, put us a length behind the other five boats, and it was only the shame of not qualifying that brought us together to win. When on the third day of racing we paddled out to the semifinals, no one expected our boatload of rookies to earn a place in the finals. Tension was high in the boat; in fact, I think we hated each other, but I knew that when we channeled that hatred into rowing the boat, we lifted it out of the water and flew. During one ten-stroke piece, Twig made us so angry that we spelled out the only ten-letter obscenity, calling one letter at each stroke. Afterward, I thought that if we could harness that energy for 2,000 meters, we could beat the East Germans. As it turned out however, we failed to qualify for the finals, and finished the next day second in the Petit Finals, or eighth in the world. I left Yugoslavia wanting to get back to my friends at Yale, but mostly eager to start training for the 1980 Olympics.

The Feathers

A Forgotten Centre of Early British Rowing

Tim Koch

ALTHOUGH IT IS LITTLE DOCUMENTED, IT IS GENERALLY ACCEPTED that the sport of rowing by "gentlemen amateurs" grew up in the late eighteenth and early nineteenth centuries around the schools of Eton and Westminster and the universities of Oxford and Cambridge.

However, competitive and often highly remunerative professional rowing by working-class watermen, boatbuilders, and the like had existed in many parts of Britain long before this, providing both a spectacle and a gambling opportunity for all social groups.

When not racing, thousands of London watermen and lightermen were rowing people and goods along the Thames, a trade that generated much work for boat builders and their yards.

Thus, when gentlemen amateurs began to take an interest in rowing for pleasure and sport, the potential was already there. In *The Brilliants: A History of the Leander Club* (1997), Geoffrey Page wrote:

> *The banks of the Thames, upstream of Old London Bridge, were lined with dozens, if not hundreds, of riverside yards, building, hiring and housing boats, and with countless watermen seeking a livelihood, ready to provide instruction to anyone wanting to learn the aquatic arts. . . . This explains why rowing, with all the necessary facilities available, got off to a flying start on the Thames in [central] London. . . . The owners of [boatyards] quickly responded to the demand*

by adding changing-rooms, club rooms and, in some cases, catering facilities.

By the 1840s however, London's heartland even with its plentiful supply of boatyards and professional watermen was becoming less and less attractive for the amateur oarsman. The Industrial Revolution brought serious problems of pollution and the rapidly increasing population made the Thames in the centre of the capital "the largest navigable sewer in the world." Increasing river traffic by all sorts of craft carrying passengers, goods, and materials made an almost impossible environment for small rowing boats, the washes of the powered craft made worse by the newly built embankments, and the buttresses of increasing numbers of bridges proving additional navigation hazards.

One positive thing that the Industrial Revolution did bring for amateur oarsmen was to provide rapid railway transport. By 1846, anyone who lived and worked in the centre of London could be in a number of rural riverside villages within thirty minutes. Thus, on its foundation in 1856, London Rowing Club could base itself in Putney, six miles from the centre of London. In *The Brilliants*, Geoffrey Page states that this "shifted the centre of gravity decisively from Lambeth to what was then still the country village of Putney, and sounded the death knell of the score or so of small private clubs which had hitherto catered for amateur oarsmen in the metropolis."

The formation of London RC at Putney was more than just a geographical move. Amateur rowing on the Thames had deteriorated between 1835 and 1855. In the words of Chris Dodd's history of London RC, *Water Boiling Aft* (2006), "An eight from the tidal Thames had not been seen at Henley for years. Was rowing for amateurs and gentlemen dead, or could it be rekindled?"

To compete against college crews from Oxford and Cambridge Universities and other "closed" clubs, the new London RC would have to be a club "on a gigantic scale" with its own boathouse and boats. When Thames RC and Leander joined London on the Putney Embankment in the 1860s, the fightback had truly begun.

As part of the move out of central London, the old Championship Course that ran between Westminster and Putney (or sections of it) was abandoned and events such as the Oxford–Cambridge Boat Race, the World Professional Sculling Championship, and the Wingfield Sculls all ran upstream from Putney, most adopting the new Championship Course, Putney to Mortlake.

Thus far, this story has followed the conventional wisdom that rowing as a sport arrived almost overnight in the fishing village of Putney—which had not seen anything of the like before. However, this is rather like those old history books that told us, "Columbus discovered America"—ignoring the fact that the people who already lived there were perfectly aware of its existence. Similarly, when the gentlemen amateurs arrive in Putney in the late 1850s and early 1860s, The Feathers Tavern and Boathouse (a.k.a. Salter's Boatyard), sited about 1,300 metres downstream of Old Putney Bridge, had been an important centre of amateur and professional rowing since perhaps the 1830s. This is a fact that is rarely—if ever—acknowledged and which this study intends to make better known.

The Feathers pub in Wandsworth was first recorded in 1755. It was sited near the mouth of the River Wandle where it entered the Thames. The Wandle is a tributary of the Thames that runs nine miles from its source in Croydon, South London.

When a short canal was built passing the Feathers in 1802, an association between the pub and boating began. In his history of Thames RC and of Tideway Rowing, *Hear the Boat Sing* (1991), Geoffrey Page says, "There was a sculling club based on Wandsworth before 1830." Frustratingly, he gives no more detail.

The part of The Feathers in the story of British rowing is associated with the three names that ran the boatyard between the 1830s and the 1880s: Salter, Clasper, and Gibson. However, their importance declines with the chronology.

The Feathers was in the hands of the Salter family for nearly forty years beginning in 1836 when James and Elizabeth Salter moved from Fulham to Wandsworth to run the riverside tavern. While their interest in rowing was possibly based on how much beer thirsty oarsmen would buy, their sons, Harry, John, and Stephen, took a much more active interest in the sport.

John and Stephen set up a boat building and hire business in Oxford in 1858 and the firm of Salters continues to be active in the boating world to this day. A short history of the company on its website says:

> [*The Feathers*] *became one of the early centres for rowing in the country and by the middle of the century Harry Salter (1822–1874) had established himself as one of the foremost rowing coaches of the era. The family were also enthusiastic competitors who entered many of the major regattas for professional oarsmen. In 1850, John and Stephen spent time with the famous Tyneside boat-builder and oarsman Harry Clasper, and, after returning to Wandsworth, the racing boats they built began to achieve considerable success in contests around the country. In 1857, they built their first eight that was used by Cambridge in the university boat race.*

A wonderfully atmospheric and gritty description of The Feathers was in a piece in the *Sporting Gazette* of 1 November 1873. Under the series title, *London Sporting Haunts* was *No.1—The Feathers Tavern, Wandsworth*. It read:

> *Anyone travelling down the South-Western loop line from Waterloo must have noticed to the right hand, just past Wandsworth Station, a low built white house standing . . . on a delta of the mouth of the River Wandle. This is "The Feathers Boathouse." . . . The landlord [is] Mr Henry Salter, more familiarly known as Harry Salter, one of the celebrated boatbuilding family of that name, and always one of the sagest trainers and best coaches on the London water. . . .*
>
> *The hostelry itself is not a very large or a very magnificent one. There is nothing of the Star and Garter about it, and ladies have never within the memory of man visited it. . . .*
>
> *You can only get to the river through the public house, and there is a total absence of the towpath and promenade which are so prominent*

*at Putney. Those who come here mean business and nothing but
business. . . .*

*[Through] a rift in the [tobacco] smoke cloud, we catch a glimpse of
. . . Old Harry Salter. . . . Why "Old" it would be difficult to say for he
is hardly passed middle age. A tall, dry, hard-faced man with a pleasant eye and speaking in a low, quiet voice. . . . [Perhaps] a bit stooped
and slow now . . . but there is enough left of his great square back and
his long, weird-like arms for you to see that he must have been . . . a
wonderful man at the end of an oar when he was young and the Salter
Brother's four was at the head of the Thames.*

*[In] the yard is a range of boatbuilding shops and as we pass we
catch a sniff of sweet, fresh pine wood and a glimpse of milk white boats
. . . as yet unbaptised and now lying deserted in knee deep shavings.*

*Further down are the dressing-rooms of the different clubs, of all
shapes and sizes. There is the little caboose of some small tradesmen's
club. . . . Further down is the square room of a minor club, run with
lockers and with a comfortable zinc bath in its corner; and the end
of the row is the long building occupied by the West London Rowing
Club, the only club of any note rowing from the "Port of Wandser" as
it habitues love to call it. . . .*

*Everything here is rough and ready, but comfortable and clean.
Towels, flannel caps . . . hair brushes, sweaters, pea jackets etc all litter
the table in the middle of the low pitched room, while the smell of hot
men is less noticeable than it otherwise would be from the fact of there
being ample ventilation from the front windows.*

That Harry Salter catered for all social classes was confirmed by the *Sporting Life* of 9 January 1861 in their review of that year's *Rowing Almanac
and Oarsman's Companion*. It noted that:

*There are . . . two very excellent chapters on training by the renowned
Harry Salter of Wandsworth who has turned out more winners than
any man of the present day. . . . The rowing men of today comprise so
many different classes, or, to be more distinct, have so many habits of*

*living, each contrary to each other . . . that it is hardly possible to define
a dietary system or course of practice that shall be common to them all.*

Some of the most important professionals of the 1840s, '50s, and '60s
trained out of The Feathers under Salter. Two of the greatest Tyneside
professionals, Robert Chamber and Harry Clasper, treated The Feathers
as their London headquarters when competing on the Thames. Tom Cole
was trained by Salter to become the Professional Single Sculls World
Champion from 1852 to 1854. After Henry Kelley had a particularly successful 1856 season, *The Era* of 7 December wrote, "We think that Harry
Salter has this year trained more winners than we scarcely have ever heard
of and had made a good ending by training Kelley."

When Harry Salter died in 1874, a sale notice for The Feathers
appeared in the *London Evening Standard*. In a listing of the clubs rowing
out of the place, the sale notice names some that were undoubtedly for
gentlemen amateurs, notably Vesta, Westminster School, The Times, and
West London.

The most important club to row out of The Feathers, however, was
not any of those mentioned above. It was in fact the Wandle Club which
had probably ceased to exist by 1858 but which can be said to have played
a vital if little-remembered role in the development of amateur rowing in
Britain as it provided many of the founding members of London Rowing
Club.

Bell's Life of 28 February 1858 carried a story that "the late Wandle
Rowing Club" had held a testimonial dinner for Harry Salter "at their old
rowing quarters, the Feathers Tavern, Wandsworth." Importantly, it lists
some of those who were formerly members of the Wandle.

At Henley, the Wandle Club had won the Silver Goblets in 1855
(A. A. Casamajor and Josias Nottidge), the Diamonds in 1854 (Herbert
Playford) and in 1855 (Casamajor). Further, wearing Wandle colours, the
Wingfields had been won by Herbert Playford in 1854 and Casamajor
in 1855. These three men were the leading founder members of London
Rowing Club: Nottidge had the vision to call the meeting that resulted in
the formation of London RC and was its first chairman; Herbert Play-
ford was its first secretary; Casamajor was its first star oarsman and its

third secretary. Other Wandle men included London's first captain, Frank Playford, its second captain, James Paine, and one of the first joint treasurers, John Ireland.

At London RC's first Henley in 1856 (where the qualification rules made London RC row as the Argonaut Club) the former Wandle men, Josias Nottidge, A. A. Casamajor, James Paine, Herbert Playford, and F. Levien won both the Stewards and the Wyfold. The same four comprised the final of the Silver Goblets with Casamajor and Nottidge beating Paine and Playford. In addition, Casamajor won the Diamonds. London RC can claim the wins, but I suggest that the Wandle Club (and also perhaps Harry Slater) can claim the credit.

In a piece on Metropolitan rowing in *The Field* of 3 December 1910, it was noted that:

> *In 1856, the London Rowing Club was founded by a combination of some half dozen or more small clubs (composed principally of finished scullers) which boated from either the Feathers at Wandsworth, a very celebrated sporting drum of the last century, or from Simmonds's (now Aylings) at Putney.*

The land that housed the boatyard belonging to "Simmonds" (actually Simmons) was originally home to Searle and Son, boatbuilders, who had been established there from at least 1851. It was bought by the oar and scull makers Aylings in 1898. Since the early 1980s, the old Aylings building has been a boat chandlery, Chas Newens Marine, with a part of it being occupied by the boat club of Putney High School for Girls since 2015.

Of the fourteen oarsmen pictured in the famous 1859 Alfred de Prades print of some of the founders of London RC, eight are definitely ex-Wandle men. This number could be higher but the only list of Wandle members that we are ever likely to find is the partial one from the 1858 *Bell's Life* story.

It is not only London Rowing Club that owes a debt to Harry Salter and The Feathers, so does their old rivals, Thames Rowing Club. In 1869, a four that included the famous "Piggy" Eyre wanted to enter the 1870

Wyfold Challenge Cup at Henley, but Thames would not back them. Thus, they trained out of The Feathers, eventually providing Thames with their first Henley win.

The years 1856 to 1866 were Harry Salter's "Glory Years" but, a short time after, The Feathers ceased to be an important centre of rowing. There were several factors that caused this: professional rowing had begun a slow decline; amateur rowing with its attendant boatbuilders, oar makers, watermen, etc was increasingly based along the more suitable Putney Embankment; Salter had become increasingly ineffective as he succumbed to alcoholism, and he committed suicide in 1874 at the age of fifty-two.

It took over a decade for it to become apparent, but The Feathers really died with Harry Salter.

After Salter's death, The Feathers passed (after a four-year hiatus) to John Hawks Clasper. Like Harry Clasper, his more famous father, John Clasper was a fine oarsman and innovative and successful boatbuilder. He had established his own boat building business in Durham in 1863 but in 1867 moved to London and soon built a name for himself working out of The Feathers yard.

While John Clasper's boat building business was going from strength to strength, his attempts to make The Feathers the centre of rowing that it had been in Harry's heyday were not so successful.

After four years in charge at Wandsworth, John Clasper decided on a major change. *Bell's Life* of 16 September 1882 reported:

The latest intelligence from Putney is to the effect that John Clasper, of the Feathers, is about to migrate from the once popular boating establishment to more aristocratic regions. A new boat house is to be built for him [at Putney].

It seems but a few years ago that the Feathers was the most popular of the hostelries amongst rowing men, but poor Harry Salter let it go down very much before he died, and Clasper does not appear to have been able to make much of what was thought at the time he became its proprietor a rare bargain.

The final owner of The Feathers pub and boathouse was Lew Gibson, a well-known professional oarsman, a former steward of London Rowing Club, and one of the last fishermen to work the Putney reach.

Gibson made strenuous efforts to restore The Feathers as a centre of rowing by holding sculling races with generous prizes but also tried to attract other sporting types by laying a running track and holding athletic events, also with big rewards for the winners.

The newspapers carried several reports on Gibson's efforts during 1884 but these then abruptly stopped. Presumably, with no boatbuilding going on following Clasper's departure, with Putney now the centre of things aquatic, and with professional rowing continuing its long decline, the "muddy water-side quarters" was no longer viable.

The Feathers finally closed in 1888. The building remained standing until 1959, sited inside the Wandsworth Council Household Waste and Recycling Centre that now occupies the site. It was a slow, sad, and undignified end for such an important centre of early British rowing.

The Eight-Oared Shell

Oliver La Farge

WHEN OLIVER LA FARGE STUDIED AT HARVARD, HE TRIED DIFFERENT sports. He had played (American) football at Groton School and wanted to continue to play football at Harvard. But weighing 150 pounds, he had no future in that sport. As a freshman, he did some rowing but realized the competition was too stiff and started high-jumping to get a chance to earn his H. Then he heard that Harvard was going to follow a few other colleges and have lighter crews. He saw his chance to start rowing again, which he writes about in this excerpt from "The Eight-Oared Shell" in his autobiography *Raw Material* (1945).

It was raw, cold, early spring. As I walked over Anderson Bridge I saw the first Freshman eights getting into the river. Some damn fool stepped into the bottom of the shell and put his feet through it. Another boat got away cleanly and started going, rolling a bit but not doing badly. I could hear the cox's commands. Some upper-class eight came downstream from Newell Boathouse and passed right under me; those fellows could row. The coach followed in his launch, megaphone in hand. What he was saying was anciently familiar. After all, what the hell was an H?

I told the track coach I was going out for rowing. He seemed to disapprove, so I told him my family wanted me to. As a matter of fact, my family wanted me to do what I wanted, but I put on an act and lied because he was a pretty decent fellow and I could not face telling him that as far as I was concerned high-jumping was the bunk, and I'd rather row in the lowest crew on the river than win letter leaping over little sticks. I went down and signed up for rowing, feeling like a man reborn. So it happened that I was in the first hundred-and-fifty-pound crew ever to take the water from Harvard.

I find, in writing about rowing, that I tend to concentrate rather technically upon the sport itself with the attendant danger of losing that very background of its relation to a boy's life which would give it validity. This is partly because the average man who reads this has played football, and many women have at least had the game explained to them and have learned how to watch it, while the essentials of rowing are widely unknown. Then, while I partook of the comradeship of my crews, there were no intimate friends among them, nothing compared to my relationship with Jones and football. More important, rowing became for me an occupation, something complete in itself into which I entered and from which I returned to ordinary life, it maintained its own, unbroken stream winding through the other currents of my existence. I believe you will find that true of anyone who is truly devoted to any game.

But it had to relate to all the rest. At Groton it brought a tolerable relationship with boys whom I respected and who carried much weight in the School; it brought self-assurance and a realization of strength; it brought the curious, traditional honours of athletes. There is a lot more to the preference of boys in most schools for athletic over academic honours than mere over-emphasis on athletics. The little, new boy, looking about him for gods, finds them at the outset of his first term in the football giants. He sees these big, self-confident, deep-voiced men in their daily goings and comings as well as in the games, among them are the holders of many other honours, Prefects of the School, leaders of this and that. . . .

Rowing at School was fun, but rowing at Harvard was magnificent. There was more of it, it was more intense, and it was better rowing. The hundred-and-fifty-pound crews were step-children, born of hesitant concessions by doubting authorities; at first they could hope for no insignia, they accepted cast-off shells and unwanted, used oars and liked them. They were made up of boys who were perfectly willing to row in a soapbox if necessary so long as they could row and count from time to time on a full-fledged race. We won recognition slowly, better boats, decent oars, a minor sports letter. Not until after my time did the lightweights get the same breaks in equipment and general treatment that less conservative colleges gave their rivals. We didn't care. For three years we rowed under the brothers, Bert and Bill Haynes, who themselves adored rowing and held it a prime part of their work to make us love it, thereby making us love them. We consciously rowed *for* them. We became a crew that could make the real Varsity stretch over a short distance, we were made use of to pace the varsity for starts and sprints, one splendid afternoon we beat the Junior Varsity handily in a regular, two-mile race.

We loved it from the bitter, all-but-winter days when ice formed on the oars to the long, grass-smelling spring afternoons when we went far upriver and then, before turning back, leaned on our oars and made the age-old jokes about going a little farther and seeing if we could stroke the Wellesley crew. The rowing after dark I remember especially; I've tried to describe it a little, I never became entirely used to the beauty of city-ringed water and the mystery of the bridges.

One night in the early spring there were a great many crews out on the Charles River Basin. We were heading upstream for home, taking it easy, and I remember how clearly the voices of coxswains and coaches, the sound of the oars, came to us from all sides. Our cox was peering ahead a trifle nervously. Presently, to one side of us, we heard a practice race coming downstream, two class crews and the coaching launch behind them, with their coxswains making lots of noise and the coach calling from time to time. To play safe we lay on our oars. It was full dark, the water around us pearly in colour because of the city lights, the distance a very dark-grey haze rather than black, the sky above having the tawny quality so common over cities. A big sign on the Cambridge bank blinked on and off, flashing a red and yellow reflection across the basin almost to the side of the boat. Against it we caught a glimpse of the racing crews, the two long, rules ink-lines of the shells and the figures in them black, small outlines in motion, sliding across the flash of light in an instant. There was some other race going on somewhere, and at a safe distance behind the class crews, several more were being given a workout.

It seemed to us that the sounds of boats and the racing were getting too close together in the darkness below us. Then suddenly we heard a coach boom out in a new kind of voice, 'Easy all, there! Easy all! Hold her all! Look out, Tech crew! Look out, you there!' And into this the cox-swains' voices shouting, and other coaches, commands, 'Hold her, Star-board! Hold her, Starboard! Hold her all! Look out for Chrissakes, look out!' There was miscellaneous yelling, and then a sound as if someone had jumped on an unusually large bass viol. It was a wonderful crash, and it was almost immediately followed by another.

Like reinforcement coming into battle the second set of Harvard races swept past us, going full tilt. The shouting broke out again, more tumult even than before, and there was a third crash. Then there were a lot of orders and questions being called in the night.

Someone said, 'What the hell?'

'They ran into a bunch of Tech crews coming out from their boathouse.'

'Let's go down and pitch in.'

Ridiculous of course, but one halfway felt like that. A wind from dis-tant, ancient seas seemed to blow across us, the sound of many oars in their locks, the shouting, the crash of galleys ramming. . . .

Cox ordered, 'Forward all!' We settled into position. It was time to row home, but the quiet paddle upstream seemed strangely tame.

In the due course of time it is given to you to row a race. Not a prac-tice race against one of your own, but the real article, and the oars of the boat taking position on your port hand are painted, not crimson, but a fine, shining blue. The feeling of it starts before then, when you take your shell down and toss her better than you ever did before, and you and the managers are in different, special communion, over the free running of your slide, the grease on your oar where it passes through the lock, the comfort of the stretcher into which your feet are laced. The love you bear each man in the boat is stronger, warmer, than it has ever been; it is posi-tive, almost visible. Each man looks smilingly at his neighbour—a curious combination, already the tension and the earnestness is on their faces, but with it comes this affection. You shove off and paddle along to the start taking it easy, perfecting your form, the cox saying just what he always says, everything ordinary, everything calming.

Starting an eight-oared race is a frightful job. There is the current, and then there will be a slight cross-wind, something you wouldn't notice if you weren't trying to hold two or more boats as light as cigar-boxes in perfect line beside each other. You jockey and jockey, the good effect of the paddle wears off. You get into position, the starter has asked 'Are you ready Harvard? Are you ready Yale?' and one of the shells swings, and it all has to be done over again.

At last you are set. A racing start is entirely different from the ordinary process of getting a shell under way. This time you want to make her fly at full speed from the first stroke, you want to develop speed just as fast as it humanly possible, and faster. You have practiced many times the series of short, hard strokes and the lengthening to the full, rhythmed swing but it remains tricky, a complex set of motions to be done so rapidly and hard that it's unreasonable to think it can happen without something going wrong.

Beyond that lies the race, the test itself. You know what a gut-wracking process it is, you are too tense about the outcome, you doubt if you can stand up to it. What's ahead of you is too much. There are many things that can postpone a start and several that can cause a race to be called back within the first ten strokes. You pray for them all to happen. You are so taut inside you twang. You are afraid, not of anything, just afraid.

The pistol cracks. You carry out those first three, scrambling strokes neatly, you begin to form the full, balanced stroke as you go on to complete the ten fast ones. All those fears and tremors are gone and you are racing. Coxswain's voice comes, internationally soothing, carrying you over into the regular swing and beat of the long-term pace your crew must set, you are eight men and you are one, the boat is going with a sizzle, smoothly through the water, and out of the corner of your eye you can see the blue blades flashing alongside you.

The effort settles down and mounts again. There are races within the race, spurts when one crew tries to pull suddenly ahead, and the other answers, the sustained, increasing efforts, the raised beats of the crew behind, the somehow easier but intense drives of the leader. Cox tells you [that] you are past the halfway mark, he tells you [that] you are near the end. The start tests a good crew, the last stretch proves it. You are tired now, everything is coming to a final settlement very soon, you must row harder, faster, and still row smoothly and well. You have got your second wind and used it up, you are pooped out and you know you are at the end of your strength, you simply have nothing left in you. The beat—the rate of the stroke—goes up. Cox is yelling, pleading, advising, cursing. And you are staying with it. On the recovery the captain grunts out something unintelligible but urgent. Near the end other men may wring out cries intended to be 'Come on!' 'Let's go!', hardly recognizable. There's not much of that, it's against your training and besides wind is too precious, but the pent-up feeling is so strong that sometimes it must have an outlet. This is a good crew, a real one. As the beat is raised, as the reserve behind the reserves of strength is poured in, each stroke taken as if it were the last you'd ever row on earth, the crew still swings together, it is still one, that awareness of each other and merging together is still present and still effective.

Three-quarters of the way through you could hear them on the referee's launch and whatever others are permitted to follow, shouting, 'Come on Harvard! Come on Yale!' Now you vaguely know that they are still shouting, but you can't really hear them. There is some sort of sound around the finish line, you do know that a great many people must be making a lot of noise, but you don't hear that eighter. You are conscious of something arching up from the banks which, without looking at it, you *see*, and you know it's cheering. Your eyes are fixed on the shoulder on the man in front of you and (I rowed starboard side) the blade of Number Seven's oar, but the one thing you do know is exactly where the other boat is. Then here it comes, the final spurt, and you cease to hear or see anything outside your business. Faint and hardly noticeable the pistol fires, then cox says, 'Easy all,' and you loll forward.

Done. Like that, done, over, decided. And you are through, you are truly empty now, you have poured yourself out and for awhile you can hardly stand the effort of your own breathing but your tradition despises a man who fails to sit up in the boat. You have known complete exertion, you have answered every trouble of mind, spirit, and being with skilled violence and guided unrestraint, a complete happiness with eight other men over a short stretch of water has brought you catharsis. You may find it in storms at sea, in the presence of your art, on a racing horse, in bed with a woman, but you will hardly find it better or purer than you have found it here.

Courtney v. Hanlan

Three Races, Three Disgraces

William Lanouette

IN HIS BOOK *THE TRIUMPH OF THE AMATEURS: THE RISE, RUIN, AND BANISH-ment of Professional Rowing in the Gilded Age* (2021), rowing historian William "Bill" Lanouette tells the stories of North America's most famous scullers. Charles Courtney from Union Springs, New York, and Edward "Ned" Hanlan, from Toronto, are both remembered for raising the sport to national and global acclaim by their ambition and talents and then for compounding its disgrace and downfall by their greed and guile. Their three scandalous races rocked the professional sport of rowing and helped bring on its demise.

Courtney's already quirky ways only worsened when he entered three infamous match races against Edward "Ned" Hanlan from Toronto, him-self a crafty competitor known for suspicious behavior and surprising outcomes. Hanlan had won with ease the professional single-sculls races at the 1876 Centennial Regatta, becoming world champ. The next year he beat Wallace Ross from New Brunswick for the Canadian champion-ship, and a year later took the American title from Pittsburgh's esteemed sculler Evan Morris.

Unlike Courtney, a six-footer with a long even stroke, Hanlan was just under five feet nine inches tall. He maximized his power by compressing—then expanding—his body in energy bursts. As one of the first professionals to master the sliding seat, this gave him extra reach and pushed the full force of his brawny legs into every stroke. "His ability to co-ordinate the strength of his whole body enabled him to defeat much larger opponents," noted *The Canadian Encyclopedia*.

"Hanlan's lower-class Irish background did not endear him to Toronto's snobbish upper- or middle-class British sportsmen who were dominant in the organization of rowing," wrote sports historian Don Morrow. Hanlan was born on July 12, 1855, to an immigrant family. His father was a fisherman who also ran a hotel on Toronto Island in the harbor, and it was there young Ned first learned to row a fishing skiff, "either in pursuit of angling or in the business of illegally smuggling rum across Lake Ontario to his father's hotel." Ned was also known as a brawler and hard drinker with a quick temper. But setting class distinctions aside, Toronto's elite formed The Hanlan Club in 1876 to organize his finances and arrange his races, leaving him free to practice and compete. Like Courtney, Hanlan could be cunning and aggressive when racing, and at Boston's City Regatta in 1877 he was barred after fouling Fred Plaisted and "Frenchy" Johnson at the turning stake.

For the first of their three unsavory races, Courtney and Hanlan met at Lachine, on the Island of Montreal in the Saint Lawrence River, in October 1878. Widely publicized, the race stirred an emotional following as a proxy struggle between the United States and Canada. Their five-mile race for $6,000 (plus a side bet between them for another $4,000) began with Courtney grabbing the lead. Both men pulled mightily, and the odds shifted minute-by-minute. Nearing the finish they were even, when across the course drifted wooden barges. Courtney stopped, then pulled on, while Hanlan darted around them to cross the line a boat-length ahead. But the barges weren't the only suspect features of this race: The *New York Times* reported that Courtney was clearly the stronger oarsman, and the "sorrowful conclusion" by his closest friends was that "he had sold the race."

One story given for a fix was that Courtney owed $2,000 on a mortgage, and this amount was his kickback for losing. A *Times* investigation refuted that rumor, blaming Courtney's loss solely on those mysterious drifting barges. The quick shift in odds for Courtney before the race, the *Times* explained, swelled from a betting frenzy that began in upstate New York, then spread by telegraph nationwide. Also, that mortgage was not due for two years. Yet, even the supportive *Ithaca Tribune* reported, "The general belief here is that Courtney sold yesterday's race," citing as evidence his erratic steering and low stroke-rate—never above thirty-two in the last mile. All this Courtney denied, blaming his loss on "rough water." The *New York Clipper* reported "an alleged dishonorable bargain" among the rowers and their backers "whereby the Union Springs sculler had bound himself to lose the race whether able to win it or not."

Press reports and rumors sustained a belief that the two oarsmen had schemed with their syndicates for Hanlan to win this first race, Courtney a second, and then either one to take a third. This three-race plot Courtney finally admitted to years later, and it helps explain how weirdly their second meeting occurred and, perhaps, also the third.

Before he could face a rematch with Courtney, Hanlan rowed two other races that proved to be shady. In the first, on the Tyne at Newcastle in June 1879, Hanlan won the English championship easily (by eleven lengths) against William Elliott. Too easily, it was soon revealed. An item on "Professional Crookedness" in *Wilkes' Spirit of the Times* reported that Elliott's backers had "weakened" before the match, and Hanlan himself secretly put up the last forty pounds of the two hundred that each side was to contribute. If Elliott had forfeited, Hanlan would have won nothing. But with Elliott rowing, Hanlan could "win all the money which a confiding and patriotic English people will bet on their champion." Even Elliott's backers put their money on Hanlan "for enough to pay for their time and trouble," leaving the betting public the losers.

Clearly, Hanlan was a preeminent sculler—when he chose to be. Beginning in 1880, he won the world sculling championship seven times; first on the Thames, then on the Tyne, and once at Point of Pines outside Boston when besting John A. Kennedy, America's second challenger.

Hanlan was feted in New York when returning with the English championship in July 1879. A three-mile flotilla greeted his steamer as it chugged into Toronto Harbor, and a Hanlan Gala Day honored him at the city's Horticulture Gardens. Wasting little time, the Hanlan Club set a match on Kempenfelt Bay near Barrie, Ontario, against the infamous James Riley [of Saratoga] in August, for what one newspaper would headline "An Aquatic Burlesque." Hanlan took the lead and held it to mid-course, but near the finish Riley was gaining on him. Abruptly, Hanlan stopped rowing. Riley stopped too, and refused to cross the line first. Riley had bet on Hanlan, and could not afford to win this race. Another account mentioned that at mid-course, Hanlan had halted when an unknown sculler crossed his path, nearly colliding. "Most of the spectators," the *New York Times* reported, "are of the opinion that the stranger was there on purpose," giving Hanlan an excuse to stop because he'd bet against himself. When the judges declared a draw, Hanlan refused a re-row and forfeited the prize money.

Both the public and the professional gamblers awaited a Hanlan-Courtney rematch, and in 1879 two wealthy gents offered a $6,000 prize for the race. One was [America's richest man] Billy Vanderbilt; the other was James Gordon Bennett Jr., enterprising publisher of the *New York Herald* and an avid sponsor of sporting events. Besides running thoroughbreds, Bennett was first to introduce polo and tennis matches to the United States, and he had won the first transatlantic yacht race in 1866. Hanlan and Courtney accepted the Vanderbilt-Bennett challenge, but from spring to summer the two sponsors bickered over details about the race, and finally withdrew their purse.

To the rescue came Asa T. Soule, head of the Hop Bitters Company in Rochester. He matched the proposed $6,000 prize and set a race in western New York on Lake Chautauqua, for October 1879. Hop Bitters was a popular patent medicine touted as "The Invalid's Friend and Hope." Compounded from hops, mandrake, buchu, and dandelion, the mix promised to cure nervousness, sleeplessness, female complaints, and drunkenness, along with all diseases of the stomach, bowels, blood, liver, kidney, and urinary organs. Hop Bitters was a grand commercial success, no doubt for another ingredient: It was 12 percent alcohol.

The course was to start and end at the lake's Fair Point by the Chautauqua Institution's busy campgrounds, run west to Mayville, and after turning stakes by the town's waterfront return to finish where it began. A rail line was laid along the lakeshore for an excursion train to follow the action. Gamblers and prostitutes and con men invaded Mayville. The New York City odds-makers Quimby & Forse set up "sentry boxes" on street corners to sell bets. A beer garden opened by the lake. And from his pulpit a Presbyterian minister warned, "The seven plagues of Egypt swarm about us and Hell's foul rays are focused upon our unhappy village."

For his part, Soule was delighted that his investment had become the nationally celebrated Hop Bitters Prize. Courtney even named his new paper shell *Hop Bitters*. A wily businessman, Soule boasted to a journalist that he squeezed commissions from the railroads, excursion and sightseeing boats, the builders of grandstands, owners of hotels and boardinghouses, and "all the games, straight and skin" [crooked] that flourished in town.

A few days before the race, Courtney went to William Blaikie, the former Harvard oarsman and New York attorney who had agreed to be referee. Courtney revealed that Hanlan's friends had urged a fix, for Hanlan to win, and had threatened his life if he reneged. After this, Courtney carried a pistol. At first the odds favored Hanlan. But with two days to go, panicky telegrams clacked in from betting parlors across the United States and Canada. As the *New York Times* explained, "All of a sudden word came that the pool-selling had stopped everywhere" in San Francisco, Denver, Chicago, Cincinnati, Pittsburgh, Philadelphia, Hoboken, New York, Boston, and Halifax. In cipher and in slang the telegrams were the same: "Give us the tip" or "How is it fixed?" or "Who is to be the winner?" or "Hurry up your pointer" or "Lots of money ready when we hear what the steer is." Something nasty was afoot, with more intrigue to come.

Courtney awoke the morning of the race to learn that during the night his racing and practice shells had been sawed in two. Both were custom-made paper boats. He rejected offers of cedar shells by Hanlan, and by his trainer "Frenchy" Johnson. The season was late, and Courtney claimed that another paper shell could not be made for two weeks. Given this situation, he withdrew. Hanlan expected to collect the prize money and rowed over the course; but Soule refused to pay, insisting on a two-man race.

Again the press was quick to spot a conspiracy. There was one rumor that Courtney had reneged on the alleged three-race deal, and was determined to win at Chautauqua, prompting Hanlan's men to ruin the shells. Another rumor was that they had sawed the shells because Hanlan was drunk the night before, and in no condition to race. But deal or no, Courtney also drew suspicion of the deed: to avoid a race he might lose. Arguing about who cut the shells thrived for years, and "Who Sawed Courtney's Boat?" became a catchphrase, a folk song, and an unanswered riddle.

Missing no chance to scorn corruption, the *New York Times* was quick to declare:

> *The moralist who has watched with dismay the steady growth of that class of crimes commonly known as "athletic sports," will be little surprised at the recent outrage committed at Chautauqua by certain rowing malefactors. It had been advertised for some time that two of the most prominent oarsmen in the country were to publicly engage in the swindling game known as a rowing match . . . for a stake of $6,000. An immense crowd assembled, and bets were made to an estimated extent of $700,000—no less than $370,000 being bet in pools alone.*

The paper reminded readers, "This is the fourth time that some unforeseen accident has prevented him [Courtney] from winning a boat-race, and it is to be hoped that this time he has made enough to enable him to live without further pursuing the profession of failing to row races."

Outrage came from other papers as well, the *Syracuse Courier* complaining about "a widespread feeling of disgust." Charles S. Francis, editor of the *Troy Times* who had been a skilled Cornell oarsman, wrote grandly, "It seems as if never since the firing on Fort Sumter did an event so arouse the anger of the American people. In every city, village and hamlet, wherever a telegraph wire or a newspaper penetrated, the storm of indignation raged." Insults and rumors lingered. Courtney revealed a letter from Soule promising him $2,000 whether he won or lost. To that, Hanlan produced a letter from Courtney offering him $3,000 to throw the race.

The "Chautauqua Lake Fizzle" dismayed both rowing's fans and financiers. But as tempers eased, and time passed, both Courtney and

Hanlan praised Soule. He, in turn, declared his continued support. The two oarsmen were famously headstrong, but for Courtney at his crankiest nothing topped his third race with Hanlan. Courtney haggled for months with Soule and Blaikie. He also bickered with Hanlan over how to split the railroad receipts. But finally a date was set, for a five-mile race on the Potomac at Washington, DC, on May 19, 1880. The Hop Bitters Prize was still $6,000, and qualms about Courtney shenanigans ran stronger than ever. His predictably erratic conduct raised new worries, among both the "sporting men" who bet on rowers for a living and the two rowers' many ardent fans.

Mocking Courtney's fickle ways, the *New York Times* proposed "a sixteenth amendment, declaring that in no circumstances shall a proposition be made to or accepted by Mr. Courtney to row a race with anybody." The popular *Frank Leslie's Illustrated Newspaper* featured a cartoon showing Courtney "fully prepared for emergencies" as he strode to meet Hanlan, bearing to the water's edge his racing shell, two oars, and a saw.

Newspapers across Canada and the United States speculated about the coming race, and both rowers were welcomed as celebrities when they arrived at Washington. Matthew Brady, the famed photographer who had chronicled the Civil War and often portrayed President Lincoln, sat Hanlan for a portrait—but was rebuffed by Courtney, who complained about not feeling well. Courtney moved into the Riggs House at 15th and G Streets NW and Hanlan set up headquarters at Willard's Hotel at 14th Street and Pennsylvania Avenue NW. The opulent Willard lobby filled with admirers, and swarmed with gamblers. The hotel even staged a gala boat-race party.

This third Courtney-Hanlan race was an extravaganza, until it became a farce. Hats and cigars were sold banded with the oarsmen's names and pictures. Banners sold in the men's racing colors: cardinal red for Hanlan, blue for Courtney. Pickpockets disguised as priests worked the crowds. Congress adjourned early. Schools let out for the afternoon, and government clerks were excused from their offices. On the course the US Signal Corps prepared to hoist red and blue balloons at relative heights every quarter-mile to display the scullers' positions. Navy launches patrolled the river, manned with armed guards to ward off any interference.

Spectators clambered onto grandstands lining Georgetown's waterfront, where the race would start and end. The shoreline downstream to the turning stake by Long Bridge (near today's 14th Street Bridge) swarmed with eager fans. A crowd estimated at one hundred thousand included President Hayes, many Cabinet members, and the British ambassador—along with political notables, business tycoons, and show-business celebrities.

William Blaikie was to referee the cancelled Chautauqua Lake race, and for months had persevered to arrange this rematch. Long resigned to dealing with Courtney, Blaikie was relieved once the contract had been inked. But he was then hardly surprised to learn, on the eve of the Washington race, that Courtney suddenly complained about a "headache." Some of Courtney's friends told newsmen he was ill, but others assured he was well rested and vigorous.

Was he ailing, or again faking to skew the odds? Blaikie had his suspicions, and later told a *New York Times* reporter,

> *When I went into Courtney's room on the morning of the race, Courtney was lying asleep, and I found his brother wiping his head with a sponge. I told him to take off the sponge and let me feel the oarsman's head. I felt of it and of my own, and I said then that Courtney's head was not as hot as mine was. But his brother declared he had a fever, and had said he was not to be called until 3 o'clock in the afternoon.*

"Not until 3 o'clock?" Blaikie asked. "Why? Was he restless last night?" Courtney's brother was silent. Again Blaikie asked, "Was he restless last night?"

"Well, no-o," the brother admitted, shaking his head.

Blaikie surmised that "if either of those men had ever been the father of a child they would know that when it has a fever it will play tag all over the bed."

Returning to Courtney's hotel that afternoon, Blaikie determined: "I couldn't see that there was any feverish look about him. His eyes were not dull at all, and there were no drawn lines or flabby looks about his face." Next Blaikie "asked the doctor, who had been called in, to take Courtney's pulse, and he did so. It was a little under 70. It doesn't strike me that that is exactly a fever pulse."

Blaikie had called Courtney's bluff, and at the Potomac Boat Club two hours later, Courtney appeared lively and determined as his hosts launched him with applause and rip-roaring cheers. To a *New York Times* reporter Hanlan appeared "plucky" and Courtney looked "fresh and in good condition." The crowds pressed toward the water as the rowers lined up under the aqueduct (by today's Key Bridge) for their race downriver and back.

At the starter's pistol shot Courtney grabbed the lead, but held it for just a furlong. Hanlan's solid and steady strokes eased his shell even. Then it pushed ahead. For two miles they raced, until. . . . What happened next surprised everyone, and no one. Courtney stopped rowing. He sat and swabbed his face and neck with water. He turned his shell around. And he pulled back up the course to his dock. There, "with hanging head and a dogged, suffering look" he heard a cheer or two, but otherwise landed amid silent glares. Once Courtney retreated to his hotel, disgusted Potomac Boat Club members flung his shells and gear into the street.

Headlining "A FARCE ON THE POTOMAC," the *New York Times* accused Courtney of faking illness "for the sole purpose of influencing betting." Courtney's own doctor admitted to a reporter that his patient had been "in fine condition" before the race, "although at first he was unwilling to announce the results of his diagnosis." The *Times* surmised: "Some declare that the man's real trouble is ineradicable cowardice, and others believe that his course is in accordance with the terms of some secret contract." Again, rumors dogged Courtney about betting against himself to pay off a mortgage, which, that year, was actually due. This third suspicious Courtney-Hanlan race left the public more disgusted than ever with professional rowing. But for the many boisterous spectators, the allure of betting and drinking and fighting at regattas held abiding appeal, and there were still a few pro rowers capable of even more outrageous exploits. This rich and rowdy sport was damaged, but not yet destroyed.

Wet Beginnings

Brad Lewis

In his book *Olympian* (2021), Brad Alan Lewis tells the story of his road to the 1984 Olympic Games held in Los Angeles (with the Olympic rowing on Lake Casitas). He had rowed in the 1980 US Olympic quadruple sculls, but President Jimmy Carter and the US Olympic Committee's boycott put an end to the American athletes' participation at the Moscow Games. Lewis decided to train for another four years to try for the 1984 Games, now in a double sculls with Paul Enquist. In the chapter "Wet Beginnings," Lewis writes how he, as a fifteen-year-old boy, rowed in a single sculls for the first time on a warm day in October 1970, in Newport Beach, California.

Sculling is a remarkably simple discipline. To learn the basics, find yourself a twelve-foot aluminum rowboat and a pair of oars. Toss the boat into the nearest lake or river or harbor. Set the oars in the locks, climb in, and blast off.

Immediately you'll notice a unique feature consistent with all rowing—you're facing backwards. While the front of the boat, the bow, points in the direction you intend to go. The rower faces the back of the boat, the stern. Thus a sculler needs an intuitive sense of direction. Some scullers twist their heads around every stroke to check for watery obstructions. Others simply point their boat down the course and hope for the best. In theory, all scullers must keep the land close to their starboard side, so that boats going in opposite direction will safely pass each other like cars on a freeway. However, no center divider exists on a winding river. Every sculler eventually collides with something—a bridge abutment, a navigational buoy—pray it is not another sculler.

You steer the boat by adjusting pressure on the oar blades. Tug harder on the port oar and the boat will angle toward starboard. That's fairly straightforward. Problems arise when you are rowing as hard as possible. The only solution to altering your course is to ease off on one side or the other. This will cause your boat to change course, which is what you want. The easing off will also inevitably cause your boat to slow down. In a race, slowing down is exactly what you not want to happen. It takes years of practice to convince your boat to go perfectly straight down the racecourse at full power.

By the way, unlike swimming, with its four unique styles, butterfly backstroke, etc., there's no designated, specified, required rowing stroke. You can row anyway you want. Among elite rowers, there's plenty of variation in terms of technique.

After a few minutes of rowing, your arms and lower back will begin to ache, and a small blister, possibly two, will form on the palm of your hand. Welcome to the world of sculling. But unlike your aluminum rowboat, a racing shell has small wheels mounted underneath a seat. The seat rolls on a pair of grooved, 30-inch long tracks. The addition of the rolling seat allows you to power each stroke with your legs, the strongest muscles in your body.

The stroke is neatly divided into two complementary segments: first the drive. Then the recovery. The drive propels the boat through the water. The recovery allows the rower to move from the end of the stroke, the release, to the beginning of the stroke, the catch. The drive is all about applying your strength, your power. The recovery is cool, subtle, a chance to take a deep breath and prepare for the next drive.

The driving effort is carefully quantified in the psyche of every practicing rower. Paddle is an easy stroll in the park.

Half-power is like walking up a flight of stairs. Three-quarter power is a brisk jog up those same stairs. Full power is the equivalent of running to the top of Mt. Whitney. Then race power. This is a special category, reserved for the ultimate in physical expression. At the completion of the final stroke of a close race, a rower should collapse over his or her oars, having spent every possible ounce of energy. Fainting from exhaustion at the finish line, although rarely seen, is greatly respected.

Newport Beach, California. On a warm Saturday afternoon, October, 1970, I drove to the Orange Coast College boathouse with my brother, Tracy, who is three years older than me. He had an appointment to meet with Steve Reichert, the team's best rower. Tracy was a strong oarsman. Unfortunately his rough technique had kept him out of the first boat. Tracy hoped that an hour's practice on the rowing machines under Steve's watchful eye could whip his technique into shape. Over time they had become close friends. Decades later they are still close friends. Rowing friendships, it seems, last a lifetime.

While Steve and Tracy practiced, I walked around the deserted boathouse, looking at the beautifully crafted eight-oared shells. The smooth, deep varnish on the skin of the wooden boats was like a mirror. As I rubbed my hand over the surface, I could see my distorted reflection trapped in the sheen. I walked to the end of the boathouse and inspected the oars, standing at attention, upright, like patient soldiers waiting for the battle to begin.

Above my head, a half-dozen single sculls hung from the rafters.

"How would you like to try sculling?" Steve asked after they had finished their workout. "You can use one of the training singles. I'll help you put it on the water."

Steve carefully lowered a red and white training single from the rafters. The shell descended from the heavens and my life was never the same. The boat, a relatively clumsy, 40-pound beast, seemed to me an impossibly sleek craft, ideal for exploring the harbor's nooks and crannies. I'd found my escape vehicle of choice, the perfect solution for a young man, not yet old enough to drive, but already searching for his freedom.

Steve and I carried the single sculls out of the boathouse, down the ramp, across the dock, finally lowering it carefully onto the water. Then Steve positioned the oars and secured the locks.

As I gingerly climbed into the boat, Steve said, "Your left hand goes over the right. Keep your thumbs over the ends of the oar handles. It's simple. Left over right. Thumbs over the ends. Use the oars like training wheels. Let the blades slide across the water between strokes. That way you won't tip over. Don't worry, I'll hold onto the stern until you get a feel for the balance."

With my bow pointed into the harbor, I practiced a few tentative strokes. The balance felt most precarious at the catch, when my oars were almost parallel to the boat. When I glanced up after a few practice strokes, I suddenly realized that Steve was now thirty feet away. He had let go of the stern. My first sculling lesson was now complete: left hand over right. Thumbs over the ends of the oar handles. Keep my head up.

I could hear Steve and Tracy laughing as I scuttled across the channel using tight little strokes. I managed to stay upright, which surprised them both. Many scullers on their first outing tip over right off the dock. Just as I was beginning to get a feel for the balance, the driver of a 45-foot motorboat opened up the throttle. Three huge waves marched across the channel, straight toward me. I barely managed to keep my boat upright through the first wave. The second wave struck before I had recovered my balance. In a blink I flipped over. I swam my boat to the OCC dock, emptied it out, and went back for more. I was fifteen years old at the time of my sculling baptism.

Sculling is well-suited for individualists, especially the single sculls. I have it in my lineage, my genes, my soul, this rare characteristic. The whole Lewis clan, brother Tracy, sister Val, mom Bernice, and dad David, are all individualists, never hesitating to march to their own drummer.

I have been blessed with an amazing, wonderful family. Dad, a Los Angeles native, worked for Transamerica Insurance, thirty-seven years, as a sales rep, commercial insurance. He was a pretty good master's runner, cranking off a 2:28.5 half-mile at the Seniors Pan Am Games when he was sixty years old. My dad rowed at UCLA for a short time after returning from the Second World War. More specifically, he rowed after returning from duty aboard the USS Fanshaw Bay (CVE-70), where he fought in the Battle of Leyte Gulf. His coach at UCLA was a young coxswain-turned-coach named Bob Hillen. When I was training for the '84 Games, Bob Hillen was still coaching. I'd often chat with him at local regattas. Great guy.

Mom, from Redwood City, worked for a time in Yosemite as a ranger. In fact, that's where my mother and father met after the war. Mom wasn't all that big on cooking or house work. Rather, she liked to put on her hiking shoes and get outside, especially long walks on the beach between Cameo Shores and Scotchman's Cove. Sometimes we ventured into the backcountry above Crystal Cove. We'd followed remote deer trails for miles on end. Those were good times.

Tracy is the hardest worker of us kids, always pulling his own weight and more. Val is perhaps the toughest, a California Highway Patrol-woman for a few years, working South L.A. at night, a challenge exceeding anything found in the world of sports.

Tracy, Val, Mom, and Dad all supported my sculling efforts. That said, as the years rolled by they became somewhat baffled by my ever increasing Olympic obsession. Once, when I was leaving for a big race, my mom said to me, "Don't hurt yourself, Brady."

I explained to her that I needed to hurt myself in order for the other guys to hurt themselves. If I could endure more pain than my opponents, the more likely it was that I would win.

"Okay, Brady," she said. "But don't hurt yourself."

All in all, without them I would not have made it to the starting line of my first race much less my last.

In the big picture, rowing comes in two flavors: sculling and sweep. In sculling, the rower uses two oars. In sweep rowing, the rower uses just one oar, as in sweeping the floor with a broom. Sweep rowing is the flavor of rowing commonly practiced by high school and college rowing teams, and occasionally seen in beer commercials.

The boat of choice for most sweep rowers is the eight-oared shell, often referred to as rowing's 'glamour boat.' My own idea of glamour was the single sculls. In truth, the concept of glamour should never be used in conjunction with any type of rowing. On every level, in every size boat, rowing is a modest sport. It is poorly suited for spectators, on TV or in person. If you were to head to South Coast Plaza with a suitcase full of money and offer every person there a $1,000 if they could name even one Olympic rower, male or female, from any country, from any Olympic

Games, you'd come away with the same suitcase full of money, (minus the cost of two or three Cinnabons). That's why I like it. Rowing is not for spectators. Never will be. Rowing is for rowers.

I learned the ins-and-outs of sweep rowing during the latter half of my junior year at Corona del Mar High School, when I joined the rowing team. We had a wild team, made up of burned-out, bored, flawed, failed, and generally cast-off athletes from water polo, football, track, basketball, cross-country. My first love was tennis. I had set my sights set on being the next Rod Laver. Unfortunately not one of my 632 muscles was of the fast twitch variety, so necessary for success in tennis. My best sporting accomplishment up until then came when I was ten years old: I taught myself to ride a unicycle.

Our coach, Mark Sandusky, may or may not have known anything about rowing, I have no idea, but he did know how to make the workouts fun and challenging at the same time. That's a pretty good trick. Our team even won a few races against second-freshman college teams.

One member of our high school team was a young shot putter-turned-rower named Curtis Fleming. Curtis and I would eventually share the sport for over a decade.

I was not a particularly gifted sweep rower. I liked it okay. I was out-doors, which I relished. Perhaps best of all, our coach couldn't call a time-out and take me out of the action in the middle of a race, as so often happened when I played on the school's basketball team my freshman and sophomore years.

Our high school team practiced at the University of California, Irvine boathouse. On many afternoons, I borrowed a single sculls from the college and paddled around the bay. The boat, an old Pocock fiber-glass trainer, had a hundred hairline cracks along the hull. By the time I returned to the dock, I was practically rowing underwater. Those were the good ol' days. I wasn't preparing for the Olympics. I sculled because I liked it. No other reason.

My grades in high school were, to put it mildly, less than ideal for a college-bound kid. Nonetheless, I eventually attended UC Irvine. I gained entrance via an athletic deferment pushed through by the UCI rowing coach, Bob Ernst. Those afternoon sculling sessions, one lone letter of recommendation from my biology teacher, Dale Geer, and an 'A' in Mr. Corey's ceramics class, saved my ass.

While at UCI, I continued to sweep row but with only marginal success. I tried hard. It didn't much matter. On my best day, I might have risen to the level of slightly above average. In my favor, I was one of the team's better runners. Plus, using only my upper body, I could climb the thick rope that hung from the high ceiling of the UCI gym several times over without taking a break.

The team had one outstanding season—1974. Coach Bob Ernst and varsity stroke Bruce Ibbetson, both future Olympians, led the team to a dozen victories. I was not in the varsity boat during those halcyon days. Instead I toiled on the lowly junior varsity. After the '74 season, Bob Ernst left UCI to coach at a better school, the University of Washington. The UCI rowing program quickly sank into mediocrity.

While at UCI, I again rowed a single sculls whenever I had a free afternoon. By this time I had moved up in terms of equipment, thanks to Duvall Hecht, who lent me the use of his beautiful wooden Pocock racing single. Duvall, the founder of UCI's crew, won a gold medal at the '56 Melbourne Olympics in the pair without coxswain event, a boat comprised of two sweep rowers and no coxswain or steersman.

I loved the simplicity of sculling. No one got mad at me when I was late for practice. If things didn't go well, I had no one to look to but myself. Best of all, the rhythm of a properly rowed sculling stroke felt incredibly satisfying to me, the intense effort of the drive, the cool of the recovery—a sensual, bordering on sexual, rhythm. It felt good.

In those days, we raced for shirts. If the race had six boats—and you won—you came away with five shirts, one from each vanquished boat. I quit rowing my senior year, having grown weary of handing over my UCI racing shirt to the guy who'd won the race. Besides, Bruce Ibbetson had graduated. There just wasn't any challenge for me without Bruce on the team.

For nearly one full year I stayed away from the sport. Then I went to the Montreal Olympic Games and saw for myself what real rowing was all about. Soon after the Games, I came back to the sport of rowing, single sculling to be specific, and began training with a vengeance.

The next year, 1977, I drove to Philadelphia for the sole purpose of racing against the fastest scullers in the country. I was perhaps the most eager, ambitious, energetic West Coaster ever to descend on the staid rowing fraternity of Boathouse Row.

My timing could not have been better. Since it was a post-Olympic year, many of the top scullers had recently retired. The door was open for new scullers like me to win a few races. I also found out how small the sculling fraternity was in the United States. At the national championships, only eleven scullers were entered in the elite competition. I finished fourth.

Toward the end of that summer, I earned a place on the national team as stroke of the U.S. quadruple sculls, four scullers in one boat. When we arrived at the 1977 Worlds in Amsterdam, I felt as though I was at Disneyland for the first time. My heroes, the legends of rowing, Alf Hansen, Joachim Dreifke, Peter-Michael Kolbe, were all around me. I watched as the East German national team marched into the boat launching area, singing their national anthem. They looked like angry robots. Iron German Discipline at its finest. I was impressed.

Eventually our quadruple sculls finished ninth at the Worlds. Ninth was better than tenth, but still a long way from the finals, much less a gold medal. But overall the whole '77 season had given me a strong sense of confidence and inspiration.

In April of the next year, 1978, I broke my right leg and partially severed the patella tendon in a foolish accident, one that I could have avoided had I used a little common sense. I was jumping down a steep grassy hill when I lost my footing. My right knee crashed to the ground. Hidden under the soft green grass was a razor sharp rock. The impact came damn close to severing my leg. In an instant, I went from preparing for the '78 national team trials to being in a full leg cast for two months, followed by a long, painful convalescence. Sheer good luck (relatively speaking), the surgeon on call at Hoag Hospital that night, Dr. Drucker, learned his craft in Vietnam, treating soldiers who had endured shrapnel wounds. He knew exactly what to do. Once out of the cast, the adhesions that had formed around my knee had to be severed. Before or since, I have never encountered anything to compare with that excruciating pain.

I finished 1978 weak, out of shape, and generally unhappy. I had to begin my rowing career all over again.

I had a wild notion the following spring that I'd be happier in Europe. One day in June, 1979, I packed up my oars and flew to West Germany. I had all of $200 in my pocket when I arrived. I wish I had taken more photos during that trip, to capture the people I met and the fun I had. I didn't win any races but I held my own. It was a good, worthy, beautiful rowing adventure.

In 1980, I rowed in the Olympic quadruple sculls. Unfortunately we never had a chance to determine our ultimate speed. President Carter, who probably never rowed a day in his life, made the unforgivable decision to boycott the 1980 Moscow Olympic Games. With an undying passion, I have hated all politics and all politicians ever since—one politician in particular, Jimmy Carter.

I kept rowing. I was twenty-five years old at the time. My best races were still ahead of me. I was sure of that.

Three years later, I raced the double sculls with Paul Enquist at the '83 World Championships. We made the finals, which was excellent. The U.S. hadn't had a boat in the double sculls finals at the Worlds in many years. Then Paul and I placed a distant sixth.

In seven years of full time training, I had made three national teams. I had never won a national championship in any boat. I had not won many races outside of California. Along the way I had acquired three single sculls, five sets of oars, a '72 Mercury Montego, and some impressive calluses on my hands. Although I did not lack for determination or equipment, my climb up the ladder of sculling success had been slow, demanding, tedious. This year, 1984, promised to be better.

To earn a place on the 1984 men's U.S. Olympic sculling team, a rower had to win the Olympic trials in the single sculls, the double sculls or the quadruple sculls. The single sculls trials were to be held in early May, with the double and quad trials in early July.

After the single trials, an official sculling camp was to be convened. The double and quad selected at this camp would then attempt to defeat any and all challengers at their respective trials. In recent years, the camp boats had dominated the trials, thanks to superior coaching, excellent equipment, and ample funding, not to mention having the best athletes. But upsets had been known to occur.

The Olympic single sculls trials, by contrast, were wide open.

The Previous Administration

Peter Mallory

IN 1989 I COMPLETED A 30-YEAR HOMERIC ODYSSEY BETWEEN MY first appearance in a shell and my first U.S. National Gold Medal, won on Lake Merritt in Oakland, California. When the regatta ended, I returned home to my metaphorical Ithaca, returned to my Penelope, my wife Susan, fat and pregnant with our unplanned second child, a girl we had decided to name Katherine Jean.

Two years earlier, Susan had won the Masters A Single Sculls event at the Nationals in Lake Placid, New York. She had never seen a shell before she met me, but she knew how to move boats. I taught her.

Susan was a Hell of a competitor. And courageous? The nine months had come and gone, and the birth pangs had begun before I had even departed from home, before the National Regatta had ever commenced.

Katie's coming! *Êtes-vous prêt?*

The day before my leave-taking, my boss at work, Don Lang, hosted a late summer gathering for the staff on his sailboat on San Diego Bay. When, in the course of polite conversation, I mentioned I was about to leave for three days to compete at the Nationals, Don's wife Karen did a Three Stooges double take, took another look at Susan's enormous abdomen, and asked her when the baby was due.

"Yesterday . . . tomorrow . . . any second, basically," replied Susan nonchalantly. Karen turned to me.

"And you're leaving, Peter? To go *row*?" Before I could even open my mouth, Susan retorted, but oh-so-politely, "A child takes only nine months, Karen. As a family we committed to this Nationals way before we committed to this baby." Only a real rower could say those words. And Susan was a real *rower*! Yessirree! Thank you, Susan. I will treasure the memory of that moment.

Karen Lang, definitely not a rower but always one to speak her mind, looked me straight in the eye and growled, "I always knew you were an a.… [*use your imagination*], Peter. This just confirms it."

At that moment, I can tell you I prayed hard that she wasn't right. At least not at that *particular* moment.

But when I returned home four days later, still our daughter remained patient and content in her mother's womb. Truly the stuff of myth, worthy even of Homer, don't you think? Katie was born the day after I returned. I was present for the event, weak-kneed and much relieved.

Another three decades and more have now gone by. More time has elapsed since my long-awaited National Championship than had elapsed between my first race on the Housatonic at Kent School and my Golden weekend on Lake Merritt!

A great deal has happened in the interim. Within a few years Karen had divorced Don. Susan had divorced me. We all said, "Goodbye! Good riddance! Hurray! Don't let the door hit your backside on your way out!" Karen is in Heaven now. So is Don. I see Susan as infrequently as humanly possible, and when her name comes up, I refer to her respectfully as "the previous administration," since I am now married to the love of my life, and her name is *also* Susan. It's coincidences like these which continue to convince me that there definitely is a God, He's definitely read *A Tale of Two Cities* and *Cat's Cradle*, He's *most* assuredly a real rower … and He must have a Hell of a sense of humor!

Didn't see my Katie growing up as much as I would have liked … she was raised by her mother. But grow up she did indeed! Now I'm trying to make up for lost time. I visit her regularly in Norfolk, Virginia, with her husband who is serving in the United States Navy. Katie has just had her own second child, and she is the calmest and most thoughtful of mothers! She says that daughters Meredith and Natalie should get the credit, being such pleasant babies and all, but I don't buy it for a second. I don't think I was ever that calm or thoughtful about *anything* in my life. Meredith and Natalie and Katie all have me beat hands down.

With so much in their futures to look forward to, we don't spend much time reliving the past, but every time we talk about the occasion of her birth on August 22, 1989, Katie reminds me:

"I waited for you, Daddy."

Yale's Eight at the 1956 Olympic Rowing

Thomas C. Mendenhall

A YEAR AFTER THE YALE CREW HAD BECOME THE 1956 OLYMPIC CHAM-pions in the eight on Lake Wendouree, City of Ballaarat (old name for Ballarat), Victoria, Australia, Yale history teacher Thomas C. Mendenhall published an account of the crew's 1956 season, *Have Oar, Will Travel, or, A Short History of the Yale Crew of 1956* (1957).

After a quick Sunday lunch in the Olympic Village—more truly a city within a city, the U.S. Olympic oarsmen took off by bus for Ballaarat, 77 miles to the northwest of Melbourne, a tiring trip over a hilly and winding road. Because of the sheltered, fast course on Lake Wendouree, Ballaarat was selected as the Olympic headquarters for rowing and canoeing. Though now a prosperous, inland city of 50,000 people, something of its stormy, frontier beginnings can still be felt. With the discovery of gold in 1851, it became the Australian Klondike. Lola Montez came to dance for the miners who even waged Australia's only civil war against the government over license fees for prospecting. Though the miners lost the battle of Eureka Stockade and the war, they sent out almost a billion dollars' worth of gold before the diggings were exhausted. But Ballaarat did not become a ghost town, for the same local industry, a prosperous agricultural hinterland, and Lake Wendouree combined to fill the gap.

A made lake in the northwest quarter of the town, dammed and dredged out of an old swamp, Wendouree is a rectangle with rounded corners, 580 acres in size, or about a mile by a mile and a half on the longer sides which run roughly east and west. The rowing course is laid out diagonally across the lake from N.E. to S.W. Five lanes wide, the 2,000 meters could just be squeezed in and the starting platform with its five bays necessitated digging away about 15 feet of the bank. The lake has no steam and is quite shallow. In order to provide maximum protection, great fields of reeds have been grown along most of the course, with room left outside for the crews to circumnavigate the lake during practice. At the finish line a jetty was built out from the west bank for the officials; on the opposite shore the temporary grand stand could accommodate 2,300 people, while the Wendouree Parade, the road and path ringing the lake shore, made it possible for over 50,000 spectators to see the races. The crews boated from four boathouses, a few hundred yards to the east of the start. The Olympic Hostel, where the oarsmen and canoeists, 550 strong, were quartered, was a short half mile to the northwest of the lake.

Through a pocket-handkerchief of a lake set among its pines and willows with the background of rolling, wooded country that gave it a homey, mid-western air, Wendouree proved an excellent course. The Yale crew, and all others used to running water, found the dead water strange and new, and at times the crews were chasing each other's tails around the shore. But good staff work, a host of outboards for the coaches, and a friendly tolerance among the oarsmen helped to ease the crowding.

Ready to settle down after ten days of movement and eager to row after the long lay-off, the Yale crew arrived at Ballaarat and Wendouree late in the afternoon of Sunday, 11 November, amid wind and rain, so cold that some of them went to bed in their new blue sweat suits, with the big U.S.A. in red letters across the front. On Monday morning, after the boats were rigged, the crew had their first outing on Wendouree. Eleven days of rowing remained before the first race, but the effectiveness of the tune-up was marred for all by the wretched weather which prevailed. Frequent rain, temperatures in the forties, and high winds made rowing a nightmare of wet clothes, back-wrenching time-trials into head winds, rolling shells, and sloppy blade work. Although the Yale crew had always liked rough water, enough is enough, especially when some of them, especially Esselstyn, began to show up with bad colds which were hard to shake under such miserable conditions. The first calm day came the

Wednesday before Thursday's first heat, and there were only two sunny days out of the entire eleven.

Rowing twice a day save for a single journey on Sunday afternoon, the crew did 12 to 15 miles a day for the first week to get back into shape, tapering off with sprints and starts as the great day approached. Again, though competition was all around and in the very air, there were no stablemates for the eight, except the American fours, so all one could do, amid discouraging conditions, was to hope that those subtle essentials of timing, control, and pace were coming back while the crew recovered its condition and raced against the clock. A slow 1,000 meters (3:06 in a cross wind) on Wednesday, 14 November, was followed the next day by the first time trial. Paced by the four who had a 40 second start in between the cloudbursts, the crew did 6:13 at a 31 rating for the 2,000 meters. For Saturday's trial the lake was so rough that Morey had to drop to 29 after the start and could only get the rating up to 32 in the closing sprint. Thus, the time (7:00) was not bad for the conditions (Australia did 7:05 earlier in the day) but slow and no real indication of how the crew was going. Another 2,000 was rowed on Monday at 24 in the rain. The final trial on Tuesday was done against a stiff head wind in the respectable time of 6:50, a heartening effort in view of Australia's 7:02 performance the same day.

Previous races, at Henley and in the Olympics, had shown low-stroking American crews to be at a disadvantage starting against European crews who stayed longer in the high 30's and usually settled higher than the Americans. Jim had tried to condition his men to rowing from behind, but they refused to give away any greater lead than was absolutely necessary. So, much of the last few days was spent practicing starts. On Wednesday, 21 November, arrangements (worthy of the U.N.) were finally concluded to take two starts over 300 meters with the Russians. The Yale crew found they could hold them for the first ten strokes, but that the Russians inevitably moved out a little as they stayed at 38 while Yale settled to 32. Once they were conditioned to expect a stern chase, rowing from behind required a certain quiet self-confidence and a willingness to sprint when the time came—both of which the Yale crew should have acquired in good measure over the last six months.

Stylistically the American rowing found itself right in the limelight at Wendouree, a flattering position however disturbing it might eventually prove for the American crews. In broken English or in some *lingua franca* of arms, shoulders, and a little bad French, oarsmen from the world over sought to plumb the secrets of American rowing while praising its accomplishments. The Japanese obtained permission to take a movie of the eight; through interpreters the European coaches held active discussions with Jim Rathschmidt over the finer points of the beginning and finish. This endless concern with style and form has always characterized any gathering of oarsmen and, to the extent that it is without solution or end, represents at once the fascination of the sport for its devotees and the curse for the outsider. At Wendouree a host of styles were on display; some self-taught; others, patently evolved out of a rowing textbook. In so far as the latter have been traditionally English, many of the styles reflected the confusion in English rowing over the last forty years—the classic orthodox at war with the more radical ideas of Steve Fairbairn. Thus, the Americans could see some straight backs taking the catch and long swings forward from the hip on the recovery, but most of the crews had "gone Fairbairn," sometimes with a vengeance, as they hit the water with a running slide, rowed light, and crouched over their oars at the finish. More often than not the compromises were unhappy or exaggerated, with the drive coming on before the blade was locked up, an exhausting lay-back, and a useless gather on the slide forward. By contrast, it was noteworthy, and indeed prophetic, that Australia, Canada, and Sweden (under the tutelage of Gus Eriksen, the retired Syracuse coach) were clearly rowing in the American style—a quick entry with no water missed, a hard coordinated drive to a comfortable finish, and a rounded recovery. To find their rowing so universally admired inevitably helped to produce a certain satisfaction, if not over-confidence among the Americans.

As a rowing camp Ballaarat had all the friendliness and enthusiasm for a common sport that might be found at Gales Ferry or Henley, with the cosmopolitan glamor of the Olympics thrown in. Never had the language requirement in far-off Yale College seemed so relevant to the Yale crew as when they lingered after meals in the dining room at the Hostel, trying German on the Russians, or French with the Poles. Each nation had furnished its competitors with a dozen or so Olympic pins, and the brisk exchange which immediately broke out with this common currency not only would have entranced a social anthropologist but also helped to break the ice with the chant of "two silver for one gold" throughout the canteen. To learn that the Romanian oarsmen relaxed by playing soccer while the Americans took naps, or the French trained on wine, the English, on beer, and the Russians soaked up Cokes, all these different ways of doing familiar things were an education in themselves for the young Americans. The dining hall at the Hostel offered every conceivable national diet as training fare: fish and rice for the Japanese, the Italian's spaghetti, and the American's steak and ice cream. Nor were the tensions of the great world absent from this rowing Elysium. Even the Russian oarsmen, with their "party line" in matters great and small and extreme cohesiveness as a group, impressed the unregimented Americans with the true significance of totalitarianism. As did a conversation after supper with an Hungarian who had just been fighting for ten days behind the barricades.

But constantly invading the aquatic idyll was the threat of the races ahead of which a steady reminder was the daily swarm of autograph hunters. The oarsmen soon became skilled in crewmanship—or the art of letting your opponent know how good you are, without either revealing your time or becoming over-impressed with his prowess in the process! As the Australians gradually loomed up as the most feared rival for Yale, the bouts of crewmanship became almost daily affairs, for the Yale crew found the Australians' open-necked friendliness most attractive, only to realize quickly the Circe-like danger in listening to the older, more experienced club oarsmen from Down Under, as heavy as Yale and definitely at the top of their form after their recent victory in the Australian championships. But Yale soon learned to give as good as they got, and the time trials at Derby became faster with every telling. A definite factor in the rising tension, particularly after the races were under way, was the Australian press. Spearheading the almost chauvinistic excitement which was sweeping the country, the newspapers screamed with prophecies of Australian victories and trumpeted whenever they came about. Fortunately Ballaarat lay outside the main tent, but it was to receive its share of this journalistic hysteria. In this atmosphere of high excitement, civic receptions for all the crews, and the crowds at Wendouree assembling for the last few practices, the old camaraderie at the Hostel or on the floats gave way to little knots of this nationality or that, herding together for courage and comfort on the eve of battle.

The 1920 Report of the American Olympic Committee and John B. Kelly's 1920 Olympic Rowing—In His Own Words

Bill Miller

AT THE 1920 OLYMPICS IN ANTWERP, JOHN "JACK" B. KELLY PERFORMED an unbelievable winning feat of two Olympic Gold Medals inside of one hour. In the *1920 Report of the American Olympic Committee*, he gives an inside description of his races. His first race was in the single sculls, winning a tough race against favored Jack Beresford, Jr., of Great Britain. After that race, Kelly immediately jumped into the double sculls with his cousin, Paul Costello, rowed to the start and raced again to capture his second Olympic Gold Medal.

After every Olympic Games, the American/United States Olympic Committee produced a large volume summarizing the activities of the United States Olympic Team with lists of officials and competitors. It contains details and results for every sport.

The 1920 volume, believed to be the first report, is very rare. The National Rowing Foundation (NRF) owns a copy and is the source for this writer. It is four hundred and fifty pages chock full of facts. In later years, the books were renamed the United States Olympic Book.

There are four entries describing the rowing events at the Olympics. The introduction, "Victories on the Water", is written by the president of the National Association of Amateur Oarsmen, James F. Fox. He describes the formation of the rowing team and the smooth voyage on the

U.S. Navy cruiser, *Frederick*, to Antwerp. The shells and rowing machines for training were carried across the Atlantic on the ship's deck.

Next are reports and results from the three medal winning boats.

The Navy Crew Report

The report was submitted by the "Superintendent, U.S. Naval Academy, To Bureau of Navigation, Navy Department". First race: "Navy steadily drew away from their hosts", Belgium. Second race: an even start for fifty yards "but from that point the American shell opened out on the French". The Grand Final stationed the U.S. Naval Academy beside Great Britain's crew from Leander Club. "At the halfway mark England led by ¾ of a length, both crews rowing in excellent form." At 1,600 meters, Navy began moving on Britain. "At 1,850 meters both crews were even ... the Americans raised their stroke to 40 and still rowing well together crossed the line a good half length in the lead of their hard fighting opponents."

Bow-Virgil V. Jacomini, 2-Edwin D. Graves, Jr, 3-William C. Jordan, 4-Edward P. Moore, 5-Allen R. Sanborn, 6-Donald H. Johnston, 7-Vincent J. Gallagher, Jr, Stroke-Clyde W. King, Coxswain-Sherman R. Clark.

The Barge Four

(No author was listed for the coxless four report)

The Pennsylvania Barge Club represented the United States in the coxless fours event. "In the semi-final, they defeated Brazil (second) and Czecho-Slovakia (third). In the finals Switzerland was first, time 6m. 54s.; United States second, time 6m. 57s.; and Norway third, time 7m. 1s."

Bow-Carl O. Klose, 2-E. H. Federschmidt, 3-K. Meyers, Stroke-F. H. Federschmidt

In his own words, John B. Kelly describes his races in the two events he entered. His report is printed here in its entirety.

Single Sculls and Double Sculls
Jack Kelly
World's Sculling Champion

The first day of the Olympic regatta was the best boat racing I ever saw. Penn Barge got to the finals by virtue of its victory over the Czechos and the Brazil four on Saturday. They were against Switzerland and Norway, and it was a great race. The Penn four pushed the Swiss so hard that they broke the record. In every event on Saturday the European record for the distance on still water was lowered. The Navy record of 6m.2 3-5s was a world record.

In the pair oared with coxswains America was not entered, but it developed into a wonderful race. Two crews collapsed within fifty yards from the finish, and Italy managed to keep going and win. Fifty yards from the finish the three crews were even to the inch.

In the double race I was a little tired, as I rowed Beresford the Englishman in single sculls a half hour before, but Paul Costello, my partner, also from Vesper Boat Club, Philadelphia, was fresh and in fine form. The Italian and French doubles, however, jumped us about two lengths in the first quarter. We stayed in the same position to the half, where the French started to come back, then we passed them and went after Italy.

We drew up alongside at the three-quarter, and after baiting them for a hundred yards we let go and broke them down. We won rather easily after that, with Italy second.

In my single sculls heat with the Swede, N. Ljunglof, on Friday I didn't encounter much difficulty and won by about three lengths of open water in 7m.44s., but D. C. Hadfield, the New Zealander, made me show something in my heat with him on Saturday.

I hopped Hadfield about a quarter of a length on the start, but he wanted to lead, so I didn't match his spurt, but settled down to a long 24. He came up and at the quarter had one-half length. He just played into my hands, as I like to row with a man's stern abreast of me. We rowed this way for the next half mile, with me stepping on his tail and trying to make him go a little faster than was comfortable. I crawled up a little in the next quarter mile, and at the mile he had about five feet advantage.

I started to make my bid here and he matched it for about 100 yards when he cracked and I won by about two lengths open.

On Sunday the English were out in force to cheer J. Beresford, who had won his previous heats and with D. C. Hadfield, was pitted against me in the finals. A great many ran with the race until they became exhausted.

At the crack of the gun I hopped Beresford about half a length and, like Hadfield, he came right up to where I wanted him, about half a length to the good. He had to row a little higher strokes than I to hold his advantage, so we rowed this way to the three-quarter mile mark.

I was a little bit afraid he might not crack soon enough, so I started to make it uncomfortable for him and, incidentally, I might add that I have had more pleasant moments in my life. At the mile we were bow to bow.

We were stroke for stroke to within 200 yards of the finish, when I raised it a little and inch by inch I moved away and went over the line about a length and a little more to the good, making, they tell me, a world record for the distance in 7m. 35s.

The people abroad never saw any one row two races so close together, and about five doctors asked permission to go over me after the race to ascertain my condition. I couldn't get dressed for two hours, as I had to sign everybody's program in Belgium.

Just when I thought I was ready to make my getaway a delegation came up from another club and asked if I wouldn't do the honor of accepting their club colors.

They took me to the club in a machine, still in rowing clothes, and I was treated to the rarest experience of my life. It took me ten minutes, with the help of a squad of gendarmes, to push through the crowd to the machine, and when I reached the car I didn't have all my clothes, as they like souvenirs.

As I walked into the club where they were going to present me with the colors they formed a bower with oars about twenty yards long, and strewed flowers in front of me as I went through.

My rowing experience, for which I was chosen to represent the United States at the Olympic Games is as follows:

Born October 4, 1890.
Started rowing with Chamounix and Montrose B. C. 1908.

Rowed first race in No. 4 seat, Montrose B. C., eight, 1908.
Joined Vesper Boat Club, 1909.
Won first race with Vesper, in Schuylkill navy regatta, 1909.
Rowed first sculling race, junior double, Harlem regatta, on Labor Day 1909.

Rowed first single race, 1910.
Have won ninety races in open regattas.
Have won six national championships.
Have won Single and double world's titles.
Have held Schuylkill navy championship since 1913.

My observations:

It is very interesting to read about Kelly's strategy in the race with Hadfield and also Beresford. He states, "I hopped Hadfield about a quarter length on the start, but he wanted to lead, so I didn't match his spurt. He came up and at the quarter [500 meters] had one-half length. He just played into my hands, as I like to row with a man's stern abreast of me". Here, Kelly shows his total confidence, though, he was wrong about his margin of victory over Beresford. The margin was one second, not "a length and a little more".

The other item to make note is the sprint victory of the U.S. Naval Academy medal race. Coming from behind was the first of a remarkable string of similar collegiate Olympic Champions (1920-U.S. Naval Academy, 1924-Yale University, 1928-University California, 1932-University California, 1936-University Washington, 1948-University California, 1952-U.S. Naval Academy, 1956-Yale University). And, like this 1920 medal race, each of these Gold Medal races needed the same strong finish to punch through the competition in the last two hundred meters for victory.

A Paean to Rowing

William O'Chee

THERE ARE FEW JOYS AS SENSUOUS AS SLIPPING AWAY FROM THE SANDY beach of Terranora Water in Australia, and feeling the reassuring lock up of my blades as I take the initial stroke on my journey to the broad and placid lake beyond. It takes me back to student days in Oxford—the rapture of being the first boat on the Isis in the morning, when the wake of a single or eight, like a tremulous skein of water on the still surface of the river, trailed like a pursuivant in the distance.

Rowing is the most perplexing of sports; it is variously idyllic and gut-wrenchingly painful. Its technical complexities give rise to a never-ending pursuit of the perfect stroke. And the friendships forged in crews from double sculls to eights, endure when those of other sports fade to dimness. Most of my oldest and dearest friends have shared with me the brotherhood of the river.

"What is that brotherhood?" you may ask.

At its most basic, rowing offers the shared friendship of a boat rowed well. Of course, this is not possible without a crew that works together, combining mind, and muscle, and spirit toward one common goal. In the single scull, it is the triumph of the will over the conundrum of balance, force, and feel to produce a boat that glides over the water with the seeming effortlessness of the gods. I suspect that beyond this there is another dimension to our satisfaction. Water is as alien a medium to humans as is the air. We were made to walk on land, and although we might learn to swim, it never takes us far from shore. For ancient Britons and many others, lakes and waterways were liminal zones between the realms of the living and of the dead. Ancient boats, crudely rowed, would have played a role in the ceremonies of these people.

Moreover, the first boats, whether paddled or rowed, freed humanity from the tyranny of the land, and allowed us to extend our vision and our imagination beyond our immediate surrounds. The sea might still have held its terrors, as it does today, but the first mariners were heroes who prevailed more often than not over the brutal forces of nature.

The galleys of the Mediterranean, with their banks of serried oarsmen, made possible the transmission of civilisation and wealth from one part of the inland sea to another. They also carried innumerable parties of warriors on journeys of conquest to other lands. It is little surprise that the earliest surviving portions of the Western canon sang the praises of these oarsmen, and the helmsmen who steered their way. In fact, in the *Iliad*, Homer used the image of dauntless oarsmen as a metaphor for the perseverance of the Trojans when he wrote:

> *With these words Hektor passed through the gates,*
> *and his brother Alexander with him,*
> *both eager for the fray. As when heaven sends a*
> *breeze to sailors who have long looked for*
> *one in vain, and have laboured at their oars at*
> *sea till they are faint with toil, even so*
> *welcome was the sight of these two heroes to the Trojans.*

In the *Aeneid*, too, Virgil invokes the image of heroic oarsmen. The funeral games for Aeneas's father, Anchises, featured a race between four galleys, in which the pluck and prowess of the oarsmen were vividly sung:

> *They next draw lots*
> *for starting places, captains stand on the sterns*
> *their purple and gold regalia gleaming far afield.*
> *And the oarsmen don their wreaths of poplar leaves,*
> *oil poured on their naked shoulders makes them glisten.*
> *They crowd the thwarts, their arms tense at the oars,*
> *ears tense for the signal; hearts pounding, racing*

with nerves high-strung and a grasping lust for glory.
At last a piercing blare of the trumpet—suddenly all
the ships burst from the line, no stopping them now,
the shouts of the sailors hit the skies, the oarsmen's arms
pull back to their chests as they whip the swells to foam.
Still dead even, they plow their furrows, rippling the sea
wide open with thrashing oars and cleaving triple beaks.

It is a scene two thousand years old, but one so ably drawn that it still rings true for every rower today. The thrill of the race endures through the ages, and with it, some echo too, of the grasping lust for glory.

Of course there are many reasons why we each took up the sport of rowing, and for most the prospect of achieving rowing glory was far from mind, if it was present at all. I was born in Australia's river city of Brisbane, and as a child I watched ships, big and small, ply their paths on the city's waterway. The tranquil slap of waves on the side of a river ferry was part of the soundtrack to my childhood.

It was at Oxford, though, that I first took to the river for sport. As a freshman at Brasenose College, I was lured by the offer of a sherry party in the rooms of the Boat Club Captain. There, amidst the oak panelled walls bestrewn with paintings, and photos, and trophy oars going back to the 1830s, stood the men of the 1st VIII. In their black blazers piped with gold silk, and their "Childe of Hale" ties of purple, yellow and red stripes, they seemed to shine with all the splendour of Trojan heroes. But it was their camaraderie that struck me as much as their dress: I wanted to one day belong to this brotherhood. And so it was, after being amply plied with glasses of golden nectar, that I signed up to appear the next day at the river for my first outing as a coxswain.

Even now I can still relive what seemed like the precarious balance of a tub pair, almost as wide as it was long, while sitting beside the Captain of Boats, as two other freshmen tried their arms, somewhat ineptly on the oars. But in the space of an hour, my metamorphosis was complete. I had succumbed to the lure of the river as surely as if the call had come from a siren herself.

In time, and after much application, I would learn to bring a deft hand and steely eye to my new vocation, but it was no easy journey. I would be the first to admit that I was probably not as gifted as others, but I made up for it with enormous amounts of tenacity. It was a good preparation for the vicissitudes of life beyond the gentle waters of the Isis.

Of course, over the years there have been many glories, and a goodly number of ignominious defeats. I should like to boast that I took the former with humility, and the latter with good humour, but that would be a terrible lie. What I do know is that the best qualities of my nature, such as I possess, were fostered by those with whom I shared a boat. Industry, courage, perseverance, and self-belief I was gifted by my friends.

Seared in my memory, also, are those little moments of excellence of which I was part. I can still see the blade of a women's four so expertly brought to the catch that the water seemed not to drop from the spoon so much as almost merge with the surface of the river as the oar was prepared. I remember the immense satisfaction of an hour's square blade rowing done well by my Lightweight Blue Boat under the tutelage of Ronnie Howard, or the great Dan Lyons setting us to do a piece with the invocation: "Remember, you guys are gods, so row like it!"

Over the last ten years I have had the privilege to document the 200-year history of the rowing club that set me on this path, the Brasenose College Boat Club. I have researched some extraordinary individuals, and had the honour of meeting a few more. Time and again, I found that they shared the same memories and experiences as I did. Whatever honours or failures we had in life after Oxford were so gladly set aside to share in the pride of having rowed for our club.

For more than two centuries, this has been exemplified in the "boat brought in safety past the college barge at last, when no hope seemed left in the Gut or on the Willows", as it has been by those who in war displayed "conspicuous gallantry and devotion to duty", or the man of whom it could be said that, "he was never known to do a mean action, and he never let down a friend." I know that rowers around the world, in their own clubs, and in their own ways, share these joys and virtues too.

As I slip away from the shore in the early morning, and lazily cleave my way over Terranora Water, I am taken back to all of this. The catch of the oars, the ringing of the puddles, the sweet chiming of the hull, banish all cares and bring to life once more the glories of the past.

Henley Royal Regatta

Rick Rinehart

Earthly glory is transitory, but there is always Henley.
——Benjamin Ivry, *Regatta*

In spring 1972, Kent School's first eight had won every high school and junior race they entered, including the Stotesbury Cup on the Schuylkill River in Philadelphia, which was regarded as the national championships for schoolboy crews, and the New England Interscholastic Rowing Association's Regatta in Worcester, Massachusetts. Hart Perry, the coach of the Kent crew, arranged that the boys—the "Men of Kent"—could travel to Henley Royal Regatta that summer to compete in the Princess Elizabeth Challenge Cup (PE). The crew's bow oar was Rick Rinehart, who wrote a book about the 1972 crew: *Men of Kent: Ten Boys, a Fast Boat, and the Coach Who Made Them Champions* (2010).

Henley is a Saxon name meaning "high enclosure" or "clearing." The town has represented an important crossing of the Thames since Roman times, its present bridge having been completed in 1774. Known throughout its early history as a popular coaching town, meaning a place where a coach and its passengers could stop for a cup of mead at the Catherine Wheel or a bed at the Red Lion Inn, it was especially favored by the likes of Dr. Johnson, Boswell, and Charles I. It was also home to England's only elected Pope, Nicholas Breakspear, elevated to the title of Pope Adrian IV in 1154. As previously mentioned, the first sanctioned crew race on the

Thames at Henley occurred in 1829 when Oxford defeated Cambridge in eight-oared "cutters" before some 20,000 spectators.

Henley's long reach was becoming so popular with oarsmen by the late 1830s that the town fathers thought that something formal should be done about it. On March 26, 1839, a Captain Edmund Gardiner suggested

> *that from the lively interest which had been manifested at the various boat races which have taken place on the Henley reach during the last few years, and the great influx of visitors on such occasions, this meeting is of the opinion that the establishing of an annual regatta, under judicious and respectable management, would not only be productive of the most beneficial results to the town of Henley, but from its peculiar attractions would also be a source of amusement and gratification to the neighbourhood, and the public in general.*

"Originally staged by the Mayor and people of Henley as a public attraction with a fair and other amusements," the official history of the regatta reads, "the emphasis rapidly changed so that competitive amateur rowing became its main purpose." The first regatta was held in the summer of 1839 and took place on a single afternoon. By the next year it was up to two days, by 1866 it was at three days, and by 1906, four. The regatta received royal patronage from Prince Albert in 1851, an honor that has been renewed by each monarch since.

Since there were few sporting organizations in the world in the mid-nineteenth century on which to model the regatta, Henley organizers, later known as the Stewards, more or less had to make it up as they went along. However, so efficient became the management of the regatta by the turn of the twentieth century that the founder of the modern Olympics, Pierre de Coubertain, adopted some of the principles of Henley's "Stewardship" in forming the first International Olympic Committee. And though the regatta plays by its own rules and traditions, it is nevertheless recognized by the governing body of rowing in England and Wales, the Amateur Rowing Association, and, more important, by FISA, the International Federation of Rowing Associations.

At the first Henley Regatta in 1839 (it was not yet "Royal") only one trophy was offered, the Grand Challenge Cup, "to be rowed for annually by amateur crews in eight-oared boats." The first competition for four-oared boats with coxswain came along in 1841 with the establishment of the Stewards' Challenge Cup, which amusingly begat a coxswainless four contest in 1869 as a response to an incident that had occurred the previous year. Evidently, according to the official Henley history, at the 1868 regatta oarsman W. B. "Guts" Woodgate on a Brasenose four had found his coxswain an "encumbrance" and had ordered him to jump out of the boat at the start. (Woodgate had figured out how to work a steering mechanism using his foot.) "Lightened by the ejection of this passenger," the citation goes on to explain, "the Brasenose four went on to win easily—only to be disqualified." The Stewards' Challenge Cup itself went officially coxless in 1873, and over the following decades trophies were added for sculls, double sculls, pairs, and several new classifications for eights. By 1972 Henley Royal Regatta offered twelve separate competitions.

Columbia University provided the first American crew to win at Henley, capturing the Visitors Challenge Cup for coxless fours in 1878, but it wasn't until 1914 that a crew from the United States, a Harvard boat, won the Grand Challenge Cup. It was also just the third foreign crew to do so in seventy-five years of competition for the Grand. Indeed, the Grand, and Henley as a whole, was dominated by English crews until competition was resumed following V-E Day in 1945. This had more to do with the paucity of foreign entrants (Kent School and a few others excepted) than the inability of the rest of the world to produce worthy crews. The international diversity of entrants increased markedly following the war, with crews from Europe, the Soviet Union, Germany, and Australia joining the United States on the engraving plate of Henley trophies. In Olympic years the regatta came to be viewed as a warm-up for the Games held later that summer.

One American Olympian who never had the chance to "warm up" at Henley was John B. "Jack" Kelly, perhaps the greatest sculler the United States has produced, and whose controversial exclusion from the regatta in 1920 may have single-handedly led to the Stewards' reconsideration of what an amateur was a decade and a half later. Born to Irish immigrant parents in Philadelphia in 1889, Kelly's was the archetypical American success story. A high school dropout, Kelly went to work for his brother's construction company in 1907, where he learned the bricklayer's trade. About two years later he started rowing out of the Vesper Boat Club boathouse on the Schuylkill; by 1916 he was the best sculler in the United States and a national champion. Upon his return from service in World War I in 1918, he started his own bricklaying company, and such was his talent for self-promotion that his business venture eventually made him a millionaire.

By the time of his application to compete in Henley's Diamond Sculls, Kelly had won six national championships and was in the midst of an incredible 126-race winning streak. Assured by the secretary of the National Association of Amateur Oarsman (NAAO), who had supposedly cleared Kelly's application in advance with the Stewards, Kelly bought himself a brand-new scull and made arrangements for passage to England. On the eve of his departure, he was shocked to receive a telegram from the Stewards that read simply: ENTRY REJECTED. LETTER FOLLOWS. As enraged as an Irishman could be after yet another seemingly typical slight by the English, Kelly took his revenge by beating the Henley sculls winner, Jack Beresford, at the 1920 Olympics.

As Kelly was one of the most famous athletes of his time, the Stewards' rebuff quickly became the stuff of populist outrage based on the wobbly conviction that his application was rejected solely because he had been "by trade or employment for wages a mechanic, artisan, or labourer." For Americans, whose passion for the little guy in such mismatches symbolized the struggle between commoner and nobility, even democracy against monarchy, this became the main story line. Facts are stubborn things, as the saying goes. The principal reason for the Stewards' rejection of Kelly's application was that they had essentially banned anyone from Vesper Boat Club from competing at the regatta after the club had publicly raised funds to send an eight over to Henley in 1905 to challenge for the Grand. This was viewed as payment to the Vesper crew, ergo professionalism. Only secondarily did the Stewards determine that "Mr Kelly was also not qualified under Rule I (e) of the General Rules (manual labour)." Still, the Kelly scandal embarrassed the Stewards into lifting the ban on Vesper entries shortly thereafter, and in 1937 all language denying applications to those who had been engaged in manual labor was expunged from the rules.

The story could have ended there, but Kelly chose to make his grudge against the Stewards multigenerational. As Benjamin Ivry recounts in his book *Regatta*, when John B. "Kell" Kelly Jr. was born, "His father vowed immediately that young Kell would vindicate the Henley Stewards' rejection by triumphing where his father had been excluded." Kell did so by winning the Diamond Sculls in 1947 and 1949. Kelly Jr. also won the U.S. single sculls championship eight times and was a bronze medalist at the 1956 Olympics.

But Jack Kelly's sweetest revenge at the Stewards may have come after his death through his actress-daughter Grace, later better known as Princess Grace of Monaco. Not only was she invited to present the trophies at the 1981 regatta, but in 2003 a women's quadruple sculls competition at Henley was renamed the Princess Grace Challenge Cup. With that, it can safely be said, the Stewards had atoned for their indelicate snub of one of America's greatest athletes.

Over its long history two distinct but comingling Henleys have evolved, one the Henley of competition on the water, the other the social pageant underway on the banks of the Thames. A *Times* of London correspondent once referred to the latter as "one week when you drift back to the Edwardian era … in spite of the advanced technology of the sport on display." Venues for viewing racing are hierarchical, from the exclusive Stewards' Enclosure at the finish line, to the slightly more casual Remenham Club farther up the course, to the anything-goes decorum of simply plopping oneself down in the grass outside the enclosures and popping a bottle of champagne. The 1972 guide to the regatta tried to dispel "the mistaken impression … that admission to the enclosures was confined to those who … had something to do with rowing." "All are welcome," it stated with an air of generosity that came to a screeching halt with the caveat, "except for the Stewards' enclosure." Mere mortals were welcome to pay admission to something called the Regatta Enclosure, which provided "an excellent view of the racing . . . licensed bars and also amusement-with-prize machines." Sounding as if it was doing the general public a favor, the brochure concluded by saying that the Regatta Enclosure had a car park "which actually adjoins it."

Because as a competitor my family was entitled to admission to the Stewards' Enclosure, the prospect of a trip to Henley had my mother and my girlfriend Liz scrambling to the dress shop and my father reviewing his fine wardrobe with particular gusto. A Web site known as the Twickenham Underground and its mysterious proprietor, "Rabbit," offers an irreverent but still helpful guide to dress code at Henley:

> *In brief the rules are fairly simple:*
>
> - *Lounge Suits or Blazers and Flannels for the gentlemen (and yes a shirt and tie is also a prerequisite for admission)*
> - *Skirts or dresses down to the knee for the ladies—no trousers, divided skirts or culottes. (Well, the rules were first designed in the eighteen forties.)—nb Remenham club doesn't require skirts to be below the knee, but you never know when you might be offered Stewards tickets, so better safe than sorry. . . .*

The Stewards' own description of its Enclosure's dress code humorlessly affirms what Mr. or Ms. Rabbit suggests here, but ends with the rather severe "Mobile Telephones are forbidden"—not simply "not allowed" but "forbidden," as if they were the invention of the devil. As Benjamin Ivry deliciously describes in *Regatta*, such transgressions of Henley correctness are often met with the words "Not at Henley, please."

Still, in presenting the trophies at the 1949 regatta, Mrs. Winston (Lady) Churchill described Henley as "This lovely pageant of English life." In between races in 1972 spectators were entertained by the Band of the Irish Guards, whose program included such disparate melodies as "Gigi," "Swan Lake," and "Mary Poppins." Following the last race of the day, the band would play a somber "God Save the Queen," for which Britons and visitors alike would immediately cease conversation and freeze in place for the duration of the anthem. It was a reminder, if anyone needed reminding, that they were indeed in England, and that no other nation's flag would be flown nor its anthem played during the regatta, even at the presentation of trophies. Not at Henley, please.

Henley is and always has been a bacchanalia of food and drink. What beer is to NASCAR, Pimm's Cup and champagne are to Henley. For the uninitiated, Pimm's Cup, particularly Pimm's Cup Number 1, is derived from gin though it has amber coloring and hints of citrus and spice. "The traditional choice," according to Rabbit's rules of Henley etiquette, is "one part Pimm's, three parts lemonade, drunk in pints. And since a healthy diet contains five portions of fruit or veg daily," Rabbit further recommends "a minimum of five pints of Pimm's per day." Pimm's can also be mixed with champagne or sparkling wine to create what is known as Royal Pimm's Cup. Accompanied by a full-blown, five-course meal or just a basket of strawberries, Pimm's and champagne are staples of the Henley picnic.

By 1972 Kent had been competing at Henley for nearly half a century and could claim a little Henley lore of its own, several incidences having to do with breaches of the regatta's singular decorum. It started rather ignominiously with Kent's first Henley visit in 1927 when Father Sill scandalously coached from a launch, evidently "forbidden" by the Stewards. (One presumes that coaching was to be done from the towpath, either on bicycle or on foot.) As recounted by Christopher Dodd in his history of the Regatta, "Nobody spoke to the boys from Kent for five days." However, Dodd explains, they nevertheless had "a warm reception at Mr. John Nugee's house at Radley," out of which contact "grew the annual exchange scheme run by the English Speaking Union," another dream of Father Sill's from earlier visit to Henley.

Take Me to the River

The Quest for a Permanent Rowing Home in Minneapolis

Sarah Risser

MINNESOTA'S FIRST AND OLDEST ROWING CLUB, THE MINNESOTA BOAT Club (MBC), was founded in 1870 by a group of motivated young men with a simple desire to row. They trained in small boats and fours, sharing the Mississippi River with steamboats and barges and stored their fleet in a leaky, covered-over, scow until they had the means to procure property on Raspberry Island, just a short walk over the Wabasha Street Bridge from the dusty bustle of downtown St. Paul. The 'Minnesotas' built their first boathouse in 1874 and immediately established an intra-club 4th-of-July Regatta tradition that quickly became as much an exclusive social as an athletic event.

Rowing was eventually organized in St. Paul's twin city of Minneapolis as part of a regional tourism and development boom. In 1877, real estate magnate Colonel William S. King built a resort pavilion on Lake Calhoun (renamed Bde Maka Ska in 2020) located just three miles south of Minneapolis. He incentivized rowing by offering the newly formed Lurline Rowing Club 'a perpetual lease on a . . . substantial building containing boat room and dressing rooms and which will admit of additions and ornamentation as the club grows . . . situated but a short distance from the Pavilion whose balconies will offer a fine chance for spectators at the future races.' King understood that the presence of competitive rowing—growing in popularity—would draw crowds to his pavilion.

King located his pavilion near the proposed street railway, which promised a comfortable alternative to horse-drawn carriages. The Lurlines postponed rowing until the train was operational. They spent 1877 acquiring a fleet of rowing shells and promoting King's Pavilion with series of galas. Unfortunately, King's finances had become strained, burdened with over $120,000 in claims. In return for debt relief, he agreed to transfer property deeds to financial advisor Philo Remington. When King was adjudicated bankrupt in late 1877, Remington subdivided and sold most of his property. Management of King's Pavilion was transferred to real estate speculator Louis Menage, and the Lurlines lost their boathouse.

Menage encouraged the Lurlines to relocate to his Lake Side Park on Calhoun's far western shore where he had platted out lots intended to become extravagant lakeside villas. The Lurlines accepted and hired architect LeRoy Buffington to design a 30' x 80' two-story boathouse 'extremely tasteful in architectural design and a decided ornament.' However, when it soon became clear that local wealthy residents preferred the shores of Lake Minnetonka to Calhoun, Menage redirected his energy toward transforming King's Pavilion into the grand Lyndale Hotel.

By 1879, the Lyndale street railway was servicing Lake Calhoun's eastern shore, and the Lurlines, newly settled on Calhoun's less-accessible western shore, felt increasingly isolated. In late 1880, they hoisted their boathouse onto jackscrews, and early the next spring they hauled it over the ice to be close to the train station, their third venue in four years. They embellished their boathouse with a 65' x 30' hall—perfect for moonlit dancing parties—and positioned it on piles to jet over the water and create space for bathing underneath.

Through the mid-1880s, the Lurlines focused most of their energy on socializing by hosting frequent 'hops' and parties. It wasn't until a few experienced oarsmen relocated to Minneapolis in 1885 that the Lurlines took a serious interest in rowing. Other developments bolstered a growing interest in the sport and kindled the Lurlines' latent competitive spirit. In 1886, the St. Paul Boat Club was founded, and train service linked St. Paul to Winnipeg, allowing MBC, the St. Paul Boat Club, and the Winnipeg Rowing Club to found the Minnesota and Winnipeg Amateur

Rowing Association (MWARA), spurring on a friendly rivalry and new competitive opportunities.

The Lurlines had a small presence at the first MWARA Regatta. However, the following year they enjoyed two unexpected wins. Top senior single sculler J. E. Muchmore finished a spectacular 15 lengths ahead of Winnipeg and St. Paul in the senior single before the Lurline junior double prevailed. The press glorified the surprising wins: 'Minneapolis don't want the earth, but it does please her when her amateur athletes begin to go to the front after years of innocuous desuetude.' Upon their return from Winnipeg a crowd gathered at the station and a band led a parade to the West Hotel where the oarsmen enjoyed a celebratory dinner. Speeches glorified their unexpected wins and became a rallying cry for a new boathouse. The growing sentiment was that the Lurlines' simple boathouse did not reflect their newfound glory nor befit the prestigious and growing nature of the club's roster.

The Lurlines were even more victorious at the 1888 MWARA Regatta, winning all five events entered and capturing the coveted Sir Donald A. Smith Cup for the regatta's signature event, the senior four. Emboldened, they attended the Mississippi Valley Amateur Rowing Association Regatta, again sweeping every event they entered before attending the Northwestern Amateur Rowing Association Regatta in Grand Rapids, Michigan. The press began referring to them as the 'Lusty Lurlines' and promoting their new desire for a new boathouse: 'The Lurlines [will] build a magnificent club house . . . one which the success of the club justly warrants.'

The Lurline boathouse was modest compared to the grand boathouses of its rivals; it didn't reflect their elite social status. In contrast MBC occupied a spacious home on Raspberry Island embellished with a lawn, running track, and tennis courts which effectively created a country club-like atmosphere. Raspberry Island could be transformed—and often was—into something magical for moonlit social gatherings. When the men of MBC returned victorious from the 1881 Mississippi Valley Amateur Rowing Association Regatta, Mayor Rice and other local luminaries celebrated with the oarsmen at the MBC boathouse. The *St Paul Daily Globe* described the scene as "charming and fairylike. . . . Chinese lanterns were swayed to and fro by the breeze like veritable fire-flies; a thousand lights danced and shimmered on the water."

The St. Paul Boat Club engaged architect J. W. Stevens to design a grand two-story boathouse intended to rival the best boathouses in the country. In addition to boat storage, the boathouse had a reception room, dressing room, bathrooms, smoking room, and a ladies' 'retiring room.' The Duluth Boat Club worked with architect Charles MacMillen to design Minnesota's most opulent boathouse on Lake Superior in 1887. Michael J. Cochran writes in his *Invincible—History of the Duluth Boat Club* (2008):

> *The ground floor contained the boat room, bathrooms, gymnasium, and closets. The second floor had a billiard room, four dressing rooms . . . a lady's toilette, and the main reception or reading room. The dressing room . . . floors were covered with rich Brussels carpets. The reading room had a profusion of comfortable easy chairs. The second-floor rooms opened onto a balcony, which ran entirely around the building. The third floor consisted of one large room for banquets and dances with a balcony running entirely around. A spiral staircase connected these floors and led to a tower, which offered a fine view of Lake Superior. . . . The clubhouse boasted a number of conveniences that were by no means common in 1887. It had plumbing, gas, a hot water heater, and a telephone.*

The Lurlines arrived at Lake Minnetonka for the 1889 MWARA Regatta buoyed by their recent wins. The press described the scene: 'Bunting and silks. Worth (sic) costumes and bare legs, beautiful women and bronzed men, a keen wind blowing across the choppy lake, the buzz of many keyed voices, the chink of money.' The Lurlines were confident that J. E. Muchmore, would trounce Winnipeg's highly regarded Fox in the senior single. When Fox prevailed, winning by a close half-length, 'There was a hush for a moment and then the Winnipeggers yelled like madmen. . . . The Canadians danced and screamed and howled and when [Fox] came to the dock they picked him up.' The defeat stunned the Lurlines. Their hearts sank with a misplaced sense of betrayal. When Muchmore rowed to the landing his teammates avoided him, suspecting him of intentionally throwing the race. They left him to carry his shell into the clubhouse alone.

The Lurlines were heavily favored to win the senior four. Their trainer, Dan Breen, had held each man in his dedicated seat all season, coaching the crew to work together as one. After the gun went off, the Lurlines moved smoothly, with synchronicity, comfortably securing a two-length lead over Winnipeg. Executing the turn at one mile, Lurline's bow oar struck the turning stake and broke, causing a drastic loss of speed allowing Winnipeg to pull ahead and prevail. The Lurlines were so agitated by their second unexpected loss they scratched their entry in the senior double, handing Winnipeg another victory by default.

Undeterred, the Lurlines continued to pursue a new boathouse. They engaged architect Foraleman to draw plans for an elegant three-story structure intended to be, 'a vast improvement over anything in the line west of Chicago.' The first story would store 36 rowing shells, incorporating every convenience for getting the shells to and from the water. Balconies would surround the second story club room, reception room, and restaurant all finished in the Queen Anne style. The third story would provide living quarters for a dedicated club chef. 'New quarters, new energy and new achievements is the motto of the blue and white for 1890,' the *St Paul Daily Globe* wrote on August 4, 1889.

The Lurlines' determination to build a grand boathouse was stymied by Charles Loring, first president of the Minneapolis Parks. Loring envisioned public access to Minneapolis's chain of lakes with their boulevards controlled by Minneapolis Parks, not held in private hands. Throughout the 1890s, the Lurlines appealed to the park board yet their prospects of building a grand boathouse on Lake Calhoun became increasingly slim. During this time, the Lurlines struggled to retain a dedicated coach. In 1899, the club finally disbanded. They tore down their boathouse and transferred their rowing shells—considered the finest collection in the state—to the newly opened Minikahda (golf) Club located on Menage's old Lakeside Park property. The Minikahda Club agreed to store the shells until the Lurlines found a more desirable venue, most likely on the Mississippi River. Proposed lock and dam infrastructure promised to transform Mississippi River Gorge from a boulder-ridden riverbed into a miles-long lake-like pool of water that would create a perfect rowing venue.

Fifty years after Colonel William S. King incentivized Minneapolis's first rowing club to draw crowds to his report pavilion, Harry S. Goldie revived the sport in an effort to market his Calhoun Beach Club (CBC) as a vibrant sports center that would showcase Minneapolis's aquatic facilities. In 1927, Goldie recruited ex-college oarsmen to found the Minneapolis Rowing Club (MRC). The Minneapolis Park Board supported the effort by creating an ad-hoc boathouse in the east wing of its old refectory, enabling rowing to return to Lake Calhoun, not to the Mississippi River as anticipated. When the CBC's development came to a sudden halt in 1930 due to financial repercussions from the stock market crash, the park board allowed MRC to continue storing boats in its old refectory.

By the mid-1950s, Lake Calhoun had become a popular aquatic sports venue, and MRC weary of negotiating its long, narrow, shells around swimmers and sail boats. MRC longed to be on the Mississippi River where they believed rowing rightfully belonged. Relocating became imperative in April 1958, when plans for a new parking lot necessitated the removal of the old refectory. Sympathetic to MRC's plight, the park board offered to help MRC find a site on the river and sold its old refectory to the rowers for one dollar. MRC was welcome to salvage materials in exchange for removing the building.

The job of relocating to their new site on 36th Street proved to be Herculean. Club members trucked salvaged lumber from temporary storage to the river and then hauled it upriver by Army Duck. They transported a bulldozer by barge from Lambert's Landing in St. Paul, through Lock and Dam #1. They procured granite paving blocks and borrowed a truck to move them. In exchange, they rebuilt the truck engine and repaired a garage. The flurry of activity concerned homeowners living above MRC's new site. They anticipated boat launchings, parties, and excessive noise and initiated a vigorous letter-writing campaign in protest. Although MRC was deemed legally entitled to stay, the rowers resigned to relocate again, presumably to avoid conflict. They appealed to the park board for a site north of the Lake Street Bridge, a request which was immediately approved.

MRC had been homeless for three years as they began clearing and hauling lumber by barge for the second time. Club members persevered, driven by a desire to row on the river. In 1963, they laid the foundation for an A-frame boathouse designed by member and industrial designer Ralph Dorr. In early 1964, they erected the frame. Each section weighed over a ton and had to be raised by winch. In the spring of 1965, six years after leaving Lake Calhoun, MRC's simple but functional Duncan Miller Boathouse was sufficiently closed in to protect the club's shells. It was finally time to row. However, in a painfully frustrating twist of fate, late-spring flooding delayed rowing yet again. In June of 1965, the club finally launched their rowing shells onto the Mississippi River Gorge, the rowing home they had been dreaming of for decades.

MRC enjoyed over 30 years of uninterrupted rowing before the Duncan Miller Boathouse was destroyed by arson. Firefighters arrived early in the morning on September 28, 1997, to 20-foot flames shooting through the boathouse roof. When rowers arrived for their 7:30 a.m. practice, only a few scarred timbers and smoldering debris remained—at least 30 boats were destroyed. MRC resolved to build a bigger, more beautiful boathouse and hired award-winning architect Vincent James to design a contemporary structure that drew heavily upon the aesthetics of rowing. James instilled a sense of dynamic, three-dimensional, space and movement with a wavy roof form which mirrored the arc of an oar in motion. He installed clerestory windows of polycarbonate glazing to make the boathouse appear as a beacon at night. MRC's Lloyd Ohme Boathouse, completed in 2001, won three architectural awards. The Minneapolis rowers had realized their historic dream of occupying one of the most unique and aesthetic boathouses in the Upper Midwest.

Ironically, the early 2000s saw a number of smaller rowing clubs spin off from MRC to train on local lakes with only simple or ad-hoc structures for boat storage. These new upstarts valued organizing and training in a manner that reflects their specific objectives over a specific venue or boathouse. The new clubs have served to diversify opportunities and participation in the sport.

For nearly 60 years, MRC's boathouse, nestled at the bottom of a bluff, has been protected from encroaching development and business interests. However, the dams that transformed the River Gorge from boulder-ridden rapids into the lake-like venue that enable rowing on the Mississippi are no longer used for navigation or commerce. The Army Corps of Engineers is actively considering their removal. MRC's advantageous rowing venue is being weighed against other interests. The environmental advocacy group, American Rivers, recently listed the Mississippi River Gorge as one of the country's most endangered rivers, and, along with a number of local environmental groups, believes removing the dams would enhance the environment by enabling the return of many long-absent native species.

MRC is currently the largest rowing club in Minnesota offering programing for all ages and abilities. They have recently organized their own letter-writing campaign, calling for the protection of their hard-won rowing venue. However, if the past is any guide, their quest for a permanent rowing home may not be over yet.

Lucy Pocock Stillwell—A Woman in a Waterman's World

Lisa Taylor

LUCY POCOCK, MARRIED NAME STILLWELL, LED AN EXTRAORDINARY LIFE FOR A *woman of her time. Her male relatives, Dick and George, have long captured the imagination of rowing historians and enthusiasts alike. Yet the focus of this talk was of course on Lucy's life. Peter Mallory and others, whose work can be found online, have begun to shine ever more light on her story and offer very thorough accounts of various areas of her life that are only touched on here. The aim was less to present new detail pertaining to Lucy's life than to view her story through the lens of social history, and to consider her role specifically as a woman within this context. I was also fortunate to be able to speak to Heidi Danilchik, Lucy's granddaughter, in the course of researching her life. I am grateful for all direct and indirect assistance.*

Lucy Pocock was born in Kingston, Surrey, in September 1887, the second of four children born to both her parents, and five to her father.

The Pococks were an established and well renowned family of boat builders and watermen, and her mother came from the Vickers family: another familiar name in boatbuilding at the time. The prominence of rowing and watermanship in the family then is perhaps unsurprising. Yet Lucy's access to the sport first for leisure and, later, as a profession is unusual. Female opportunities for leisure were contested, especially for those outside of the middle and upper classes. The specifics of rowing—its unwieldy equipment and the movements it required—represented further challenges.

Lucy was reported to have been passionate about rowing 'ever since she could lift an oar'. While her father, Aaron Pocock, worked at Eton, he would take his four children out rowing together, coxing them himself. Eton would no doubt have given her more opportunities for rowing. As well as providing access to equipment, benign water, and relatively flexible working patterns for her father, it offered privacy. A world away from the polluted, highly trafficked Thames, it offered a sheltered environment that was optimal for rowing. For women specifically, such shelter—both physical and cultural—was almost a pre-requisite for participation in sport and physical activity.

Lucy's passion for rowing was not simply about the joy of being on the water: she was a competitor. Her access to competition is a further unusual feature of her life. She appears to have raced, successfully, from the age of about 18 or 19, and ultimately she would become a champion, winning the *Daily Mirror* Sculling Championship of the Thames in 1912.

Entry to this race was only open to female family members of previous winners of the Doggett's Coat and Badge Race. The watermen themselves would be the gatekeepers to the boats required to race and their female relatives would not, in all likelihood, have been able to enter themselves without their backing.

This rule had two important functions. One was as an important practical filter, guaranteeing some degree of skill or experience. Such a de facto guarantee of competence was perhaps a prudent choice for a race on a difficult stretch of water. Yet in men's professional racing, competence was of course no guarantee of safe or sportsmanlike behavior. This was a contest run by a newspaper, with the intention of generating money and interest. The Doggett's Coat and Badge Race was a well-known and highly regarded event and this would put watermen's family names—an important asset—at stake in a new way. The link would create good publicity opportunities, as would recruiting former winners as coxes, and sculling champion Ernest Barry as a judge.

The second was to locate participants within the particular social and cultural context of a working-class community of tradesmen. This was important because the legitimacy of physical exertion and strength, for women, varied significantly according to class. Working class women were constructed as more physically robust than their middle- and upper-class counterparts; and while this physicality was often construed as a negative, it also meant the ideological barriers to physical exertion were less among the working class. Working class women showed less conformity to conservative feminine ideals by the very fact of their class. Their transgression of these ideals was, correspondingly, less.

Whatever the stipulations of the race, it proved popular and highly competitive. Qualification was required even for the heats, and some 25,000 people were reported to have lined the banks to watch the final. According to Lucy's granddaughter, Heidi Danilchik, Lucy's opponent, Miss Brady, had been put forward to race by her family, who had heavy financial stakes in her win. She also suggested that a rematch between the two of them would be raced on 'double or nothing' terms, implying a strong financial imperative. This does not seem to have been the case for Lucy. While her prize money facilitated subsequent travel to the United States, there is no indication that financial gain was an integral part of her decision to race. This highlights an element of privilege to Lucy's position: her participation was more driven by sport for sport's sake than for financial security or opportunity.

At the end of the first race between these two, Lucy is reported to have fainted, and her opponent to have gone 'immediately to her assistance to bring her round': although competitive during the race, the constitution of the winner could bear no more. It's a compelling narrative drawing on sporting morality and sexual norms: the race loser sculling to the aid of the woman who beat her, the feminine impulse to care and nurture unchanged despite the competitive tussle. In the rematch, reports claim that Miss Brady fainted, having lost, and that Lucy provided similar support to her. Coincidence? Perhaps—yet the symmetry of this storyline, and the degree of fouling and match-fixing common in men's professional racing, should give us some pause. Such explicit display of weakness also offered a useful way to communicate ideas about femininity and women in sport as well as providing more sensational headlines. Reports could reiterate middle-class gender norms surrounding female physiological capacity and exertion, appeasing readers with more conservative views on women racing on the river.

This desire to appease conservative audiences is evident in more general reporting on the race. The 'form' of many of the competitors is characterised as 'indifferent when compared with the form of the average male sculler'; the form shown by Lucy, however, is described as 'a revelation to most oarsmen of what a woman sculler can do' (*The Citizen*). A different article portrays Lucy as 'the picture of athletic girlhood', and 'the centre of interest for a huge crowd as she stepped ashore—a little woman for such a big task' (*Hendon and Finchley Times*). In fact, Lucy was over six foot tall; she was 25 in 1912, so hardly a girl; and images of her don't easily align with this written description. I would suggest that rather than a lack of journalistic observation, this was an intentional reshaping of the facts, driven by the need to sell papers; part of long tradition of 'fake news'.

On winning the sculling rematch, Lucy's prize money—supplemented by bets placed by her father—enabled her, her father, and sister to join her younger brothers, Dick and George, in the USA. Dick and George had left the UK for Vancouver, Canada, in 1911, and in 1912 moved to Seattle, having been invited to build boats for Hiram Conibear of the University of Washington (UW).

Shortly after her arrival, Lucy began to work as a cook for the UW men's rowing team, and was subsequently employed to coach rowing and the related, prerequisite skill of swimming. Women had rowed at UW since 1903, in competitive racing from 1907, and employed coaches there were not unusual. Yet women's involvement in rowing at this time at UW was in flux. American society, like British society, was conflicted about the extent to which it was appropriate for women to exert themselves. The frontier feel of Washington State might have created a more liberal mood—certainly when compared to Oxbridge or the Ivy League—but the university still exhibited fairly conservative impulses when it came to women's sport.

Despite her reported popularity, Lucy only appears to have coached for one season. Her granddaughter suggested that she resigned from the club when it became clear that women would no longer be permitted to pursue competitive training under a new Gymnasium Director. After she left UW, Lucy appears to have continued to scull for pleasure; and the story goes that her husband to be—James Stillwell, a contractor working on the waterfront—saw this graceful, accomplished sculler skimming across the water, and the rest, as they say, being history. They were married, had children and grandchildren, and led a long and happy life together, Lucy taking a step away from more active, public life, and back towards the domestic sphere.

Lucy's life story thus exhibits an intriguing mix of conformity to, and disruption of, gendered norms in terms of work, sport, and home life. On the one hand, here was a woman who was a champion athlete, in a sport dominated by men, both professionally and among amateurs; a woman whose athletic successes allowed her and her family to emigrate to a place she made a life in; and a woman who was paid to coach competitive women's sport in 1913. On the other, we can see her in much more conventional vein: as a young, single woman she participated in competitive sport; she worked in order to support her parental family group and, on getting married, quietly disappeared from the sport and from public life.

Both versions are incomplete; neither is straightforwardly true or false. I believe the second does her a disservice, but that the first overlooks the extent to which her achievements were facilitated by men, and—importantly—by men that all had stakes in her success, from her father and brothers, to the University of Washington and even the *Daily Mirror*. She undoubtedly possessed exceptional athletic talent, but the specifics of her family life—a famous rowing name, the financial and domestic opportunity to emigrate, the serendipity of her brothers establishing themselves in a rowing community that would accept women—meant unusual opportunities were there for her to take.

A Memorable Race at Henley
Women's Regatta

Thomas E. Weil

In rowing, there are many matches, but few real races, and many winners, but few real champions. I recently had the privilege of following a race from the umpire's launch at Henley Women's Regatta. It was a battle for the ages, and it showcased eighteen young champions.

Boat racing is pretty straightforward and unforgiving, sheer repetitive hard labor from start to finish. If each boat rowed every stroke at equal intensity from beginning to end, you could theoretically know after the first one who the winner would be. Every stroke contributes a little, more or less, to the result, and that is how the contest unfolds. The outcome of most other team sport events can be changed instantly with one or two swings of the foot, the bat or the stick, or one or two throws of the ball. This is rarely the case in rowing, at least not on the upside—one bad stroke can cost you the race, but it takes the cumulative hundreds or thousands of good individual strokes to win one.

Yes, there is the always exciting start, with high rates for varying periods. There may be currents and wind gusts, and errant steering and collisions. There may be power tens and the rising din of spectators on the banks. There may be the occasional equipment breakage, or debris, or the collapse of a rower. There may be favored lanes. But when all is said and done on the Henley reach, there are two boats trying to get to the finish line first. Barring unusual circumstances, the work is done by putting the oar in the water and pulling, over and over, unrelentingly. The outcome is often predictable before the contestants are half way down the course.

Boat races tend not to be events pregnant with excitement until the last moment.

Even in the 2012 Henley Women's Regatta finals, by which time the heats had pretty much sorted out the slower boats, and left two of the best of the entries to vie for the medals, the average margin of victory (counting a verdict of "Easily" as only four lengths, which decreases the actual margins) was almost exactly two lengths. Only nine (of 27) contests had separations of less than one length. Only four were closer than a half length at the finish. Two races over the 1,500 meter course ended with the crews two feet apart. I was in the umpire's launch for one of them.

The 25th Henley Women's Regatta was memorable for much more than reaching the quarter century history mark. Torrents of rainfall in the preceding weeks had left the Thames in an engorged state, with high, fast water that could quickly amplify a small steering error and made the upstream course a real struggle, especially for the smaller boats. Those conditions were further aggravated by headwinds that gusted throughout Saturday, June 16, at well over 25mph, but eased off somewhat for Sunday's rowing.

Event 358, the junior eights final for the Peabody Cup, was scheduled to go off at 3pm. It was an all-American match, pitting New Hampshire boarding school Phillips Exeter Academy against the Lerro boat from Mount Saint Joseph Academy of Philadelphia.

Their respective paths to the finals varied somewhat. Exeter was scheduled to race Pangbourne College (a high school in Reading) on Saturday, but Pangbourne declined to go on the water because of the marginal conditions, leaving Exeter with a bye for the day. The Mount, on the other hand, rowed a Saturday heat against Sir William Borlase's Grammar School from Marlow, dispatching them by two lengths in 6:39.

Semi-final heats for the junior eights were set for Sunday morning, with the finals scheduled for the afternoon. Exeter went off at 10:40 in its morning heat, and defeated Headington School from Oxford (who had won the Junior Eight in the UK National Schools Regatta in May) by two lengths in 5:50. The Mount's heat followed at 10:45, and that crew took special pleasure in beating Green Lake of Seattle by three and a quarter lengths in 5:44, since Green Lake had been listed as fifth in the

US school crew rankings, while The Mount was placed ninth. (That The Mount's Sunday morning time was almost a minute faster over the same course than their Saturday afternoon time is indicative of how truly awful Saturday's winds and current were.)

Then the decisive Sunday afternoon was upon us. Events on the course delayed the start of the final race for the Peabody Cup, but even when the boats were on the starting platform below Temple Island, which lies mid-river to the right of the starting area, Father Thames was still playing his games. Exeter had the left hand Berkshire (Berks) station as we headed upstream, and The Mount the right hand Buckinghamshire (Bucks) slot. Just upstream from the start, the Berks bank has a concave curve. As the fast current sluiced down the bank, it would dip into the curve, and then rush back out into and across the stream, so that, with sterns being held at the starting platform, bows were pushed towards Temple Island, more so on the Berks than Bucks side. Needless to say, it was frustrating for both the crews and the umpire to try to straighten the boats and then get them off before the bows were swept out of line again.

Two Mount families, one Exeter family and I had the good fortune to be seated in the elegant long umpire's launch then idling behind the starting platform. The umpire, dressed in blazer, stood attentively in the bow, the launch driver sat amidships at the great engine console, and radio commentator Judith Howell stood in the stern, providing a running race report to spectators and officials alike. Built 99 years before by Hobbs and Company, who still ply their trade above Henley bridge, our boat was one of several similar craft used at the regattas that are iconically emblematic of Henley rowing. Every picture down the course of a regatta race along the reach shows the same essential ingredients—the long lines of booms which define the lanes, the two boats in the event, and the umpire's regal launch following watchfully behind. There are few greater thrills for a regatta spectator than to be perched on those polished mahogany seats running fore and aft inside the hull, to feel the engines kick in as the race starts, and to witness the entire contest from beginning to end.

"Attention," cried the umpire. With a quick downward swipe of her red flag, and a shout of "Go!", the boats leapt off. The Mount's racing start held at over fifty strokes a minute, for much longer than Exeter's, which gave The Mount an initial lead of a few seats. Exeter's earlier settle was powerful, however, and ate up the river as the two boats battled it out. The Mount eventually settled their rating, and the duel was on.

At the outset of the struggle, The Mount still maintained a higher rate than Exeter, propelling their shell with a seemingly continuous and unbroken cycle of catch, drive, release and recover, while Exeter pounded away at a lower rate—catch, drive, *release and send*, and recover. Which style would prevail?

It was not possible to tell from the seats in the launch, especially with the other passengers sitting directly in front of me, whether the crews took tens, or when one boat might have had a few seats on the other. My frame of reference was principally the two sterns ahead of us, the flash of blades at release, recovery and catch, and the roiling puddles left in their wake. The race provided none of the drama that comes from a major break in tempo, a surge, or a crab; at one point the umpire warned Exeter back into its lane, but no clash appeared imminent. Instead, the tension and excitement that built in the launch was driven by the rising crescendo of every stroke taken by the two crews as each strained for an advantage while the distance to the finish grew inexorably shorter.

It was obvious from the start that these very evenly matched boats were there to race. Two of the clearest measures of intensity in rowing are the grimaces and concentration written over and in a competitor's face, and the controlled fury with which the blade takes the water, levers the boat past the point of the catch, and comes out hungry for the next stroke. Racing at times at the same rating, sixteen women pulled as one, neither boat giving any quarter, every stroke in both shells exploding into and out of the river, two batteries of port and starboard howitzers firing full bore in close proximity, power coated with grace, and flaming desire, confidence and pride sending the thin hulls flying up the course.

For those in the launch, it would have been normal, and desirable, under other circumstances, to have paid some attention to the fabled venue, to the cheering spectators, to the tents, and to the festive and historic atmosphere that makes Henley such a magical experience. That is one of the great privileges that a launch ride offers. And there are always the historic distance markers to note on the way down the reach—the Women's Regatta passes The Barrier, the Bushes, Fawley, and the Remenham Club. But the magnetic draw of the monumental struggle taking place in front of us left no wish or time for such distractions. All eyes were fixed on the race.

Like great presses hammering down the declaration, "Here we come. What are you going to do about it?", eighteen women fought for every inch of reach, and every inch of run. We sat mesmerized in pursuit, not daring to miss a single instant of what was a classic contest, watching two snarling jaguars stretching to catch the same prey. It was a display of furious athletic drive, skill and competition at its finest.

Stroke for stroke, the two crews surged up the Thames in cadence, each throwing down its best, neither able to break the other. Side by side, head to head, bow ball to bow ball, they raced 1,500 meters together to the finish.

At first just a blur on the Berkshire bank, the white crown of the finish line judges tent came quickly into focus, and the excitement of the first five minutes of racing turned into the gripping tensions of hopes and uncertainty, of the last few strokes, of the deciding push. Each of us in the launch had been transported into one or the other of those two boats, teeth clenched, fists tight, eyes fixed on the shells, willing the outcome. Let it be . . . The Mount . . . or Exeter!

Then the line flashed by. Oars which had a moment before been savagely ripping the river now trailed listlessly in the water. The shells drifted to a halt. The umpire raised her white flag to indicate a clean race.

Who had crossed first? None of us in the launch could tell. Indeed, in the moments before the finish line judges announced the result, a spectator could bask in the pleasure of the realization that this had been a very special occasion, and that, while there would have to be a winner, there was no loser. We were privileged to have seen greatness unveiled in this memorable, flashing, all-consuming charge up the Henley reach.

Each of the two crews had earned the title of champion before the contest was done and the outcome settled.

And then the announcement came. Exeter had won by two feet in 5:33.

The launch trip back down to the boarding point at the start was one of murmured commiseration and congratulations, all tucked gently into the wrappings of pride and admiration for what both boats had accomplished. We shared a sense of awe and gratitude for having been able to witness this memorable spectacle at such close and intimate quarters. It takes two great crews to serve up a great race. This was a truly superb race between two extraordinary crews.

How special was it? The 5:33 finishing time for these schoolgirl eights, filled with 16–18-year-olds, was remarkable under the prevailing conditions. Only two finals had faster times, the elite quad, in which Leander defeated Vesper in 5:29, and the elite eight, in which Radcliffe was beaten by a British composite in 5:20. The time achieved by both Exeter and The Mount in their junior (i.e. high school) final was faster than the final times in the other 24 Women's Henley events, including the senior (i.e. university) eights, the intermediate A (i.e. academic/university) eights and the intermediate C (i.e. club) eights.

Now *that* was racing, and that Sunday, on the River Thames in Henley, every woman in each of those two boats earned the title of champion.

The crew of Mount Saint Joseph Academy (Lerro), from bow to stern: (bow) Kiera McCloy, (2) Rose Ehrlich, (3) Julie McGlynn, (4) Dana Zielinski, (5) Darian DiCianno, (6) Kathleen O'Connell, (7) Emily Carbone, (stroke) Dana Lerro, (cox) Mary Raggazino. Coaches Megan Kennedy and Mike McKenna.

The crew of Phillips Exeter Academy, from bow to stern: (bow) Cory Johnson, (2) Cassian Corey, (3) Emily Ball, (4) Forrest Barker, (5) Catherine Closmore, (6) Kerrick Edwards, (7) Jennifer DiPietro, (stroke) Mary Reichenbach, (cox) Jessica Michaels. Spare Millicent Dethy. Coach Sally Morris.

POETRY/SONGS/PLAY

A Regatta Rhyme (On Board the 'Athena', Henley-on-Thames)

Joseph Ashby-Sterry

I like, it is true, in a basswood canoe
To lounge, with a weed incandescent;
To paddle about, there is not a doubt
I find it uncommonly pleasant!
I love the fresh air, the lunch here and there,
To see pretty toilettes and faces;
But one thing I hate—allow me to state—
The fuss they make over the Races!
I DON'T CARE A RAP FOR THE RACES!
MID ALL THE REGATTA EMBRACES
I'M THAT SORT OF CHAP, I DON'T CARE A RAP,
A RAP OR A SNAP FOR THE RACES!

I don't care you know, a bit how they row,
Nor mind about smartness of feather;
If steering is bad, I'm not at all sad,
Nor care if they swing altogether!
Oh why do they shout and make such a rout,
When one boat another one chases?
'Tis really too hot to bawl, is it not?
Or bore oneself over the races!
I DON'T CARE A RAP FOR THE RACES!—
MID ALL THE REGATTA EMBRACES

I'M THAT SORT OF CHAP, I DON'T CARE A RAP,
A RAP OR A SNAP FOR THE RACES!

Then the Umpire's boat a nuisance we vote,
It interrupts calm contemplation;
Its discordant tone, and horrid steam moan,
Is death to serene meditation!
The roar of the crowd should not be allowed;
The gun with its fierce fulmination,
Abolish it, pray—'tis fatal, they say,
To pleasant and quiet flirtation.
I DON'T CARE A RAP FOR THE RACES!—
MID ALL THE REGATTA EMBRACES
I'M THAT SORT OF CHAP, I DON'T CARE A RAP,
A RAP OR A SNAP FOR THE RACES!

If athletes must pant—I don't say they shan't?
But give them some decent employment;
And let it be clear, they don't interfere
With other folks' quiet enjoyment!
When luncheon your o'er, 'tis really a bore
And I think it a very hard case is
To have to look up, from pâté or cup,
And gaze on those tiresome Races!
I DON'T CARE A RAP FOR THE RACES!—
MID ALL THE REGATTA EMBRACES
I'M THAT SORT OF CHAP, I DON'T CARE A RAP,
A RAP OR A SNAP FOR THE RACES!

The races, to me, seem to strike a wrong key
'Mid dreamy delightful diversion:
There isn't much fun when men in the sun
All suffer from over-exertion!
In sweet idle days, when all love to laze,
Such violent work a disgrace is!

Let's hope we shall see, they all will agree
To next year abolish the Races!
I DON'T CARE A RAP FOR THE RACES!—
MID ALL THE REGATTA EMBRACES
I'M THAT SORT OF CHAP, I DON'T CARE A RAP,
A RAP OR A SNAP FOR THE RACES!

Eton Boating Song

William Johnson Cory

Jolly boating weather,
And a hay harvest breeze,
Blade on the feather,
Shade off the trees,
Swing swing together,
With your bodies between your knees,
Swing swing together,
With your bodies between your knees.

Skirting past the rushes,
Ruffling o'er the weeds,
Where the lock stream gushes,
Where the cygnet feeds,
Let us see how the wine-glass flushes,
At supper on Boveney meads,
Let us see how the wine glass flushes,
At supper on Boveney meads.

Thanks to the bounteous sitter,
Who sat not at all on his seat,
Down with the beer that's bitter,
Up with the wine that's sweet,
And Oh that some generous "critter",
Would give us more ducks to eat!

Carving with elbow nudges,
Lobsters we throw behind,
Vinegar nobody grudges,
Lower boys drink it blind,
Sober as so many judges,
We'll give you a bit of our mind.

"Dreadnought" "Britannia" "Thetis",
"St George" "Prince of Wales" and "Ten",
And the eight poor souls whose meat is,
Hard steak, and a harder hen,
But the end of our long boat fleet is,
Defiance to Westminster men.

Rugby may be more clever,
Harrow may make more row,
But we'll row for ever,
Steady from stroke to bow,
And nothing in life shall sever,
The chain that is round us now,
And nothing in life shall sever,
The chain that is round us now.

Others will fill our places,
Dressed in the old light blue,
We'll recollect our races,
We'll to the flag be true,
And youth will be still in our faces,
When we cheer for an Eton crew,
And youth will be still in our faces,
When we cheer for an Eton crew.

WILLIAM JOHNSON CORY

Twenty years hence this weather,
May tempt us from office stools,
We may be slow on the feather,
And seem to the boys old fools,
But we'll still swing together,
And swear by the best of schools,
But we'll still swing together,
And swear by the best of schools.

A Racing Eight

James Lister Cuthbertson

Who knows it not, who loves it not,
The long and steady swing,
The instant dip, the iron grip,
The rowlocks' linked ring,
The arrowy sway of hands away,
The slider oiling aft,
The forward sweep, the backward leap
That speed the flying craft?

A racing eight of perfect mould,
True to the builder's law,
That takes the water's gleaming gold
Without a single flaw.
A ship deep, resonant within,
Harmonious to the core,
That vibrates to her polished skin
The tune of wave and oar.

A racing eight and no man late,
And all hearts in the boat;
The men who work and never shirk,
Who long to be afloat.

The crew who burn from stem to stern
To win the foremost place,
The crew to row, the boat to go
The eight to win the race.

The Oarsman's Song

Steve Fairbairn

The willowy sway of the hands away
And the water boiling aft,
The elastic spring and the steely fling
That drives the flying craft.

The steely spring and the musical ring
Of the blade with the biting grip,
And the stretching draw of the bending oar
That rounds the turn with a whip.

And the lazy float that runs the boat,
And makes the swing quite true,
And gives the rest that the oarsman blest
As he drives the blade right through.

All through the swing he hears the boat sing
As she slides on her flying track,
And he gathers aft to strike the craft
With a ringing bell-note crack.

From stretcher to oar with drive and draw,
He speeds the boat along.
All whalebone and steel and a willowy feel—
That is the oarsman's song.

Putting on the Garment of Water and Light

Philip Watson Kuepper

It was as though a moment
of actual magic had taken hold.
The air had taken on a golden glow,
as though light was about to become
a form one could touch.

Henley-on-Thames, early morn,
just after the first wren had sung
dawn into being,
and the still, still world
was yet to waken.

To that perfection he brought
his shell to lay upon the water,
slip into it like a sleek garment,
take up his oars and row
into the brightening light.

He was watched by a presence, spiritual,
by the ghosts of all
the rowers who had rowed before him.
He felt the spectral
breath upon his back.

He felt the spectral
oars pull him forward,
felt the pulse of the spirit
beating in the hallowed
air through which he rowed.

He left behind the fair song of the wren,
swept past the boatsheds
edging the Thames, like embroidery
on a school's scarf,
past the watchful windows

Of the buildings of the town
waking, one by one,
as the light touched them.
by the spirits of all the rowers
gone before him, he was pulled

Forward toward the point
where he turned
to row back to where
he began, to realize,
each morning, his benediction.

Style and the Oar

R. C. Lehmann

To sit upon a seat
With the straps about your feet,
And to grasp an oar and use it, to recover and to slide,
And to keep your body swinging,
And to get the finishing ringing,
And to send the light ship leaping as she whizzes on the tide;

To make the rhythm right
And your feather clean and bright,
And to slash as if you love it, though your muscles seem to crack;
And, although your brain is spinning,
To be sharp with your beginning,
And to heave your solid body indefatigably back;

Not to be a fraction late
When the rate is thirty-eight;
To be quick when stroke demands it, to be steady when he's slow;
And to keep a mind unheeding
When the other lot are leading,
And to set your teeth and brace your back and just to make her go.

And when she gives a roll
To swing out with heart and soul,
And to balance her and rally her and get her trim and true;

And while the ship goes flying
To hear the coxswain crying
"Reach out, my boys, you'll do it!" and, by Jupiter, you do!

To seek bed at ten,
And to tumble out again
When the clocks are striking seven and the winds of March are chill;
To be resolute and steady,
Cheerful, regular, and ready
For a run upon the Common or a tramp up Putney Hill;

To sink yourself and be
Just a unit, and to see
How the individual withers and the crew is more and more;
And to guard without omission
Every glorious tradition
That the ancient heroes founded when they first took up an oar;

In short, to play the game
Not so much for name or fame
As to win a common honour for your colours light or dark—
Oh! It's this has made your crew-man
Such a chivalrous and true man
Since the day that Father Noah went a-floating in the Ark.

The Broken Oar

Henry Wadsworth Longfellow

Once upon Iceland's solitary strand
A poet wandered with his book and pen,
Seeking some final word, some sweet Amen,
Wherewith to close the volume in his hand.
The billows rolled and plunged upon the sand,
The circling sea-gulls swept beyond his ken,
And from the parting cloud-rack now and then
Flashed the red sunset over sea and land.
Then by the billows at his feet was tossed
A broken oar; and carved thereon he read,
"Oft was I weary, when I toiled at thee";
And like a man, who findeth what was lost,
He wrote the words, then lifted up his head,
And flung his useless pen into the sea.

It's a Great Art, Is Rowing

George Pocock

It's a great art, is rowing.
It's the finest art there is.
It's a symphony of motion.
And when you're rowing well,
Why, it's nearing perfection.
And when you reach perfection
You're touching the divine.
It touches the you of you's
Which is your soul.

Steve Fairbairn

R. E. Swartwout

A Palinode

All ye whose style is Orthodox,
Who nobly ply the oar
With a firm, columnar swinging
As your fathers did before,
Who reach right out and drive it through
With solid body-heave,
Sink ancient animosities
And give a cheer for Steve!

We know that curious style of his
Is most completely wrong;
But for all his leg-drive heresy
His boats *do* get along!
It must be subtle wizardry,
So, whatever we believe,
Here's to "the best of coaches"—
Come, give a cheer for Steve!

The Sculler

John Taylor

JOHN TAYLOR WAS A MAN OF THE OAR AND THE PEN AND NAMED HIM-
self the "Water Poet." Taylor was a waterman on the River Thames in
London for most of his life, but he also traveled and then wrote about
his journeys in pamphlets, which he published with the help of subscriptions. His first collection of poetry came in 1612 with the full title *The
sculler rowing from Tiber to Thames with his boate laden with a hotch-potch,
or gallimawfry of sonnets, satyres, and epigrams. With an addition of pastorall
equiuocques or the complaint of a shepheard.* Here is Epigram 29 from the
collection.

Epigram 29

I That haue rowed from Tyber vnto Thames,
Not with a Sculler, but with Scull and Braines:
If none will pay my fare, the more their shames,
I am not first vnpaid that hath tane paines.
Yet Ile be bold if payment be delayd,
To say and sweare your Sculler is not payd.

Rowing for the World Championships

Ed Waugh

HENRY "HARRY" CLASPER (1812–1870), A PROFESSIONAL ROWER AND boatbuilder, was a real Geordie who lived and worked close to the banks of the River Tyne in northern England. Harry—by his fans called "Hadaway Harry"—became a champion sculler on the Tyne, and he also won several races with his brothers in a coxed four-oared boat. On April 1, 1845, Harry's younger brother, Edward, died at the age of twenty-five. As Harry and his brothers were going to race for the World Championships at the Thames Regatta in London on June 26 that year, they needed to find a substitute. Harry picked their uncle, forty-two-year-old Ned Hawks, fondly known as the "Old 'Un," as Edward's replacement. For the race Harry had built a new boat for his crew, the *Lord Ravensworth*. Competing for the championships were also two other crews, one led by the Thames champion Robert Coombes and one by W. Pocock, who led the so-called London crew. In 2015, Ed Waugh's two-act play *Hadaway Harry*, which can be played by one or two actors, premiered at Maritime Trust (Boathouse) in South Shields, England. In 2021, the play was published in *Geordie Plays* with two other plays by Ed Waugh. The following is an excerpt from act 2, when Harry, at stroke, and his brothers Robert (cox), William, and Richard, with Uncle Ned, are sitting ready on the start line on the Thames.

HARRY: Well, this is it, lads—cast your minds back to January, those dark, cold days when this was a distant dream—this is what you've put in the sacrifice for.

And remember, they have the home crowd, so they'll keep coming back at us. (*energetic*) Are we ready? (*beat*) Good—gan to the netty first!

Visual: route map of race Putney to Chiswick Eyot.

PATHE MAN (V/O): The Thames presented a scene of gaiety unprecedented as to excite universal admiration.

Harry puts his towel around him and drinks from a bottle.

PATHE MAN (V/O): Myriads of persons, both on water and on shore, awaited with feverish impatience along all 2.5 miles from the start at Putney Bridge to the finish at Chiswick Oyet.

ANNOUNCER (V/O): Start lining up gentlemen, please.

PATHE MAN (V/O): Would the London watermen retain their well-earned laurels as champions of the world or yield them to the gallant and enterprising men of the Tyne?

GEORDIE MAN (V/O): Hadaway Harry, hadaway lads.

Harry salutes them.

HARRY: The Geordies in London had turned up en masse from the docks to cheer us on. The noise was deafening. We knew exactly why we were here.

Cheering.

Harry waves as he comes stage front, kneels, looks out and around and pours water over his head from bottle.

GEORDIE MAN (V/O): Gan on Harry.

He mops up water with towel, waves, and sits on trunk.

ANNOUNCER (V/O): Line up chaps, that's good.

HARRY: The clear, unpolluted water of Putney contrasted starkly with the brown, smelly sludge of the Tyne. Oh, the beautiful Tyne; she might be dirty but she was ours—and we were going to make her proud.

We'd been drawn in the middle, with Coombes on the advantageous inside. We'd have to cut them off before the all-important Surrey Bend. The leader there generally wins.

My heart's pounding. I'm sure Coombes crew can hear it even above the din. They share a joke . . . is it confidence or bravado?

I look back for re-assurance . . . wor William, wor Robert, and Uncle Ned. I wink to appear relaxed. They smile back sheepishly and grip their oars.

Wor Richard, crouched like a jockey in front, a lesson in concentration . . . will he navigate us successfully this time? I know the experience of last year still haunts him.

He catches my eye, pats my shoulder and smiles. I grab his leg in acknowledgement. The adrenaline surges. I get a boost of much-needed confidence.

Putney Bridge just behind us is crammed with thousands of people, all shouting and waving. I want to say "right lads, remember, we're running our own race—controlled and disciplined" but there's no point, it's too late for a team talk.

We're in our start positions now.

Legs and arms bent, hands clasping the oar.

Back straight. Ready to go.

Crowd noises.

HARRY: We're only eight and a half minutes away from the dream.

ANNOUNCER (V/O): Are you ready?

HARRY: (*shouts*) For Edward!

ANNOUNCER (V/O): Attention—

HARRY: Hey! (*to audience*) The Coombes crew pull out early.

Gun fires.

HARRY: The crowd erupts.

Crowd noises.

HARRY: Richard bellows (*shouts*) draw. The first stroke, that all-important first stroke—no ripping, don't rip it, lads—just take up the pressure and press long. (*shouts*) Go!

Harry rows from here to the end of the race.

HARRY: I squeeze the blades into the water . . . every moment feels like an eternity . . . the boat moves . . . it's smooth . . . it's a good start.

A race can be won or lost in the first minute, that initial sprint—everyone must be in it together.

We kick in at over 50 strokes a minute . . . the pain soon builds, we're all taking short and deep breaths.

Coombe's boat comes closer to our side looking for faster water . . . we need to hold the main line of the stream, the middle's where the water's deepest and the current the fastest.

Richard steers us straight, he's not giving an inch this time.

All three boats are together, matching stroke for stroke. (*shouts*) Rhythm, hold.

After 400 yards, I drop the rate of striking to 45, we enter our race rhythm—and glide further between each stroke. It's a marginally more sustainable pace, preserving vital energy for when it's needed. The steamers moored at Putney Embankment fly by and we soon leave the euphoria of Putney Bridge behind.

Stroke for stroke—all three crews are in tandem.

The crowds cheer, their detail becomes less and less defined as sweat fills my eyes . . . only their noise can be heard above the sound of our oars dipping into the rough water stretch as we pass Fulham on our left-hand side, and head towards Hammersmith.

The summer wind blows against the incoming flow of the tide . . . water from the blades sprays across us but the rhythm, it feels good.

COMMENTATOR (V/O): Half a mile gone and Coombes' crew are beginning to inch ahead.

HARRY: Just opposite the Craven Cottage, Coombes take the lead—only half a length up but if they break clear now they'll be hard to catch, especially if they get the inside on Surrey Bend—but that's a mile away and we're oar to oar with Newell.

They come too close. . . . (*shouts*) How, man, bugger off.

Richard steers us . . . again, he's still not giving an inch.

I call on the lads. (*shouts*) Up strokes.

Hu, hu, hu.

We lift ourselves from the already painful rhythm to a faster one . . . it works. We're soon a seat up on Newell and quickly move away to three-quarters of a length—Coombes is nearby, just ahead, I can hear their cox urging them on.

I call on ten big strokes.

In two, in one (*shouts*) ten full!

Hu, hu, hu.

The surge of power is unbelievable as all four of us commit our full strength.

We take off . . . I can sense Ned's frame shaking with the full force he's sending down . . . we begin to leave Newell behind . . . another 200 yards . . . we ease off slightly.

We're tailing Coombes by half a length. It's good though . . . they know we're there . . . they can hear us . . . let *them* feel the heat.

The Crabtree pub is coming up on our left.

We're just past half way. Richard shouts.

RICHARD (V/O): (*shouts*) Big push at Crabtree.

COMMENTATOR (V/O): And the men of the Thames are edging the Tynemen.

HARRY: In two, in one (*shouts*) twenty full!

Hu, hu, hu.

This time 20 big ones are unleashed and we're pressing Coombes.

I catch him out of the corner of my eye. He's digging in now. He looks up and we glance, momentarily . . . at that moment he's my enemy and I detest him.

COMMENTATOR (V/O): And the Tyne team are level with Coombes.

HARRY: Two hundred yards later, I call on the lads again.

In two, in one, (*shouts*) twenty more!

Hu, hu, hu.

Another power surge and we're edging ahead.

All the time I'm wondering how much Coombes' crew have in them. They'll have been training in the cold winter months for this an' all.

Never underestimate your opponent.

We could have overtaken them there but with just under a mile to go it was too early to make for home—I wanted us to have enough in the tank for that final burst.

COMMENTATOR (V/O): In response the Coombes crew up their stroke.

HARRY: Bugger!

COMMENTATOR (V/O): Both boats fly under Hammersmith Suspension Bridge—12,000 people on the edifice are cheering and stomping as the rowers pass below.

HARRY: Surrey Bend's up ahead . . . that all-important Surrey Bend (*shouts*) ten.

Ten big strokes through the bridge—then out into the wide expanse of the Thames.

There's dozens of boats on either side, crammed with spectators. A deafening roar goes up as the crowd get their first view of us emerging from under the bridge.

I call another (*shouts*) ten.

And we're pulling away from Coombes . . . only inches per stroke but it's enough.

We pull half a length ahead.

It soon becomes a length and they're in full view behind us.

I see their oars splashing into the water . . . their cox shouting for more effort.

Newell's crew fall even further back further—it's between us and Coombes now.

Two hundred yards to the long, meandering Surrey Bend and the two-mile marker . . . we're still a length up.

Six minutes in, most races are decided by now.

What *have* they got left?

Never ever underestimate your opponent.

Richard sees the Surrey Bend and shouts.

RICHARD (V/O): (*shouts*) Defend the bend, defend the bend.

HARRY: It's worth a length at least if we make them work harder on the outside.

I call again (*shouts*) twenty.

Richard is animated, screaming out instructions.

RICHARD (V/O): Pull . . . legs, legs, sit up, sit up, pull, pull.

HARRY: My *beautiful* lads respond with twenty of the biggest strokes of our life . . . the feeling is indescribable, I get tingles down my spine.

But it only serves to encourage Coombes' crew who start to creep up on the inside.

Richard turns the rudder to cut into them – forcing them off their line. I look at him, he winks . . . the naughty bastard!

Richard imparts more instructions.

RICHARD (V/O): (*shouts*) Spring off, spring off.

HARRY: I call for another ten. The lads respond again . . . we're that all-important length ahead.

Richard steers us to the inside of the bend.

He wants more from us.

RICHARD (V/O): (*shouts*) Move it.

HARRY: I call again (*shouts*) ten.

The lads respond again.

The boat feels like it sprouted wings . . . we cut inside . . . it's magnificent, truly magnificent.

We've got the Surrey side . . . we've got the inside! Oh, you beauty, Richard!

We force Coombes to come on the outside, they lose valuable ground and energy.

We all lean even more weight on the oar and push our legs harder.

We're keeping tight on the bend . . . they're pushing on again, straining to keep up with us.

We concede no ground but every time I force my legs down harder, the pain increases, my arms ache more.

Still holding the bend . . . on our right is St Paul's School . . . we're two lengths up now . . . hold them here and we've won. . . . Robert, pumping away behind, knows it. He lets out an encouraging scream and we all send down even harder strokes.

We come out of the bend—it's rough water but straight again.

Two lengths ahead. . . . Richard nods, he can see the green island of Chiswick Eyot ahead in the distance.

But never, ever underestimate your opponent.

It's 600 yards away . . . only 600 yards to the finishing line.

This is our chance to move further ahead . . . we've planned to break them here.

I look at Richard and nod. He screams.

RICHARD (V/O): (*shouts*) Edward!

HARRY: It's the final signal.

Four voices echo him (*shouts*) Edward!

Twenty huge power strokes. I'm counting down inside, nineteen, eighteen, seventeen. . . . I know the others will be too.

Four pistons work harder to increase the speed.

Boat and crew as one.

Perfect harmony.

Surging between strokes.

This is what it's all aboot!

COMMENTATOR (V/O): And the Tyne crew have increased their lead to two and a half lengths.

HARRY: Whatever Coombe's crew have left, they've got to throw it at us now—their final push, it has to be! We've got them on the ropes. You hope they've got nothing . . . surely they'll crumble now—they can't keep up with us.

But they push again, moving slowly but steadily back on us . . . we're now only two lengths ahead. (*shouts*) Ten.

More power strokes, we push them back again . . . but they just keep coming.

I hear ear-splitting screams—cheers and boos rise from the bank to almost deafen us.

They're gaining on us . . . they must be gaining on us.

We dig our oars in against the pull of the current and every muscle strains with the load.

We take long strokes . . . we're still together . . . our oars cut into the Thames, gripping the water more effectively.

I've seen these lads in training, giving their all, I envisage Robert gritting his teeth and William, mouth agape, searching for breath, pumping his arms—but this is the real thing . . . how much have we left?

To my left, I see Coombes coming back into contention.

Our pace isn't slacking, though—the lads are pulling their hearts out, stroke after stroke after stroke.

Four brothers and Ned willing to sacrifice everything for this race. I'd never been so proud of these boys.

The rowing's smooth, powerful and flowing . . . hypnotic.

Four of us as one.

Sweat drips and stings, blurring vision.

But now, Coombes' bow comes level with our stern. We're only a length ahead.

I move the stroke rate up again—I worry whether the lads'll respond this time. (*shouts*) Ten.

I hear three "howay lads" in different groans—Ned sounds the weakest ... the lads are coming with me, though ... (*excited*) they're coming with me ... and the old boy's still hanging in there—please don't falter, Ned.

My heart lifts with every stroke, we inch further ahead. Our big moves have worked ... it's beautiful ... we can do this ... we can do this.

I want to shout out "listen lads, can you hear it? It's singing ... *the boat's singing!*"

But I'm too exhausted.

Richard gets animated and points.

RICHARD (V/O): (*screams*) Cheswick Eyot, Harry, Cheswick Eyot.

HARRY: 250 yards to go. I summon up the final ounces of my energy. (*shouts*) Go!

The final sprint, we're back up to 50 strokes.

Two hundred yards. My lungs feel as if they're filled with acid. I taste blood—I'm on the verge of passing out. I'm searching for breath ... pumping my arms ... it only needs one of us to crack and it's game over.

But we're all as one—no-one daring to let the side down. Pain surges through my body. I'm searching for oxygen with short rapid breaths. My heart's thumping in my chest.

RICHARD (V/O): 30 seconds. Pull, pull.

HARRY: I hear Richard demanding more from the lads.

Our oars tear the water into lumps of foam.

The pain's blinding.

My heart's pounding, at over 200 beats a minute this is heart attack territory—but you can't take it easy or catch your breath.

A boxer could go down at this stage but there's nowhere to hide in a boat.

Stay together lads.

RICHARD (V/O): 29 ... 28.

HARRY: His voice seemed to float away—we're two lengths up and in our heads we're all counting down ... 27 ... 26.

Belief runs through the crew ... each and every one of them fighting their own inner battle for the greater good.

25 ... 24 ...

Then I hear their cox ... "more power". He's getting louder and louder, screaming (*loud*) "more power, more power".

They're gaining.

The rhythmic sound of their oars ... they try to finish us.

There's silence but we communicate without words ... all putting in similar huge effort, not wanting to let the side down.

23 ... 22 ... 21 ...

They haven't taken any advantage.

Fewer calls come from inside their boat ... they're now deep in pain territory.

RICHARD (V/O): (*shouts*) Stay together.

HARRY: Richard's voice calms us.

The rhythmic thump of their finishes gets less pronounced.

They're tiring, they have to be.

RICHARD (V/O): (*shouts*) 50 yards ... take it home, lads—up two.

HARRY: Up two! I can't!

I'm already sending down everything I have. Above the din I can hear Ned gasping in loud croaks, there's nothing left in his tank ... only the burning desire not to let us down is driving him past breaking point.

Keep going, Ned, please keep going.

Dig deep, lads, dig deep ... but I'm now too far gone—my legs scream "no more", my lungs beg for mercy and my head feels as if it's about to explode.

The mind, it's now all in the mind—will it be strong enough to keep pushing on or will it break?

How much do you want this Harry? How much, do you want it?

18 . . . 17 . . . 16 . . .

The crowd noise stops.

HARRY: I no longer hear the screaming crowd, darkness is descending.

My body screams (*loud*) STOP!

His rowing is out, distorted.

HARRY: (*He's disorientated, emotional*) Uh, uh . . . then suddenly the rowing's no longer in sync. (*panicing*) The boat feels loose. Why have we stopped racing?

I look back. Ned's head's dropped, his hands by his side, he's slumped forward . . . motionless.

I try to shout "Ned" . . . but nothing comes out.

I see wor Robert flopped over his oar, desperately gasping for air.

William lies back on Robert's lap, his chest bellowing as he groans and sucks in oxygen.

What's happened?

I try to swallow. I can't. All my senses have stop working.

Why did we throw the race away so close to home?

And then Richard leans forward and kisses iz on the forehead.

RICHARD (V/O): We won, Harry, we won! We're the champions of the world!

HARRY: (*beat*) I see he's bawling his eyes out. He's always been a soft shite.

Tears well up in my eyes and I cry . . . like a little bairn . . . tears of joy flood down my cheeks . . . I cry uncontrollably. I muster all my strength to look behind again. Through the veil of tears, I see wor Ned—eyes rolled back into his head, chest heaving, groaning, frantically trying to suck oxygen into his gasping mouth.

Robert, arm on the gunwale, is gasping for air. He's ashen . . . as white as a ghost. He looks up and stares at iz, eyes vacant from fatigue, he tries to smile, but his bottom lip just trembles.

I try to communicate but nothing happens. Wor William . . . now bent forward, being sick. Between retches he groans—but he's alive.

Knowing the lads are safe, I slump forward for what felt like an eternity, but it must have only been a few seconds. I try to remember the last fifty yards but they're a complete blank.

As my senses return, I see people . . . the sheer number is overwhelming . . . the banks have erupted . . . hats are being waved and thrown in the air. Those who aren't clapping and cheering are pointing.

(*to lads*) Hey lads . . . lads . . . look, they're pointing at us.

Visual of rowing crowd cheering.

Contributors

Aquil Hashim Abdullah, born in Washington, DC. Rowing advocate. Aquil began rowing in his senior year at Woodrow Wilson High School in Washington, DC, and was recruited to row at George Washington University, where he majored in physics. After finishing his studies in 1996, he trained at Potomac Boat Club and became the first African American male to win the US National Championships in the single sculls. In 1999, Aquil rowed in the Diamond Challenge Sculls at Henley Royal Regatta, but in his second heat he broke his foot stretcher and lost the race. Later that year, Aquil took a silver medal in the single at the Pan American Games. The following year, he lost the Olympic Trials by 0.33 second and missed out on a spot on the 2000 US Olympic Team. Aquil returned to Henley in 2000 and won the Diamonds, the first African American to claim the title. In 2001, he published *Perfect Balance* (with Chris Ingraham). Between 2000 and 2004, he competed for the United States at the international level in the quad, single sculls, and double sculls. He (and Henry Nuzum) placed sixth in the A final in the double sculls at the 2004 Olympics. Aquil was the first African American male to represent the United States in the sport of rowing at the Olympic Games; he thereby followed in the footsteps of Olympians Anita DeFrantz and Patricia Spratlen-Etem. After retiring from elite rowing, Aquil became involved in increasing diversity in rowing and now works with Arshay Cooper and the A Most Beautiful Thing Inclusion Fund, the National Rowing Foundation (NRF), and the Black Coaches and Rowers Association. In December 2021, Aquil was elected as a Steward to Henley Royal Regatta.

Andy Anderson (a.k.a. Dr. Rowing), born in Syracuse, New York. Rowing coach, columnist and teacher. Andy saw his first rowing race at age four and has been entranced with the sport ever since. Discovering to his dismay that most oarsmen weigh more than one hundred pounds, he turned to coxing in high school despite considering himself a "big guy." At Trinity College, Hartford, Andy continued to cox despite growing to be the tallest coxswain in the country and towering over three of the four strokes he shared the stern with. He has coached gold medal boats at school, college, national, and world championships. In 1997, Andy was inducted into the National Rowing Foundation's Rowing Hall of Fame. He has been a teacher and coach at Groton School in Massachusetts since 1980, and he has been a columnist for various rowing magazines since 1994. Andy published his book *The Complete Dr. Rowing* in 2001.

Joseph Ashby-Sterry (1835–1917), born in London, England. Poet, novelist, and journalist. Ashby-Sterry started out his career as a painter and did oil paintings and drawings for *Punch* and other magazines. However, journalism and writing soon took over, and it is said that he was one of the most read journalists of his time. Ashby-Sterry's collection of poetry, *Boudoir Ballads*, was published in 1876. His contributions appeared in *Punch*, and he also wrote the "Bystander" column in *The Graphic* for eighteen years. He was art critic for the *Daily Graphic* between 1891 and 1907.

Toby Ayer, born in Burlington, Vermont. Teacher in physics and rowing coach at Salisbury School, Connecticut. Toby rowed for four years at MIT while studying physics and linguistics, and his crews won a "Division 2" national championship and the Club Eight at the Head of the Charles. As a Rhodes Scholar, he continued studying linguistics at Oxford and rowed for the University, twice in the Isis boat, in 1997 and 1998, and twice in the Blue Boat, in 1999 and 2000, beating Cambridge in 1998 and 2000. After a year as Harry Parker's assistant coach at Harvard, Toby began teaching freshman physics at MIT while continuing to train out of Newell Boathouse. During this time, he taught linguistics at both Harvard and Northeastern and coached the boys' team at Brookline High School. He also won the Head of the Charles Club Fours in 2004 and the 30+ division at the CRASH-Bs in 2005. He spent the summers of 2006 and 2007 at Penn AC, winning gold at Canadian Henley and silver at the Elite Nationals. Toby has coached at the Craftsbury Sculling Center and continues to compete both on the water and on the erg. His book *The Sphinx of the Charles: A Year at Harvard with Harry Parker* was published in 2016.

Ralph Henry Barbour (1870–1944), born in Cambridge, Massachusetts. Novelist and short story writer. Barbour was a prolific author of boys' sports fiction, but he also wrote romance and adventure books. Many of his sports book for boys dealt with baseball, (American) football, and other sports, including rowing. He produced more than one hundred novels and a great number of short stories, which were published in *The American Boy*, *Sport Story Magazine*, and *Boys' Life*. Barbour also wrote under the pseudonym Richard Stillman Powell (together with L. H. Bickford).

Frans G. Bengtsson (1894–1954), born in Tossjö, Scania, Sweden. Poet, translator, essayist, biographer, and novelist. Bengtsson began his studies at Lund University in 1912 and read far beyond the literature list than his courses required. Not seeing an urgent need to finish his studies, he spent his time writing poems and playing chess. A kidney disease from childhood forced him home in 1915, but it did not stop him from studying. Back in Lund in 1919, Bengtsson graduated with a degree in English in 1920 and in philosophy and history of religion in 1921. He earned a licentiate degree in English literature in 1931. Bengtsson started his literary career as a sonneteer, becoming a master of the genre. He translated Henry David Thoreau's *Walden; or, Life in the Woods*, John Milton's *Paradise Lost*, and the French poem *La Chanson de Roland*. Bengtsson also translated several of Eric Linklater's novels, including *The Men of Ness* (1932), which would inspire him to write his own Viking novel in the 1940s. In addition to publishing books with essays reflecting on his interest in men of letters and military men, he published a two-volume biography on the Swedish King Charles XII, in 1935 and 1936. Bengtsson's most famous work, the novel *Röde Orm*, was published in two volumes in 1941 and 1945. The novel about Orm, who was called *röd* ("red") due to the color of his hair and beard, became extremely successful and was translated into numerous languages. In 1954, the novel was published in a wonderful English translation by Michael Meyer, *The Long Ships*.

Mark Blandford-Baker, born in London, England. Bursar of St Edmund Hall, Oxford. Mark worked as Home Bursar of Magdalen College, Oxford, between 2001 and 2021 and is now an emeritus fellow. His introduction to rowing was delayed when his school's boathouse burnt down. He took up rowing at Cambridge '99 Rowing Club when he arrived to work in Cambridge in 1983; Mark occasionally rowed for St Catharine's College and later Jesus College, where he worked, respectively. While playing rugby and having little time for rowing training, Mark took his British Rowing's umpire license in 1991 and passed his FISA umpire exam in 2001. He enjoys umpiring whether it's a two-lane river course or a World Championships (most recently at the Championships in Račice in 2022). Mark has also lent his umpiring skills at two Olympic Games, in 2012 and 2016. He is a member of Leander Club and has served on the club's committee and on the Board of British Rowing. Mark is the treasurer for the National Schools' Regatta, and a Chairman's Assistant at Henley Royal Regatta. He has an extended collection of about five hundred rowing books and has occasionally contributed articles to British Rowing's *Rowing and Regatta*, *Row360*, and Hear The Boat Sing (HTBS). In 2009, Mark published *Upon The Elysian Stream: 150 Years of Magdalen College Boat Club, Oxford.*

Daniel J. Boyne, born in Stevens Point, Wisconsin. Teacher, writer, yoga instructor, and rowing coach. After graduating in 1982 from Trinity College in Hartford, Connecticut, where he rowed, Daniel has been primarily connected to Harvard University since 1986. He received an MEd in adult literacy from Harvard in 1998. He subsequently worked with undergraduates at the college as a teaching fellow and later received a Certificate of Distinction in Teaching from the Derek Bok Center for Teaching and Learning. Daniel has written several essays for magazines, including *The Atlantic, Harvard Magazine,* and *Grays Sporting Journal.* Published works include *Essential Sculling* (2000); *The Red Rose Crew: A True Story of Women, Winning, and the Water* (2000; 2nd ed. 2005), which won a Miller Lite Sports Journalism Award; *Kelly: A Father, a Son, an American Quest* (2007; 2nd ed. 2012), a book that won first prize in the Premier Book Awards in the category of biography in 2008; the autobiography

The Seven Seat: A True Story of Rowing, Revenge, and Redemption (2019); and the novel *Body of Water* (2023), a rowing detective story, which takes place on the Charles River in Boston, Massachusetts.

Göran R. Buckhorn, born in Malmö, Scania, Sweden. Writer, editor, and a fidgeting rowing historian. Göran had a mediocre career as a rower at Malmö Roddklubb (MRK) in his teens but had better luck as a novice and women's coach; president of MRK between 1990 and 1993, he is a lifetime member of the club. Göran cofounded a rowing club in 1992 at his alma mater, Lund University, where he had studied literature and culture science; he also did postgraduate study at the University of Wales, Lampeter. He worked as an editor at a Swedish publishing company for fourteen years. He cofounded the Swedish rowing magazine *Svensk Rodd* in 1990 and coedited it for ten years. After moving to the United States in 2000, Göran was a contributing editor to the magazine until it ceased to exist in 2014. In the United States, he has worked in a few different positions at Mystic Seaport Museum, including being the editor of the museum's magazine for nine years. Göran has written numerous articles on rowing for books and magazines. For a short stint, he wrote a rowing history column for British Rowing's publication *Rowing & Regatta*. In 2009, he founded the rowing history website Hear The Boat Sing (HTBS), for which he is still the editor. Göran is one of the directors of Friends of Rowing History. He has edited several books and written two books on rowing: an essay collection in Swedish, *En gång roddare . . .* (2000, "Once a Rower . . .") and *A Yank at Cambridge—B.H. Howell: The Forgotten Champion* (2015).

Rebecca Caroe, born in London, England. Strategic marketing specialist, podcast host, and advocate for Masters rowing. Rebecca was spectacularly unsporty at school, but when she studied at Pembroke College, Cambridge, she began rowing after she had attended a university recruitment cocktail party. A coxswain approached her and said, "You're tall—you should row." So she did. Rebecca's rowing accomplishments include rowing in the winning Blondie Cambridge crew in the 1986 Women's Boat Race. She has won several Head of the River races and has taken medals at the National Championships and Henley Women's Regatta. She competed but never won at Henley Royal Regatta. For eighteen years she was the head of Rowperfect UK. Rebecca moved to New Zealand in 2009. She now hosts the *RowingChat* podcast and runs Faster Masters Rowing, where she advocates for Masters rowing around the world. Since 2017, Rebecca has been the publisher for the annual rowing anthology *Rowing Tales*.

William Johnson Cory (1823–1892), born **William Johnson** in Great Torrington, Devon, England. Educator and poet. He studied at Eton and then went on to King's College, Cambridge, where he won the Chancellor's Medal for an English poem on Plato in 1843 and, the year after, the Craven Scholarships. After graduating from King's College in 1845, Cory became an assistant master at Eton, where his pupils gave him the nickname "Tute" (for tutor). He wrote poetry in both Latin and English. Cory's "Eton Boating Song" was performed the first time in 1863. He was forced to resign from Eton in 1872 after an "indiscreet letter" that he had written to a pupil was reported to the headmaster. He changed his name the same year to Cory and emigrated to Madeira for health reasons in 1878. There, he married and had a son. Cory returned to England in 1882 and published his maybe most-known work, *Ionica*, in 1891.

Francis "Frank" Cunningham (1922–2013), born in Lowell, Massachusetts. Educator, rowing coach, and writer. Cunningham started to row at Noble and Greenough School in Massachusetts in 1937 and continued to row at Harvard in the 1940s, though his rowing career was interrupted by World War II, when he served in the Marine Corps. After graduating, Cunningham tried out a couple of different jobs before he got a teaching degree at the University of Washington and started a thirty-year long career as an educator. He founded the junior rowing program in the Seattle Park system in the late 1940s and coached there until 1968, when he began coaching at Lakeside School, where he taught English. Throughout his career as a coach, he repaired racing shells, usually wooden ones, and most of those built by Pocock. In 1980, Cunningham started to row and coach at Lake Washington Rowing Club. He came to coach many of the United States' most prominent scullers, including some Olympians. Cunningham was inducted into the Rowing Hall of Fame in 1975 as stroke of the 1947 Harvard eight. He received the USRowing's Medal of Honor in 2010. His *The Sculler at Ease* was published in 1992 and a collection of his articles, *Ask Frank*, came out in 2006.

James Lister "Cuthy" Cuthbertson (1851–1910), born in Glasgow, Scotland. Poet and schoolteacher. Cuthbertson was educated at Trinity College, Glenalmond, Perthshire, where he played cricket, and then went on to Merton College, Oxford, where he rowed. In 1875, he joined the staff at Geelong Grammar School in Victoria, Australia, as a classical master and was also assigned to be in charge of the school's rowing. Cuthbertson founded the school's publication *School Quarterly*, for which he wrote poems, including rowing poems; one of the pupils helping him with the school magazine was Steve Fairbairn. In 1879, the school published his *Grammar School Verses*. He returned to England in 1882 to finish his studies at Merton College and graduated in 1885. Cuthbertson then went back to Australia to rejoin the staff of Geelong Grammar. In 1893, his *Barwon Ballads* was published in Melbourne. In 1912, two years after his death, a memorial edition of his poetry, *Barwon Ballads and School Verses*, was published by his old pupils at Geelong Grammar School.

Greg Denieffe, born in Carlow, Ireland. Accountant, rowing historian, and collector of rowing memorabilia. Greg received his formal education by the Christian Brothers in Carlow, which ended when he turned seventeen. At twelve, he joined the local rowing club and raced cadet (U-15), learning to lose gracefully before turning his hands to coxing the adult crews. He then played hurling for a couple of years before slipping back into a boat. Greg has lived and worked in England since 1986 and claims to have missed only two Henley Royal Regattas since then, once because his back gave up on him minutes before leaving for finals day and another due to the imminent arrival of one of his daughters in 2009. A member of the HRR Stewards Enclosure, he has rowed for and been the treasurer of both Carlow Rowing Club and Milton Keynes Rowing Club. His first foray into writing was as Carlow's press officer, penning a weekly column for the local newspaper. In 1984, he edited a brief history of Carlow Rowing Club, published to celebrate the club's 125th anniversary. He regularly contributes articles to the rowing history website, Hear The Boat Sing (HTBS). Greg has a keen interest in history, regularly watches hurling and rugby matches, and has been known to expound at great length on the virtues of Bob Dylan.

Christopher "Chris" Dodd, born in Bristol, England. Rowing journalist, writer, and historian. Chris has written about rowing for more than forty years. His inglorious competitive rowing career ended in his freshman year at Nottingham University in favor of editing the student newspaper. After thirty years as a *Guardian* journalist, he turned freelance in 1994 when his crazy scheme to set up the River & Rowing Museum in Henley-on-Thames attracted a sponsor. The museum opened in 1998 and has won awards for its content, education programs, and architecture. Chris is a board member of the Friends of Rowing History (FoRH) and has lectured at FoRH's Rowing History Forums in England and the United States and at World Rowing conferences. He was a member of FISA's media commission from 1990 to 2002 and was press chief at the World Championships in Nottingham (1986) and Indianapolis (1994). He edited the rowing content of *Olympic News Service* in Atlanta (1996) and was in charge of the media center at the 2002 Commonwealth and World Student Games regattas in Nottingham. Chris was the founding editor of Britain's *Regatta* magazine, FISA's *World Rowing* magazine and cofounder of *Rowing Voice*. After leaving the *Guardian*, he continued as rowing correspondent until moving to the *Independent* in 2004, where he stayed until the said title, to its shame, lost interest in rowing. His books on rowing include: *Henley Royal Regatta* (1981), *The Oxford & Cambridge Boat Race* (1983), *Boating* (1983), *The Story of World Rowing* (1992), *Battle of the Blues: The Oxford and Cambridge Boat Race from 1829* (ed. with John Marks; 2004), *Water Boiling Aft: London Rowing Club, the First 150 Years 1856–2006* (2006), *Pieces of Eight: Bob Janousek and His Olympians* (2012), *Bonnie Brave Boat Rowers* (2014), *Unto the Tideway Born: 500 Years of Thames Watermen and Lightermen* (2015), *More Power—The Story of Jurgen*

Grobler: The Most Successful Olympic Coach of All Time (with Hugh Matheson, 2018), and *Thor Nilsen: Rowing's Global Coach* (2020).

Stephen "Steve" Fairbairn (1862–1938), born in Toorak, Melbourne, Australia. Oarsman, rowing coach, and writer. Fairbairn got his first taste of rowing at Geelong Grammar School, where he also played cricket and Australian football. Like his four older brothers, he was sent to Jesus College, Cambridge, where he read law (later, his younger brother was also sent to Jesus). All the Fairbairn brothers (and six of their cousins) rowed at Jesus. Fairbairn rowed in the Cambridge Blue Boats in 1882, 1883, 1886, and 1887, winning the latter two races. He also won cups at Henley Royal Regatta: Wyfold Challenge Cup in 1882, Grand Challenge Cup in 1885, and Stewards' Challenge Cup in 1886. In 1897, Fairbairn raced in the Diamond Challenge Sculls but was kicked out in the first round. The following year, he and his friend Arthur M. Hutchinson, "Old Hutch," lost in the final of the Silver Goblets & Nickalls' Challenge Cup. Fairbairn coached at Jesus, some Cambridge Blue crews, Thames Rowing Club, and London Rowing Club. He coached the crews to use an effected blade work and leg-drive and not to focus on how to move their bodies according to the Orthodox style. Fairbairn insisted that he taught his rowers a new method, which came to be called "Fairbairnism", and not a new style. He initiated the Head of the River Race for eights on the Thames in London in December 1926 and organized a head race on the Cam in 1929 for the Fairbairn Cup. Fairbairn wrote several works on rowing: *Jesus College Boat Club Rowing Notes* (pamphlet 1904; also known as *Notes on Rowing*), *Rowing Notes* (pamphlet 1920, 8 pp; 1926, 12 pp; 1929, 12 pp; more editions were published but were undated), *Rowing Notes* (ed. Arthur Eggar, 1926; 2nd ed. 1928; 3rd ed. 1930), *Fairbairn's Rowing Annual, Season 1927–28* (1927), *Slowly Forward* (ed. Frederick Brittain, 1929), *Oar, Scull and Rudder* (1930, written by Frederick Brittain, introduction by Fairbairn), *Some Secrets of Successful Rowing* (1930; 2nd ed. 1931), *Fairbairn of Jesus* ([ed. Frederick Brittain] autobiography 1931), *Chats on Rowing* (ed. Buddy Gross, 1934; 2nd ed. 1948; 3rd ed. 1949), *Rowing in a Nutshell* (ed. Tom B. Langton, 1936), *On Rowing* (ed. Ian Fairbairn; includes Steve Fairbairn's works above except *Fairbairn's Rowing Annual* and *Fairbairn* *of Jesus*; two texts, "Don't Exaggerate" (1936) and "The Endless Chain Movement" (1937), were published for the first time; 2nd ed. 1990; 3rd ed. [ebook] 2014, ed. Peter Mallory).

Mark Helprin, born in New York City, New York. Novelist, short story writer, essayist, and columnist. He was raised on the Hudson and in the British West Indies. He holds degrees from Harvard University (BA 1969) and Harvard's Graduate School of Arts and Sciences (MA 1972) and did postgraduate study at Princeton, Columbia, and Magdalen College, Oxford. He has served in the British Merchant Navy, the Israeli infantry, and the Israeli Air Force. He is the author of novels, including *Winter's Tale*, *A Soldier of the Great War*, and *Paris in the Present Tense* (2017), as well as three collections of short stories, including *The Pacific & Other Stories* (2004), and three children's books. A former contributing editor of the *Wall Street Journal* and adviser in defense and foreign relations to presidential nominee Robert Dole, he has published in the *New Yorker*, the *Atlantic Monthly*, the *Wall Street Journal*, the *New York Times*, the *National Review*, and many other newspapers and magazines. A senior fellow of the Claremont Institute for the Study of Statesmanship and Political Philosophy, fellow of the American Academy in Rome, and former Guggenheim fellow, he has received various prizes, including the National Jewish Book Award, the Prix de Rome, the Peggy V. Helmerich Distinguished Author Award, and the Henry Salvatori Prize.

Ron Irwin, born in Buffalo, New York. Teacher and writer. Ron learned how to row at the West Side Rowing Club in Buffalo and continued to row at Kent School in Connecticut. After Kent, he went on to row in a number of winning crews at the collegiate level. Ron holds an MA in literary studies, an MA in creative writing, and a PhD in media studies and is currently a senior lecturer in the Center for Film and Media at the University of Cape Town in South Africa. Ron's first novel, *Flat Water Tuesday*, which was published in 2013, is loosely based upon his experiences as an oarsman at Kent School. This novel has been optioned to film. Ron's *My Side of the Ocean: A Novel* was published in 2023.

Jerome Klapka Jerome (1859–1927), born in Walsall, England. Writer, novelist, essayist, playwright, and humorist. He attended grammar school, but when he was twelve, his father died and his mother the year after. He tried different occupations, including acting. This gave him material for his book *On the Stage—and Off* (1885), which was followed by a collection of humorous essays, *Idle Thoughts of an Idle Fellow* (1886). Jerome married in 1888, and the honeymoon was spent on a boat on the Thames. F. W. Robinson, editor for the magazine *Home Chimes*, asked Jerome to write "the story of the Thames" for his publication. The story was to give the readers of the magazine sceneries and the history of the river, dotted with humorous passages, but the latter took over. Robinson cut out most of the historical, serious parts and kept the funny parts, and Jerome gave it a new title, *Three Men in a Boat (To Say Nothing of the Dog)*. The episodes were published in *Home Chimes* from August 1888 to June 1889. In September 1889, the publisher J. W. Arrowsmith preserved it between covers, and it became an instantaneous bestseller and a classic. Other works by Jerome include the essay collection *Second Thoughts of an Idle Fellow* (1898), the novel *Three Men on the Bummel* (1900; also known as *Three Men on Wheels*), and several other novels. Since the second edition of *Three Men in a Boat*, in 1909, the novel has never been out of print.

Robert Treharne Jones, born in Surrey, England. MD, medical technology consultant, and rowing commentator, known as "The Voice of Rowing." Robert started rowing at medical school and has since been a competitive member of fourteen different clubs, including the captaincy of two and the chairmanship of a third. He is now president of Castle Dore Rowing Club in Cornwall. Robert has been commentating on the sport for more than forty years and has provided course-side commentary for countless World Championships; the Olympic and Paralympic Games in Beijing, London, Rio, and Tokyo; as well as the Boat Race on BBC Radio 5. As head of Commentary at the National Schools Regatta, and previously at Regatta Radio in Henley, he has trained aspiring commentators, and many graduates of this program have gone on to commentate at the national and international levels. In addition to his commentary skills, he is also an experienced rowing journalist, historian, and photographer.

Robert was press officer for Henley Royal Regatta for fifteen years and also at Leander, where he was one of the contributing authors and photographers for *Leander Club, the First 200 Years* (2018).

Stephen Kiesling, born in Austin, Texas, and grew up in Los Altos, California, where he raced bicycles and played football. He followed his sister Jennie onto the crew at Yale (class of 1980). As a sophomore, he was named to the All-Ivy League First Team. As a junior, Stephen was in the Yale crew who were the runner-up in the 1979 Grand Challenge Cup at Henley and in the coxless four who placed eighth at the 1979 World Championships. As a senior, he was selected for the 1980 US Olympic Team, which boycotted the Olympic Games in Moscow. His senior thesis, "The Shell Game: Reflections on Rowing and the Pursuit of Excellence," was first published by William Morrow in 1982. Stephen moved to New York City, where he launched two magazines, *American Health* and *Spirituality & Health* (where he continues to write). He also wrote *The Complete Recreational Rower & Racer* (1991) and *Walking the Plank: A Year aboard the Pirate Ship Whydah* (1994). Stephen has also written on rowing for the *New Yorker*, *Sports Illustrated*, and *Outside*. He continues to row and competed in the 1984 and 2008 USA Olympic Trials, as well as rowing in a Gillette commercial in the 1990 Super Bowl and in Netflix's documentary *The Andy Warhol Diaries* (2022). In 1998, Stephen launched the Ashland Rowing Club (now Rogue Rowing), which won the USRowing Club of the Year in 2017. He lives in a boathouse filled with whitewater kayaks and singles at Ti'lomikh Falls on the Rogue River in southern Oregon. He competes each year with team Etats Unis at the Head of the Charles.

Tim Koch, born in Cornwall, South West England. Rowing coach, historian, writer, and photographer. Tim started rowing at Auriol Kensington Rowing Club in Hammersmith, West London, in 1985. Having rapidly developed an interest in the sport of rowing's history and heritage, he soon took on the self-invented and self-appointed role of "historian and archivist" of his club. Several seasons of enthusiastic but not particularly triumphant rowing were followed by slightly more successful periods as a cox, club secretary, regatta secretary, and club captain. In late 2009, Tim sent a "one off" contribution to the rowing history website Hear The Boat Sing (HTBS). This has turned into at least one article a week for the past fourteen years. His association with HTBS has given him privileged access to the great and the good of the sport, and every year he writes about the sport's most iconic events in England: The Oxford–Cambridge Boat Races, Henley Royal Regatta, Doggett's Coat and Badge Race, and the Wingfield Sculls. Tim published a booklet, a biography of Kensington RC's most famous oarsman, the 1912 Olympic champion, "Wally" Kinnear, *W. D. Kinnear: World Amateur Sculling Champion*, in 2012. He has researched the legendary "Dead Heat" 1877 Boat Race and its finishing judge, "Honest" John Phelps, which led to a twenty-eight-minute video documentary on YouTube and an article in the 2014 Boat Race program. Tim can still be found on the River Thames in London, now as a coach at the children's rowing charity, Fulham Reach Boat Club. Tim is one of the directors of Friends of Rowing History. He says that one day he may get bored with rowing or run out of things to write about it—but there are no signs of this happening yet.

Philip Watson Kuepper, born in Burlington, Iowa. Poet who is working at a library in Mystic, Connecticut. Philip earned a BA from St. Francis College, Brooklyn, New York, in 1981. He has published poems in *Poetry*, the *Washingtonian Monthly*, *Promise Magazine*, and *RFD* and in a number of anthologies. He has also published an essay on friendship in the *New York Times*. Though not a rower, since 2010, he has published hundreds of poems on the rowing history website Hear The Boat Sing (HTBS). Philip's collection of poems, *A Sea to Row By—Poems*, was published in 2015.

Oliver La Farge (1901–1963), born in New York City, New York. Writer and anthropologist. Studied at Groton School, Massachusetts, and took a degree from Harvard University in 1924. He rowed both at Groton and Harvard. As an anthropologist, La Farge explored sites in Mexico, Central America, and the American Southwest. He wrote several nonfiction books, mostly about Native Americans, as well as novels and short stories.

He won the Pulitzer Prize in 1930 for his novel *Laughing Boy* (1929). When La Farge's memoirs *Raw Material* was published in 1945, he was serving as a major at the US Transport Command.

William "Bill" Lanouette, born in New Haven, grew up in North Haven, Connecticut. Bill took up rowing at Fordham College in New York City and continued the sport with the New York Athletic Club, the London School of Economics Boat Club (University of London), the Potomac Boat Club in Washington, on the Charles while a fellow at Harvard's Kennedy School, and at the San Diego Rowing Club. He was a journalist on the staffs of *Newsweek*, the *National Observer*, and *National Journal* and was Washington correspondent for the *Bulletin of the Atomic Scientists*. In a second career, Bill was a senior analyst for energy and science issues at the US Government Accountability Office, the investigative agency for Congress. His first book, *Genius in the Shadows: A Biography of Leo Szilard, the Man behind the Bomb* (1993) was a *New York Times Book Review* "Notable Book of the Year." He has reported about rowing for *Newsweek*, *Sports Illustrated*, the NAAO (now USRowing), *Rowing News*, *Rowing Guide*, and *Smithsonian Magazine*. Bill's book, *The Triumph of the Amateurs: The Rise, Ruin, and Banishment of Professional Rowing in the Gilded Age*, was published in 2021.

R. C. (Rudolph Chambers) "Rudie" Lehmann (1856–1929), born in Sheffield, England. Rowing coach, poet of light verse, writer, editor, and politician. Lehmann was educated at Highgate School in London and Trinity College, Cambridge. At Cambridge, he rowed for First Trinity Boat Club. Twice he rowed in the Trial Eights, in 1876 and 1878, but did not manage to make the Light Blue boats. Lehmann was not successful at Henley Royal Regatta; of the ten races he rowed in between 1877 and 1888, the crews did not win a single race. He was called to the bar in 1880. He cofounded *The Granta*, Cambridge undergraduates' magazine, in 1889 and became its first editor. The same year, he had his first article published in *Punch* and later became a member of the editorial staff of the magazine, where he worked until 1919. Lehmann coached Oxford, Cambridge, Brasenose College Boat Club, Leander Club, Trinity College

Dublin, Berliner Ruder-Club, and Harvard. He was honorary secretary of the Amateur Rowing Association in 1893–1901 and captain of Leander in 1894–1895. Lehmann was editor of the *Daily News* in 1901, high sheriff of Buckinghamshire in 1901, and member of Parliament (Liberal) 1906–1910. He was the first to write Sherlock Holmes parodies, which were published in *Punch*, collected between covers titled *The Adventures of Picklock Holes* (1901). Writing light verse on rowing, he became known as the "Poet Laureate of Rowing."Among his books on rowing are *Rowing* (1898) and *The Complete Oarsman* (1908).

Brad Alan Lewis, born in Los Angeles, California. Rower and writer. Lewis rowed in a single sculls for the first time in 1970 and continued to row sweep at Corona del Mar High School and at University of California, Irvine. After witnessing the Olympic Games in 1976, he decided to go in for sculling. Training in a quadruple sculls for the 1980 Olympic Games, Lewis was horribly disappointed about the US Olympic Committee's boycott of the Games. He still has not forgiven President Carter despite many years later receiving a Congressional Gold Medal together with 460 athletes who were forbidden to compete in Moscow. At the 1984 Olympic Games in Los Angeles, Lewis, together with Paul Enquist, became the champions in the double sculls, the first American Olympic gold medal in rowing since 1964. He is still rowing and sees similarities between training in the single and writing: both are practiced alone. "Countless strokes no one would ever see; countless pages no one will ever read. Exactly as it should be." Lewis has written several books, among them some on rowing: *Assault on Lake Casitas* (1990; 2nd ed. 2011), *Wanted: Rowing Coach* (novel, 1995; 2nd ed. 2007), *Lido for Time 14:39: My Training Journal from October 1983 through the Olympics in August 1984* (2011), and *Olympian* (2021; a reworked edition of *Assault on Lake Casitas*).

Henry Wadsworth Longfellow (1807–1882), born in Portland, Maine (then a part of Massachusetts). Poet, educator, and translator. Longfellow studied at Bowdoin College and then spent three years in Europe to study French, Spanish, and Italian. After returning to the United States, he took a position as a language professor at Bowdoin. In 1834, Longfellow was offered a professorship in modern languages at Harvard College with the condition that he spend a year in Europe. There, he studied German, Dutch, Danish, Swedish, Finnish, and Icelandic. He returned to the United States in 1836 to take up his position at Harvard. In 1839, he published his first collection of poems, *Voices of the Night*, which was followed by *Ballads and Other Poems* (1841). He left Harvard in 1854 to concentrate on his writing. Among his most famous works are *Evangeline* (1847), *The Song of Hiawatha* (1855), *Paul Revere's Ride* (1860), and the translation of Dante Alighieri's *Divine Comedy* (1867).

Peter Davis Mallory, born in New York, New York, is a direct descendant of the shipbuilders of Mystic, Connecticut. He was a volunteer, a so-called mud angel or *angelo del fango,* in the aftermath of the catastrophic Florence flood of 1966. After beginning his rowing career as an intramural coxswain at Kent School, he stroked the University of Pennsylvania Lightweights and spent half a century rowing and coaching for clubs around the country, including six stints as a US National coach. Peter has won multiple Canadian and US championships as a rower and as a coach. He is a member of San Diego Rowing Club in the United States and Leander Club in the UK. Peter continues to scull regularly from his own boathouse in the New Jersey Pine Barrens. For thirty years, he has written and edited articles, blogs, and books on rowing history and has spoken on the subject around the world. Among Peter's published works are *An Out-of-Boat Experience . . . or God Is a Rower, and He Rows Like Me!* (2000, 2002, 2017), his masterwork *The Sport of Rowing* in four volumes (2011), *Fairbairn on Rowing* (ed. 2017), *Rowing Tales* (ed. 2017 and 2018), *Leander Club, the First 200 Years* (contributing author, 2018), *More Than Rowing, Kent School Boat Club, The First 100 Years* (2022), and *Life Is a Metaphor for Rowing* (www.row2k.com, 2022–2023).

Thomas C. Mendenhall II (1910–1998), born in Madison, Wisconsin. Professor of history, college president, and rowing historian. Mendenhall studied at Andover and Yale and attended Balliol College, Oxford, on a Rhodes Scholarship from 1935 to 1936. At Balliol, he was captain of the boats at the college boat club. After returning to Yale, Mendenhall rowed on the Berkeley College crew and received his PhD in history in 1938. He was appointed instructor in history at Yale in 1937 and associate professor in 1946, and he had several different positions at Yale between 1937 and 1959, including master of Berkeley College. For twenty-two years, Mendenhall served on the Yale Rowing Committee. He was professor of history and president of Smith College during 1959–1975. Mendenhall was a very productive author of books on history matters, and he also wrote numerous rowing articles for *Yale Alumni Magazine* and *The Oarsman*. Among his books on rowing are *Have Oar, Will Travel, or, A Short History of the Yale Crew of 1956* (1957), *A Short History of American Rowing* (1981), and *Harvard–Yale Boat Race, 1852–1924, and the Coming of Sport to the American College* (1993).

William "Bill" Miller, born in Taunton, Massachusetts. Rowing coach, rowing historian, and NRF director. Bill played basketball in high school but swapped the ball for an oar when he went to Northeastern University, where he became captain of the Varsity team; he was inducted into the Northeastern University Athletic Hall of Fame in 1982. Bill raced in the coxed pair at the 1968 Olympic Trial, was a member of the US National Team in 1969 and in 1971–1975: rowing in the coxed pair at the 1969 European Championships and the 1974 and 1975 World Championships, coxed four at the 1971 Pan American Games and the 1972 Olympic Games, and the eight at the 1973 European Championships. He coached the MIT Lightweight Varsity in 1974–1978 and Boston University Varsity in 1979–1986. He was elected Eastern Association of Rowing Colleges (EARC) Coach of the Year in 1981. Bill coached crews going to Henley Royal Regatta in 1981, 1986, and 1988, and coached the US National Men's Lightweight Eight in 1982. Other positions Bill has had in rowing include US team manager in 1977 and 1979, member of the Men's Olympic Rowing Committee in 1977–1980, USRowing regional technical director in 1988–1991, and director of the Northeast Rowing Center in 1989–2011. Bill cofounded Friends of Rowing History in 1992 and is the organization's website manager. Since 1999, he has been a director of the National Rowing Foundation (NRF) and since

2014 NRF's master of the induction ceremony. Bill cofounded the Duxbury Bay Maritime School in 2000.

William O'Chee, born in Brisbane, Queensland, Australia. Rowing historian and writer. He learned rowing at Brasenose College, Oxford, where he coxed the men's 1st VIII for three years and coxed the Oxford Lightweight Blue Boat in 1987. After returning to Australia, William became the country's youngest federal senator at the age of twenty-four and served more than nine years in the Australian Parliament. During that time, he founded a rowing club in Cairns and coached the 1st VIII of the Canberra Girls Grammar School, as well as putting together a cross-party parliamentary quad to scull on Lake Burley Griffin. William is also a former officer in the Australian Army and has devoted much of his time to veteran welfare. The governor of Queensland appointed him a trustee of the ANZAC Day Trust in 2014. William is still involved in rowing, though he describes himself as a "fat cox, slow sculler and tortured writer." He is a member of Leander Club, Nephthys Boat Club, a life member of Griffith University Surfers Paradise Rowing, and founder of Cairns Rowing Club. William's other sporting passion is skeleton, and he spent thirteen years representing Australia in World Cup and World Championship events and achieving two tour wins. More recently, he has turned his mind to rowing history and is the author of a history of the Brasenose College Boat Club from 1815 to 2015, *The Pinnacle of Fame* (2023). He has also developed an expertise in rowing history of the seventeenth, eighteenth, and nineteenth centuries.

George Yeoman Pocock (1891–1976), born in Kingston upon Thames, England. Waterman, boat designer, and builder. Pocock was an apprentice to his father, Aaron Frederick Pocock, who was a boathouse manager for Eton College. George, his brother Dick, and their sister Lucy all successfully raced for money, becoming champions. Dick won the Doggett's Coat and Badge Race in 1910. The Pocock brothers left England in 1911 to emigrate to Vancouver, Canada. The year after, they moved to Seattle to build boats for the University of Washington's crews after having received an invitation from the Huskies' coach, Hiram Conibear. During World

War I, George and Dick worked for the aircraft manufacturer Pacific Aero Products (in 1917, it became Boeing). In 1922, George left Boeing to continue to build boats for the University of Washington, forming a company under the name Pocock Racing Shells, while Dick took up residence as boatman at Yale. George became the prime shell builder of America and built state-of-the-art watercraft for many US Olympic crews. He was appointed boatman to US Olympic crews in 1936, 1948, 1952, and 1956. George writes about these Olympic Games, how it was to grow up at the River Thames at Windsor and Eton, and dialogues he had with famous American coaches in his unpublished memoirs. Rowing historian Christopher Dodd writes in an eight-part article on the rowing history website Hear The Boat Sing (HTBS) in 2022 that "George was a reader and a deep thinker, and he was an excellent writer."

Rick Rinehart, born in New York City, New York. Executive book editor. Rick started to row at Kent School for Hart Perry and was the bow oar on his school's 1972 eight that swept the juniors competition in the United States, winning NEIRA and Stotesbury Cup championships. The crew also went on to win the 1972 Princess Elizabeth Cup at Henley Royal Regatta, beating the Canadian national champions. He told the story of the crew in his book *Men of Kent: Ten Boys, a Fast Boat, and the Coach Who Made Them Champions* (2010). In 2022, Rick and others from his 1972 crew participated in a "row-past" at Henley to mark the fiftieth anniversary of their win, as well as the hundredth anniversary of rowing at Kent School. He has lived in a variety of places such as Colorado, Ohio, Florida, and Arizona, and he has rowed recreationally and has enthusiastically promoted the sport of rowing at all levels. Rick has enjoyed a forty-year career in book publishing and continues today as executive editor at Globe Pequot, the trade division of Rowman & Littlefield, which has published several rowing books by Toby Ayer, Daniel J. Boyne, William Lanouette, and Peter Mallory.

Sarah Risser, born in Minneapolis, Minnesota. Freelance photographer and writer. Sarah became interested in rowing while captaining her high school Nordic ski team, looking for an effective cross-training option. She

joined the Minneapolis Rowing Club before pursuing collegiate rowing at Wesleyan University. After a twenty-year hiatus, Sarah returned
as a Masters athlete and began training on the Mississippi River with
local Twin Cities rowing clubs. Since 2009, Sarah has competed at local,
regional, and national regattas in the single, double, four, quad, and eight.
More recently, Sarah has focused on training in the single sculls at the
historic rowing venue of Lake Elmo. She also rowed with the Genesee
Rowing Club in upstate New York, enjoying several wins in the women's
50+ eight. After earning her BA from Wesleyan, Sarah earned a master's of environmental management from Yale University before complet-
ing an MBA at the National University of Singapore. She has worked
with various nonprofit environmental organizations. After tragically losing her eighteen-year-old son in a vehicular crash, Sarah directs most of
her energy toward road-safety advocacy but continues to make time to
explore rowing history. She has published articles in *Minnesota History*
and *Ramsey County History*.

R. E. (Robert Egerton) Swartwout (1905–1951), born in New York
City, New York. Coxswain, writer, poet, and cartoonist. Swartwout rowed
and coxed Middlesex School in Concord, Massachusetts, from which he
graduated in 1924. He took a bachelor of fine arts in 1928 at Trinity College, Cambridge, where he coxed the Cambridge Blue boat to victory in
1930, and took a master's in literature in 1931. Swartwout contributed to
Granta and *Punch* and did crossword puzzles for *The Spectator*. He wrote a
few books, including two with connections to rowing: *Rhymes of the River*
(1927) and the novel *The Boat Race Murder* (1933).

John Taylor (1578–1653), born in Gloucester, England. Writer, poet, and
waterman; dubbed himself the "Water Poet." He attended both elemen-
tary and grammar school but never finished his formal education. After
finishing an apprenticeship as a waterman and serving in the fleet of Earl
of Essex, Taylor spent most of his life as a waterman on the River Thames
in London and became the clerk of his guild. In his poems and pamphlets,
he wrote about disputes the watermen had with theatre companies, which
moved from the south bank to the north bank in 1612, depriving the

watermen of business. The watermen also lost income with the development of horse-drawn carriages, which he addressed in *An Arrant Thief* (1622) and *The World Runnes on Wheeles* (1623). Taylor was one of the most read poets in Stuart England and published more than 150 publications, including some of his popular travel writing. Thanks to subscriptions, he managed to print his works, among them *The sculler rowing from Tiber to Thames with his boate laden with a hotch-potch, or gallimawfry of sonnets, satyres, and epigrams. With an addition of pastorall equiuocques or the complaint of a shepheard* (1612). Many of his publications were gathered in *All the Workes of John Taylor the Water Poet* (1630). The literati at the time, including Ben Jonson, criticized his poor and unsophisticated language.

Lisa Taylor, born in Oxford, England. Rowing historian, writer, and editor. Lisa learned to row at Selwyn College, Cambridge. After a year of college rowing, she was selected to row for Blondie, the women's reserve crew, for the University Boat Races in 2005. She was women's captain and club president of the Selwyn College Boat Club from 2005 to 2006. In 2011, Lisa was offered a Stewards' Charitable Trust scholarship to undertake a master's degree and work part-time for British Rowing on participation and development initiatives. During this time, she coached junior athletes at Weybridge, Walton, and Guildford Rowing Clubs and supported projects including an adaptive rowing program at Guildford RC, indoor rowing at the Surrey Youth Games, and delivery of testing for Start (GB Rowing's talent identification program). She coached full-time at the Lady Eleanor Holles School from 2013 to 2016. Lisa was awarded funding for a PhD focused on the history of women's rowing in partnership with the River & Rowing Museum, Manchester Metropolitan University, and Sporting Heritage in 2016. She completed her studies in 2020 with her dissertation "Stride: A History of Competitive Women's Rowing in Britain, 1945–2000."

Ed Waugh, born in Newcastle upon Tyne, England. Playwright, writer, and journalist. Ed earned a BA in history and politics from Sunderland Polytechnic (now Sunderland University) in 1980. With Trevor Wood, Ed cowrote fourteen plays from 2002 to 2015, including the international hits *Dirty Dusting* and *Waiting for Gateaux*. Other sporting hit plays are *Good to Firm*, about the Grand National (the horse race in the UK), and *Alf Ramsay Knew My Grandfather*, about a team of County Durham miners who won the first soccer World Cup in 1909. Ed and Trevor's film script *The Liquidator* won "Best Comedy Script" at the Gotham Film Festival in New York in 2010. Ed has written a trilogy of one-man plays about working-class sportspeople. *Hadaway Harry*, about the boatbuilder and professional rowing world champion Harry Clasper, premiered at South Shields boathouse in 2015 and has had three separate tours in London, Newcastle, and the North East of England. *Carrying David*, which premiered in 2019, is about the boxer Glenn McCory and how his terminally ill brother David inspired him to win the world cruiserweight title in 1989. This play was performed in the North East of England, Northern Ireland, and London. *Wor Bella* premiered in the spring of 2022 and is about the female soccer star Bella Reay, "Wor Bella", and the female munitionettes who worked sixty hours a week in the grueling arms industry during World War I to maintain the war effort. These women played soccer on weekends to raise money for injured war veterans and orphans. *Hadaway Harry*, *Carrying David*, and *The Great Joe Wilson*, the latter a play about Joe Wilson, the "Bard of Tyneside," are contained in the book *Geordie Plays, Vol. 1* (2021).

Thomas "Tom" E. Weil, born in Kabul, Afghanistan. Rowing historian, writer, speaker, and collector. He is a US Navy Vietnam veteran and a recovering lawyer. As his father was a diplomat, Tom has lived in India, Korea, England, Turkey, and the United States, but he has only rowed in the United States (at Andover, Yale, and the New Haven Rowing Club) and in England and Ireland, an activity he put aside more than fifty years ago to take up researching the sport. Tom has been writing and speaking on rowing and rowing history; assembling a large collection of rowing art, artifacts, literature, and archives; and donating much of that to the River & Rowing Museum in Henley (where he served twenty years as a trustee), the National Rowing Foundation (where he is still a trustee), Mystic Seaport Museum, and Marist College. He is a founding member of the Friends of Rowing History, and a life member of USRowing,

Leander Club, the Yale Crew Association, and the North American Society for Sport History. In addition to numerous articles and book chapters, Tom is the author of *Beauty and the Boats—Art and Artistry in Early British Rowing* (2005). He creates doggerel, that is, unsophisticated verse written by the inept for the entertainment of the easily amused. T. S. Eliot is his first cousin twice removed and the only Nobel laureate in his family. So far.

David Michael de Reuda Winser, known as **David Winser** (1915–1944), born in Plymouth, Devon, England. Poet, oarsman, author, doctor, and soldier. Winser was educated at Winchester College where he proved to be a good marksman and oarsman. While he studied at Winchester, he was awarded the King's Gold Medal for English verse. Winser earned a scholarship to Corpus Christi College, Oxford, where he rowed in the Blue boat in 1935, 1936, and 1937; the latter year, Oxford won the Boat Race. At Oxford, Winser continued to write poetry, and in 1936, he won the prestigious Newdigate Prize for his "Rain." After Oxford, he was awarded a Commonwealth Scholarship to study medicine at Yale University for two years, 1937–1938 and 1938–1939. Back in London after Yale, Winser did his clinical training at Charing Cross Hospital. He was a stretcher-bearer in the beginning of the war before he became a Medical Officer in the 48th Royal Marine Commando. He was awarded an M.C. for gallantry for tending wounded soldiers during D-day. Winser was killed in November 1944 during Operation Infatuate, the Battle for Walcheren, in the Netherlands, probably by "friendly fire." He wrote poetry and articles for magazines and also novels, *A Gay Goodnight* (1937), which has some rowing in the story; *Time to Kill* (1939); and the short story "The Boat Race Murder" (1940). Under the pen-name John Stuart Arey, he published poetry and three more books, the novels *Night Work* (1942: Am. title *Night Duty*, 1943) and *There Was No Yesterday* (1943); and nonfiction *Students at Queen's* (1944).

Permissions Acknowledgments

"The Pineapple Cup" is from *Perfect Balance* by Aquil Abdullah (written with Chris Ingraham) published by Potomac Sculling Publishing in 2001. © Aquil Abdullah. Reprinted with permission of Aquil Abdullah.

"The Legend of the Japanese Eight, Part I and Part II" by Andy Anderson (a.k.a. Dr. Rowing) were first published in *American Rowing* magazine, part I in November/December 1994 and part II in November/December 1995. The articles were also later published in *The Complete Dr. Rowing*, Bend the Timber Press, 2001. © Andy Anderson. Reprinted with permission of the author.

"A Regatta Rhyme (On Board the 'Athena', Henley-on-Thames)" by Joseph Ashby-Sterry was published in *Punch* on 10 July 1886.

"Training with Harry Parker" by Toby Ayer is an excerpt from chapter 6, "On This One," in *The Sphinx of the Charles: A Year at Harvard with Harry Parker*, published by Lyons Press in 2016. Reprinted with the permission of Lyons Press.

"At the Mile" by Ralph Henry Barbour is an excerpt from chapter 26 of *Captain of the Crew*, published by D. Appleton and Company, 1901.

"Henley behind the Scenes" by Mark Blandford-Baker was first published in the June 2018 issue of *Row360*. © Mark Blandford-Baker. Reprinted with the permission of the author.

"Orm's Beard" by Frans G. Bengtsson is an excerpt from chapter 5, "How Krok's Luck Changed Twice, and How Orm Became Left-Handed," of *The Long Ships* (1954), translated by Michael Meyer. Publisher:

16, 2021, and "Michael Dillon Revisited" on November 30, 2021. © Greg Denieffe. Reprinted with the permission of the author.

"Downfall of Rowing's Master Class" by Christopher Dodd has been published in different forms through the years. This is an updated version from 2022, which was written specially for this anthology. © Christopher Dodd. Published with the permission of the author.

"The Oarsman's Song" by Steve Fairbairn was first published in *Chats on Rowing*, without a title, by W. Heffer and Sons Ltd., 1934, and Nicholas Kaye Ltd., 1948; with the title "The Oarsman's Song" in *On Rowing*, ed. Ian Fairbairn, Nicholas Kaye Ltd., 1951; in *The Complete Steve Fairbairn*, ed. Ian Fairbairn, The Kingswood Press, 1990; *On Rowing: The Complete Series*, ed. Peter Mallory, ebook, Rowperfect, 2014.

"Palais de Justice," from *Ellis Island and Other Stories* by Mark Helprin. Copyright © 1976, 1977, 1979, 1980, 1981 by Mark Helprin. Used by permission of Brandt & Hochman Literary Agents, Inc. All rights reserved.

"The First Meeting of the Crew" is an excerpt from *Flat Water Tuesday* by Ron Irwin. Copyright © 2013 by Ron Irwin. Reprinted by permission of Thomas Dunne Books, an imprint of St. Martin's Press. All Rights Reserved.

"Early Boating Recollections" is an excerpt from chapter 15 of *Three Men in a Boat (To Say Nothing of the Dog)* by Jerome K. Jerome, published the first time as a book by J. W. Arrowsmith in 1889.

"One Hundred Years from Now" by Robert Treharne Jones was published in the 2007 Oxford–Cambridge Boat Race program. © Robert Treharne Jones. Reprinted with permission of the author.

"A Different Symphony" by Stephen Kiesling is the last chapter in his *The Shell Game*, published by William Morrow in 1982; Contemporary Books in 1983; Nordic Knight Press in 1994; and Kindle (2019). © Stephen Kiesling. Reprinted with the permission of the author.

"The Feathers: A Forgotten Centre of Early British Rowing" by Tim Koch is a reworked piece from a three-part article about The Feathers Pub and Boatyard. These pieces were published on the rowing history website Hear the Boat Sing (HTBS), "The Feathers: A Forgotten Centre of Early British Rowing. Part I: Preamble" (May 5, 2022), "The Feathers: A Forgotten Centre of Early British Rowing. Part II: The Salters and the Glory Years" (May 6, 2022), and "The Feathers: A Forgotten Centre of Early British Rowing. Part III: Decline" (May 7, 2022). © Tim Koch. Reprinted with the permission of the author.

"Putting on the Garment of Water and Light" written by Philip Watson Kuepper in July 2012 was published in his *A Sea To Row By—Poems* in 2015. © Philip Kuepper. Reprinted with permission of the author and HTBS Publication.

"The Eight-Oared Shell" by Oliver La Farge is an excerpt from an essay with the same title in his autobiography *Raw Material*, published by Houghton Mifflin Company in 1945 (a shorter version of the essay was published in *Harper's*, July 1942). Copyright Oliver La Farge. Used by permission of Frances Collin, Literary Agent.

"Courtney v. Hanlan: Three Races, Three Disgraces" by William Lanouette is an excerpt from chapter 11, "Courtney v. Hanlan," in *The Triumph of the Amateurs: The Rise, Ruin and Banishment of Professional Rowing in the Gilded Age*, published by Lyons Press in 2021. Reprinted with the permission of Lyons Press.

"Style and the Oar" by R. C. Lehmann was first published in *Punch* on March 26, 1902. The poem was later published in Lehmann's *Selected Verse* (1929).

"Wet Beginnings" by Brad Alan Lewis is chapter 2 of *Olympian*, published by Shark Press in 2021. *Olympian* is a reworking of Lewis's *Assault on Lake Casitas* (1990). © Brad Alan Lewis. Reprinted with the permission of the author.

"The Broken Oar" was written by Henry Wadsworth Longfellow in 1876, later published in his *A Book of Sonnets*.

"The Previous Administration" by Peter Mallory was published in a slightly different version in *An Out-Of-Boat Experience . . . or God Is a Rower, and He Rows Like Me!*, published by San Diego Writers' Monthly Press, 2000; 2nd ed. 2002; 3rd ed. 2017; 4th ed. Rowperfect, 2022. © Peter Mallory. Reprinted with the permission of the author.

"Yale's Eight at the 1956 Olympic Rowing" by Thomas C. Mendenhall is an excerpt from *Have Oar, Will Travel or A Short History of the Yale Crew of 1956*, published by The Yale Crew Association in 1957. Reprinted with the permission of the Mendenhall family and The Yale Crew Association.

"The 1920 Report of the American Olympic Committee and John B. Kelly's 1920 Olympic Rowing—In His Own Words" by William Miller was written in 2022 for this anthology and is included with the permission of the author. © William Miller.

"A Paean to Rowing" by William O'Chee was written in 2022 for this anthology and is included with the permission of the author. © William O'Chee.

"It's a Great Art, Is Rowing" by George Pocock is reprinted with the permission of George Pocock's granddaughters, Kathryn M. Kusske and Sue Pocock-Saul.

"Henley Royal Regatta" by Rick Rinehart is an excerpt from chapter VII, "Temple Island to Home" in *Men of Kent: Ten Boys, A Fast Boat, and the Coach who made them Champions*, published by Lyons Press in 2010. Reprinted with the permission of Lyons Press.

"Take Me to the River: The Quest for a Permanent Rowing Home in Minneapolis" by Sarah Risser is a shorter version of her article "Take Me to the River: Establishing a Rowing Home in Minneapolis," which was published in the fall 2019 issue of *Minnesota History*, an academic journal published by Minnesota Historical Society. © Sarah Risser. Reprinted with the permission of the author and the Minnesota Historical Society.

"Steve Fairbairn" by R. E. Swartwout is from *Rhymes of the River*, published by W. Heffer and Sons Limited in 1927.

"The Sculler" is an excerpt from John Taylor's *The sculler rowing from Tiber to Thames with his boate laden with a hotch-potch, or gallimawfry of sonnets, satyres, and epigrams. With an addition of pastorall equiuocques or the complaint of a shepheard*, which was first published in 1612.

"Lucy Pocock Stillwell—A Woman in a Waterman's World" by Lisa Taylor is an abridged version of a talk she gave at the River & Rowing Museum, Henley-on-Thames, on International Women's Day, March 8, 2018. © Lisa Taylor. Published with the permission of the author.

"Rowing for the World Championships" by Ed Waugh is an excerpt from act 2 in *Hadaway Harry*, a play first performed in 2015. Waugh's plays *Hadaway Harry, Carrying David,* and *The Great Joe Wilson* were preserved between covers in *Geordie Plays, Vol. 1* published by Tyne Bridge Publishing in 2021. © Ed Waugh. Reprinted with the permission of the author.

"A Memorable Race at Henley Women's Regatta" by Thomas E. Weil was first published on June 22, 2012, on Row2k.com. © Thomas E. Weil. Reprinted with the permission of the author.

"The Boat Race Murder" by David Winser was first published in Great Britain in 1940 in the anthology *Detective Stories of To-Day,* edited by

Raymond Postgate. In the United States, it was first published in 1942 in *Sporting Blood*, edited by Ellery Queen. The story has been published in several crime anthologies since then. Reprinted with the permission of David Thompson and Annie Newark, executors of the Estate of David Winser.

Milton Keynes UK
Ingram Content Group UK Ltd.
UKHW011349271023
431448UK00020B/162